The Struggle for Eden

Community Gardens in New York City

MALVE VON HASSELL

Library of Congress Cataloging-in-Publication Data

Hassell, Malve von, 1957—
The struggle for Eden: community gardens in New York City / Malve von Hassell.
p. cm.
Includes bibliographical references (p.) and index.
ISBN: 979-8-9899277-1-5
1. Community gardens—New York (State)—New York. 2. Urban beautification—New York (State)—New York. 1. Title.

Copyright © 2025 by Malve von Hassell

Library of Congress Control Number: 2025906423

NO AI TRAINING: Without in any way limiting the author's exclusive rights under copyright, any use of this publication to "train" generative artificial intelligence (AI) technologies to generate text is expressly prohibited. The author reserves all rights to license uses of this work for generative AI training and development of machine learning language models.

Original publication:
The Struggle for Eden: Community Gardens in New York City, by Malve von Hassell, was originally published in hard cover by Bergin & Garvey, an imprint of ABC-CLIO, LLC, Santa Barbara, CA, 2002. Copyright © Malve von Hassell. All rights reserved.

Copyright acknowledgments

The author gratefully acknowledges permission for use of the following material:

Excerpts from "Solidarity Forever," based on original words by Ralph Chaplin and adapted by Lisa Van Guard, Cherry Tree Association, Inc. Reprinted by permission of Lisa Van Guard.

Excerpts from a letter written by Santa Gomez to Mayor Giuliani, June 1999. Reprinted by permission of Santa Gomez.

Excerpts from an anonymous poem, written by one of the gardeners, appearing in the brochure prepared by the organization Earth Celebrations for the annual Winter Candle Lantern Pageant, January 28, 1995. Reprinted by permission of Felicia Young, Director of Earth Celebrations.

ACKNOWLEDGMENTS

There are countless images and ideas of urban community gardens—as many as there are gardeners. Indeed, this is their essence and strength. Urban community gardens epitomize the possibility of urban spaces in which individuality in all its myriad forms can exist in the context of a community without being subsumed by it. This book does not claim to offer more than a reflection of fragments of these images and ideas, filtered through my own personal subjective lens. Furthermore, any written description is necessarily frozen in time, while the story is in continuous movement. Gardens and the efforts on their behalf literally are works in progress—or, to use a proclamation on a mural on the Lower East Side, "La Lucha Continua/The Struggle Continues." Since the writing of this book, the community garden movement in America has continued. Many gardens are thriving. There are currently approximately 29,000 gardens in cities across the countries. Some gardens are no longer in existence, and some of the organizations I reference are also gone. However, new ones have sprung up, and many cities now embrace the notion of community gardens as an integral element n their urban planning. This paperback edition of the original hardcover offers a slice of history and as such might help to inspire community gardeners, urban planners, and readers. If any descriptions and common themes represented in my writing ring true, it is because of the generous help and assistance given to me by many individuals throughout the process of research and writing. In particular I would like to express my gratitude to Shelby Allen, Jennifer Baird, Sam Beck, Sally Booth, Howard Brandstein, Jeffrey Cole, Catherine Creedon Sandell, Jon Crow, Michael Draper, Joe Eisman, Sarah Ferguson, Margarita Fernandez, Andrew Fisher, Ellen Goolsby, Ayo Harrington, Paula Hewitt, Adam Honigmann, Aresh Jhavadi, Jennifer Kaslow, Claudia Keel, Julie Kirckpatrick,

Diane Signe Kline, Stanley Kogan, Kathy Kreutzburg-Enos, Joel Kupferman, Jill Florence Lackey, Lenny Lebrizzi, Don Loggins, David Lutz, Anna Magenta, Ross Martin, Miranda Martinez, David Maynard, Sally McCabe, Margaret Moore, Carmen Pabón, Carolyn Ratcliffe, Federico Savini, Trudy Silver, Jac Smit, Jackie Smith, Andy Stone, Edie Stone Tshering, Peter Suzuki, Erika Svendsen, Sylvia Syracuse, Phil Tietz, Lisa Van Guard, Alysse Waterston, Jane Weissman, Haja Worley, Cynthia Worley, and Felicia Young. I am deeply grateful for their interest, patience, and their helpful, critical, and supportive comments; however, any errors are mine. I also am grateful for all I have learned over the years as a member of a virtual community of urban garden supporters—who engage in information exchanges, debate, criticism, and encouragement over the Internet—a rich medley of voices that turns into a roar at times of adversity. Finally, I would like to acknowledge and express my gratitude for the help and assistance extended to me by Jane Garry, senior editor of the Greenwood Publishing Group; Maureen Melino, copyrights editor; Shana Grob, production editor; and Linda Robinson, copy editor, for incredibly efficient, quick, and courteous help at all levels during the preparation of the original hardcover edition of this work.

I included a few snapshots made during my fieldwork in this second edition of my work. Meanwhile, there are many wonderful and compelling images of community gardens widely available on the Internet.

Please note that the index includes only the names of those gardens referenced in the text, not all the gardens that appear in the necrology.

Wolf Ulrich von Hassell
September 10, 1913—March 3, 1999

"You are beautiful, but you are empty," he went on. "One could not die for you. To be sure, an ordinary passerby would think that my rose looked just like you—the rose that belongs to me. But in herself alone she is more important than all the hundreds of you other roses: because it is she that I have watered; because it is she that I have placed under the glass globe; because it is she that I have sheltered behind the screen; because it is for her that I have killed caterpillars (except the two or three that we saved to become butterflies); because it is she that I have listened to, when she grumbled or boasted, or even sometimes when she said nothing. Because she is my rose."

The Little Prince (Saint-Exupéry 1995:138)

Contents

Introduction 1

History of Urban Community Gardening 39

The Frog and the Rooster: Urban Community Gardening
and Community-Based Grassroots Initiatives 89

Primavera, Father Winter, Gaia, And Other Restless
Spirits: Cultural Constructions of Community 141

The Rediscovered Amaranth: Patterns of Production,
Distribution, and Consumption in Community Gardens 179

Conclusion 217

Photos 243

Necrology 249

Bibliography 253

Index 273

About the Author 295

Introduction

Our Gardens Make Us Strong

When the Gardens' inspiration through the people's blood shall run,
there can be no power greater anywhere beneath the sun
Yet what force on earth is weaker than the feeble strength of one
But our Gardens make us strong!

The Earth is being murdered by the greed of man alone
They dug the mines and rape the fields and spread the cancer stones
Now it's time to stand together to defend our only home
And our Gardens make us strong!

If there's some we hold in common is the love we hold for Earth
We reclaim the vacant lots and grow tomatoes and the herbs
Is there anything left to us than to grow the food we eat
And feed our neighbors too!

They tax us untold millions that we don't know where it goes
They cut down on public spending and then they raise the rent
So, nothing's left to do now than to organize and fight
And our Gardens make us strong!

We the people own the government and they work for us you know
We have made a Constitution, it's the only Law to know
It's our Freedom toward more justice for red, black, white and yellow
and the Gardens make us strong!

In our hands is placed a power greater than the World Wide Web Stronger
than the market forces by which we never will be led
We can bring to birth a new world from the ashes of the old
And the Gardens make us strong!

Chorus:
Solidarity forever Solidarity forever Solidarity forever
*For the Gardens make us strong!*1

The Struggle for Eden

The above lyrics were sung to the rousing tune of "John Brown's Body" by members of the More Gardens! Coalition and other garden activists at a public hearing about the fate of community gardens in New York City on February 10, 1999. It evokes essential elements of the struggle for community gardens—a resistance to the market economy and to social economic injustice, a concern with the destruction of the environment, a belief in the power of a democratically organized grassroots movement, and the embrace of a vision for the future. This particular episode in the struggle for community gardens is an instructive sample of the colorful and imaginative style of garden activists in New York City and part of the rich and complex history of urban community gardens.

A city dweller unfamiliar with community gardens in New York City most likely would be surprised when walking into such a space on a summer day. There are community gardens in all boroughs of the city. Open to visitors as long as garden members are inside, the best times to visit are in the evenings after work and on weekends. Some gardens have fences decorated with elaborate metal sculptures, most have simple wire fences with a padlock gate. With the roar of the city still ringing in his ears, a visitor might find himself walking through the gate underneath a vine-covered pergola into a space where a goldfish pond is surrounded by flowers. In the late summer, gardens are awash with flowers and ripening vegetables. On mild evenings people sit in the common area, while others walk around with watering cans filled from a rain barrel. Scents of flowers and herbs get more pronounced in the evening. A chicken might be pecking at the compost heap, clucking with irritation. Children run in and out of the garden, occasionally admonished by an adult to keep from trampling onto the plants. Sounds of the city recede, and, if the visitor is lucky, he might see a datura gradually opening into the dusk.

Introduction

Urban community gardens come in all sizes, from dark and narrow lots between buildings to larger pieces of land, several lots, or even a portion of an entire street block. A few gardens extend across several acres. Most community gardens are situated on city-owned land with insecure tenure at best. In the 1980s and 1990s many gardens were lost, as the land was taken back by the administration for various purposes, including commercial and housing development. Some gardens have been in existence for a brief time period only, with plants barely covering the debris left behind in the wake of a demolished apartment building; others have been in existence for decades and are filled with mature trees and plants.

Individual garden histories, internal organization, and internal politics are equally variable. Membership populations range from highly diverse groups in terms of class, ethnic, and racial backgrounds to more homogeneous groups, largely reflecting the demographics of the respective neighborhoods. Some gardens are run and operated by children and teenagers in the neighborhood; in others members include seniors and children and all age groups in between. Generally gardens will have a mix of individual member plots and common areas. Some gardens are planted entirely with flowers and decorative plants, others are filled with vegetables and fruits, and many contain a mix of these. The single unifying factor is that these gardens have been formed and are maintained by people in the communities.

In this book I portray the history and present of urban community gardens on the Lower East Side in New York City. This involves a consideration of cultural, political, and economic factors and dynamics within individual community gardens, at the level of neighborhood garden coalitions, and at the level of city-wide struggles on behalf of the gardens. I concentrate on the last two decades of the 20th century in this portrayal of a social movement that seeks to impact urban environments both in social elements of programs half-heartedly begun during earlier administrations, building maintenance and inspection programs, and to step up the process of privatization are reflected in housing data reported in 1997 (Thrush 1997).[2] The continuation of this process is evident in the eagerness with which landlords of buildings with expiring Section 8 subsidy contracts are choosing to opt out of public funding in order to rent out these same apartments on the open market. Another indicator is the city's focus on divestment and on shifting the responsibility for apartment buildings to the private sector; for instance, the Asset Sales Program launched in 1997 involves an accelerated process of selling buildings. Given a vacancy rate in 2000 of 3.19 percent, the declining number of affordable housing units and housing subsidies, the increasing number of units in need of repair, and more than 75,000 households severely overcrowded (more than 1.5 people per room), the housing crisis is not looming; it is fully entrenched.

Meanwhile, young professionals are flocking to the Lower East Side in search of housing; many of these newcomers to the area think that a one-bedroom apartment for $1,695 on Orchard Street is a bargain. In the area south of Houston Street, a portion of the Lower East Side renamed Loho by real estate agents, commercial or mixed-use buildings are being converted into rental apartments with prices as high as $3,000 a month for a studio (Hamilton 2000). Apartments that landlords chose to keep vacant in the 1970s are now being renovated as rentals in a market of skyrocketing rents.

On the Lower East Side, Puerto Ricans have been particularly affected by these developments. Historically Puerto Ricans in the United States and in New York City have been subject to a limited and discriminatory labor market and housing. This is a process of long standing, beginning with capital flight and the contraction of manufacturing during the late 1950s, with severe job losses in

Introduction

industries such as garment trades, small manufacturing, restaurants, and hotels with large numbers of low-paid workers (Sánchez 1986). Mele traces the history of gentrification of the Lower East Side and the displacement pressures and concomitant disenfranchisement of Puerto Ricans over the past forty years (Mele 2000).[3] For this population group grassroots-based housing initiatives and community gardens provided the means for regaining a sense of control over their lives and staking a claim to the neighborhood.

Names of community gardens—Esperanza, Paraíso, Amigos, De Colores, All Peoples, Miracle, Tranquilidad (Hope, Paradise, Friends, Many Colors, Tranquility) to name a few—on the Lower East Side are evocative of visions for a community (von Hassell 1998). These visions differ, reflecting a diversity of constructs of "community." A statement of purpose of the Green Oasis Community Garden, founded in 1981, clearly spells out the founders' vision.

First, to create something beautiful that would change the way the community felt about the neighborhood. Second, to encourage members of the community to become involved, allowing for an opportunity for all to share in a common positive experience and community responsibility. And third, to provide a safe space for the youth, an alternative to the streets.

Green Oasis was constructed on five building lots and contains a theater, a playground, a grape arbor, a barbecue pit, a pond housing goldfish and a turtle, birdhouses, vegetable plots, slate and marble pathways for wheelchair accessibility, a gazebo, and beehives providing honey. Its founding fathers, Reinaldo Arana and Norman Vallee, were artists. Their goal was to create an alternative to the streets for the neighborhood youth. Twenty years later the garden stages regular theater productions and runs art and theater workshops in cooperation with local schools and city programs. The garden's active board of directors reflects the

The Struggle for Eden

diversity of the neighborhood; among other activities, the board engages in fundraising campaigns in order to expand existing programs and to develop new activities. A junior board of directors, consisting of children and young adults, operates alongside the adult board of directors, with active involvement in the running of the garden and the decision-making process.

Another example of such a statement of purpose is the more personal description by Carmen Pabón, the founder of the Jardín Bello Amanecer Borencano.[4]

> "I begin the garden Bello Amanecer in 1984 by the month of June. The purpose of this garden was for elderly people and children of the neighborhood. I have a group of elderly working with me, planting flowers, having activities, having ministry once a week on Wednesday by Diane Dunne, Ministry of Hope for the Future for the homeless people, feeding them three times a week. Monday night and Wednesday at 3 P.M., we have bible study, food orientation, housing. Saturday 1:30 to 6 P.M. we provide food, clothes pantry for the elderly for the weekend. Thursday exercise in the afternoon. Friday we get together in the garden with all the elderly to have workshop" (Carmen Pabón, Jardín Bello Amanecer Borencano).

Carmen Pabón came to the United States in 1946; she worked in a sewing factory in the Bronx. Living in a public housing apartment on Houston Street from the 1950s on, she raised eight children and became a very active member in the community—in her children's school, in the church she attended, and in the community board. She was concerned with the inadequacy of social services for poor people and the need for affordable housing. She started the garden in 1984, after she had retired. The community organizations Charas and Adopt-A-Building supported her efforts and helped her to obtain a lease from Operation Green Thumb, and homeless people whom she knew

Introduction

helped her to clear the garbage-filled lot. Carmen Pabón tended and operated the garden with assistance by a few friends and volunteers. It contained many sitting areas with chairs and tables underneath trees, a few planting areas along the side, and a small *casita* in the back. Its main use was as an outdoor space for social activities, not necessarily specifically linked to gardening. The Jardín Bello Amanecer Borencano was partially bulldozed on February 15, 2000. Only a thin sliver on the side with the colorful mural was saved. In view of the forthcoming construction next to it, the "Beautiful Dawn of Puerto Rico" will be little more than a dark alley between two building walls.

These two gardens, successful in their different ways, are examples of the diversity of character and focus of the gardens on the Lower East Side. They also illustrate some of the demographic factors of the Lower East Side. Thus, founding members of Green Oasis were part of a contingent of predominantly white educated middle-class residents who came to the Lower East Side in the 1960s and thereafter and became involved in various types of activism on behalf of the neighborhood. The founder of the Jardín Bello Amanecer Borencano is one of many Puerto Rican working-class women who came to the Lower East Side in the 1940s and who got involved in community activism and gardens and became leaders in their community. At times in the history of community gardens on the Lower East Side, these demographics and attendant social and economic class dynamics have exacerbated divisions. However, just as often such divisions have been overcome, as individual groups find common ground in the struggle for community gardens and ultimately for the right to determine the future of their own community.

Community gardens on the Lower East Side have been described as "dreamy." An anthropologist who has researched and written about the area for decades mentions the gardens in connection with a list of initiatives on the Lower East Side since

the 1970s:
> "Other similarly dreamy ideas had already been put into action: a communal apartment house on East Eleventh Street heated with solar power, a portion of its electricity supplied by a sleek windmill; communal urban gardens that were beginning to take shape amidst the ruins of burned-out buildings, providing shade, beauty, and fragrance, and often vegetables to boot—many of them crowned with *casitas*" (Sharff 1998: 83).[5]

Perhaps these gardens are indeed based on "dreamy ideas," yet, they have proven to be remarkably resilient, persisting in the face of a largely unsupportive and eventually actively hostile city administration. While the history of community gardens on the Lower East Side is not transferrable to other cities, elements of this resilience, creativity, and an increasing degree of organization and activism are replicated to differing degrees in community garden initiatives in cities across the United States. A portrayal of the history of community gardens on the Lower East Side cannot claim to represent urban community gardens in all of New York City or across the nation; for that matter, such a history cannot claim to represent all gardens on the Lower East Side, given the diversity at all levels among them. However, a focused portrayal and analysis can serve as a magnifying lens and a foundation for a consideration of the history and significance of urban community gardens in the country.

In the mid-1990s a gardener in the El Sol Brilliante community garden on the Lower East Side was asked to describe the garden's contents in terms of plants and animal life: "We have a peach tree, two plum trees, a fig tree, two apple trees. People grow all types of vegetables from corn and sunflowers to lettuce and okra. We have two resident cats in the garden, lots of birds and squirrels, and I recently found a bat." This gardener like other gardeners on the Lower East Side knows every plant in the garden,

Introduction

is intimately familiar with the garden's contours, and knows at what times of the day sunlight can reach past the surrounding buildings into the garden. Such statements by gardeners describing their gardens ring with a jubilant sense of pride and a sense of staking a claim to something created by their own hands. They reflect a delight in signing their work and taking responsibility for it. An expression of individuality, proclaimed in this statement as much as in the physical structure of gardens with their individual plots, coexists with an identification with a group, "we," which may include all members of a particular garden, all gardens in a community, or even all gardens in New York City. Community gardens provide a unique linkage between individual existence in urban environments and experiences within a group context and at the level of the entire city.

CONCEPTUAL THEMES RAISED BY URBAN COMMUNITY GARDEN INITIATIVES

It is an interesting commentary on the perception of community gardens by social scientists that a recent volume on the anthropology of landscape contains no more than a passing reference to allotment gardens (Hirsch 1995: 3). Yet that volume is concerned, among others, with perceptions of space and place and the way in which such perceptions are played out in the "relationship [here] between an ordinary, workaday life and an ideal, imagined existence, vaguely connected to, but still separate from that of the everyday" (Hirsch 1995: 3). Community gardens bridge that distance. Rooted in the everyday life of people in cities, community gardens are the embodiment of a concrete "praxis" of claiming the city landscape, literally reshaping it, recycling it, eating it.

The Struggle for Eden

Community gardens have important stories to tell as individual instances of social history and as keys to urban history. Community gardens have provided a context for the development of ideas and concepts relevant to our understanding of urban shifts and dynamics over the past decades as well as in the future. The ideas and concepts can be considered from three angles.

Community gardens are points of junction, expression of, and battleground for the emergence of new sets of ideas of living in cities, providing a setting and context for a new praxis of urban community activities, community action, citizenship, and activism.

Community gardens as individual entities and as part of larger whole are points of intersection for the dynamics of politics (racial, cultural, class), economics (housing, development, poverty), the environment (open space, cities of the future, ecological systems), technology (biotechnology, pollution, urban agriculture), and gender roles (in gardens' internal organization and in coalitions and activism on behalf of the gardens).

Finally, community gardens, individually and as a group, can be seen as a form of revitalization movement. A revitalization movement, a deliberate attempt to create a new way of life for a society or group, can take many forms, with different degrees of religious and political emphasis. Such movements generally arise in the context of rapid changes, feelings of loss and powerlessness, and the experience of some form of domination. On the Lower East Side, community garden initiatives have represented a central component in the struggle to construct an entire way of life as a response to poverty and attendant social ills, in resistance to the anomy and alienation in urban life, and in partial rejection of the market economy.

Urban community gardens have arisen in the context of a market economy. In New York City in particular, the political economy of corporate concentration, the real estate market, and

Introduction

labor market shifts have been instrumental in creating vacant land, which was then turned into community gardens by neighborhood people. The same processes contributed to increasing pressures on these spaces in the form of investment capital and a city administration bent on returning these spaces to the tax rolls. A related set of processes, part and parcel of efforts to make the city safe and attractive to corporate capital, revolves around increased efforts by the city administration to control public space and discipline the poor and middle class alike (street vendors, jaywalkers, community gardeners, artists). For community gardens this has meant privatization and bulldozing of gardens.

The market economy and dynamics of power and capital provide the base and context for the conflicts in the realms of ecology, poverty, housing, education, and community that are played out in community gardens and in the struggle over their continued existence. The conceptual themes raised by community garden initiatives must be understood in this context. These themes are as follows: a concern with sustainability of cities in the context of a burgeoning environmental movement, the development of visions for an alternative society, an eclectic and amorphous set of beliefs loosely labeled eco-feminist spirituality, the power and uses made of the media in conjunction with new forms of communication, and shifting conceptualizations of individuality and individuals in society. These themes are defined, limited, and caused by the market economy, however, in the context of the history of urban community gardens they have also given rise to new forms of negotiating life in cities and new levels of community organization and activism.

The Struggle for Eden

Sustainability

A key term in environmental activism is sustainability. Initially derived from the notion of an equilibrium within a closed loop in an environmental cycle, it has come to represent a complex social-cultural and economic proposition in relation to the environment. According to Nijkamp and Perrels, sustainability in urban environments refers to "cities where socio-economic interests are brought together in harmony (co-evolution) with environmental and energy concerns in order to ensure continuity in change" (Nijkamp and Perrels 1994: 4). In the late 20th century the notion of an environmental equilibrium has given way to new approaches in ecological thinking, with a focus on non-equilibrium dynamics, spatial and temporal variation, complexity, and uncertainty (Scoones 1999). In community garden initiatives, individuals are confronted with such a more dynamic perspective on ecology on a daily basis, making them aware of the impact of human actions on the environment, the complexity and changing nature of the environment, and the fragility of initiatives in social and political terms.

Wekerle (1996) distinguishes between two dominant discourses on urban sustainability. One discourse is centered on a so-called eco-systems approach that seeks to integrate ecological principles into urban planning by incorporating scientific, technical data on environmental degradation and the environmental impacts of development and growth. The other discourse is concerned with the dynamics of global restructuring and the role of global capital and transnational corporations in ongoing competition among cities to maintain prosperity through growth. According to Wekerle both of these discourses are flawed and partial perspectives. Both in different ways leave out or ignore space for agency of individuals or even individual organizations. A third and alternative discourse on urban sustainability derives

Introduction

much of its impetus from mobilizations of social movement groups.

Taking a holistic approach, this discourse links economic growth, environmental health and social equity. Decent jobs, adequate living conditions, and democratic decision-making are seen as compatible with urban environments that are free from contamination and pollution. Urban sustainability is viewed as the outcome of urban policies and programs that are community-based and decentralized in their decision-making, with a goal of eliminating existing hierarchies of power and domination. The transformation of social relations and the democratization of everyday life are viewed as the essence of sustainable cities. This discourse from the grassroots is fundamentally different from the emphasis on eco-system sustainability that is rooted in an ecological model or the global restructuring model that posits the juggernaut of global capital forces (Wekerle 1996: 138).

An example of this discourse can be found in the work by Daly and Cobb, who discuss their ideas for sustainable economic welfare in an attempt to offer "realistic alternatives to capitalism and socialism (both growth economics)" (Daly and Cobb 1989: 2). They argue that the scale of human activity has become too large relative to the biosphere and that only a radical revision of all social and economic organization on the basis of the principle of sustainability would help to stave off a looming environmental and ultimately human disaster. To this end they argue in favor of decentralization of political and economic power, ownership or participation in the management of the means of production, and the subordination of the economy to social goals (Daly and Cobb 1989: 15).[6]

Community garden initiatives represent such attempts to work toward urban sustainability. This is reflected in gardens' internal organization and in activities such as food production, waste management, land use, and efforts to recycle everything from old truck tires to brownfields. In community gardens the embrace of the concept of sustainability represents challenges to key tenets of the market economy. By their actions community gardeners propose a departure from the market economy's principle of "après moi le deluge" of unchecked growth, leaving behind wasted environments and wasted generations for whom there is no place in the profoundly transformed labor market of the late 20th century. Instead gardeners, by engaging in a praxis that emphasizes democratic organizational forms, urban food production, cooperative entrepreneurship, education, and an awareness of the fragility of the environment, struggle toward a notion of stewardship of the environment and individual possibilities and choices within that context.

According to Williams a fundamental distortion in people's perception of their lives arises in the course of urbanization. An essential fact of human existence—food production—is displaced and viewed as marginal and associated with the past and distant lands (Williams 1973: 300). Community garden initiatives reflect an appreciation for this essential fact of human existence. They go further than that. Not reducible to quaint illustrations of what a radish looks like in the ground or bean sprouts in a school experiment, the horticultural equivalent of a petting farm, community garden initiatives touch upon patterns of production, distribution, and consumption, transforming day-to-day lives of members at multiple levels of meaning.

A vision of a sustainable city and sustainable communities is expressed in a description of the Banana Kelly Street project on Kelly Street in the South Bronx. This project, begun in the early 1970s, involved a combination of housing rehabilitation and construction and community gardening as the result of grassroots community activism (Fowler 1996). The first housing project involved a family of eight; in addition to increasingly sophisticated housing initiatives, Banana Kelly then went on to the creation of a

Introduction

food cooperative and a recycling center as well as a community garden in a vacant lot. According to Fowler this counters what he calls ecologically and socially destructive agriculture.

"The connection to the examples of Banana Kelly and urban farming is clear: a healthy city form (or countryside) comes from the performance of basic economic activity—growing food, building shelter—collectively at the most local level" (Fowler 1996: 228).

Fowler's description is idealistic to the point of being oblivious to the political context and the history and development of Banana Kelly over time (von Hassell 1996). Like many other community development initiatives, Banana Kelly has been fraught with conflicts over leadership, goals, and strategies to achieve those goals, has been subject to increasing distance between leadership and clients, and has involved manipulation of and imposition of values upon those people whom it was to serve—hardly "like ecosystems undisturbed by humans" (Fowler 1996: 225). However, the ideas involved—the linkages between housing, work, food production, and community gardens as means of redressing social inequities and providing building blocks for community organization—have informed many initiatives in the following decades.

The concept of sustainability as it is embraced by community garden activists also involves national and global perspectives. Community gardeners have drawn my attention to publications such as the *Earth First Journal*, a publication that is as much concerned with the destruction of the environment at a global level as with social inequities enacted and sustained by corporate capital and the market economy. Concerned about gene manipulation of seeds, chemical fertilizers, herbicides and pesticides, and the domination of urban food supply by large corporate chains, community gardeners make linkages between the micro environment of a community garden and national and global issues and between social activism and environmental activism.

Visions of an Alternative Society

> "The emerging radical culture of the near future will focus on the values and experiences of hunters, gatherers, gardeners, and free peasants in the "excluded zones" marked for neglect or simple expropriation by Capital. This culture will involve a strong neo-shamanic movement on a much wider and more popular level than now Gardening will emerge as one of the major economic forces of this resistance, but also as a central cultural focus. If there is to be a "War on the Zaibatsus" (whether violent or non-violent), it will be fought in part for a cause that is both symbol and substance of the reality envisioned in the very act of resistance: the garden. Grow your own world" (Wilson 1999: 33–34).

This text is from the introduction of a publication called *Avant Gardening*, a collection of essays about community gardens in New York City, in particular on the Lower East Side, by gardener, artists, writers, and activists. It reflects the eclectic syncretism of ideas that has been the characteristic of activist thought in environmental initiatives. It also reflects the fact that for many individuals community garden initiatives represent more than the wish to grow tomatoes and marigolds in vacant lots; instead, they have become central components in a critique of civilization and in the development of alternative visions for society.

Wilson (1999) speaks of a need "to resist the triumph of global capital," arguing that global capital and its effects on daily life leave no room for the imagination. He makes an analogy to the notion of a generic apple, an apple perfect in appearance but devoid of taste, the sterile product of industrial farming. According to Wilson, global capital has an effect on life that is similar to the creation of the generic apple, erasing vitality, creativity, and imagination. Gardening is seen as a way to counter this domination, transforming everyday life and reinjecting place-based meaning into daily activities of production, distribution, and consumption.

In alternative visions for society encountered in community garden initiatives, nostalgic notions of the past are wrapped into and transformed within a modernist vision. The nostalgia is for envisioned previous "golden ages," which of course never existed. Williams reminds us that reference to an idea derived from the past is not reducible to a merely nominal continuity. A recurrence of a concept cannot be treated as an illusion simply to be contradicted or exposed—"it has power as such" (Williams 1973: 292).[7] Indeed, ideas and concepts when divorced from their original context can acquire even greater power.

Williams makes a distinction between insiders who live directly within a landscape and outsiders who entertain an objectified concept of it; one is rooted in nature, the other in an existence defined by commercial life, where everything including the land can be alienated. According to Hirsch this falsely splits the two modes of experience as if they were mutually exclusive (Hirsch 1995: 13). However, Williams also shows precisely how these two modes of experience are interrelated. That is, language and thought are fragmented in the modern experience, and the perspectives of the insider, caught in the immediacy of the experience, and the objectifying outsider are wrapped into a single complex and conflicted vision of urban and rural landscapes. "These fictions of cities of the future interact, in the mind, with the long fictions of the pastoral" (Williams 1973: 277).

Community gardeners seek to restore the possibility of experiencing one's environment in an immediate fashion; at the same time they are rooted in and defined by the market economy and are critical observers of it. Urban community gardens are not attempts to escape the city, but rather attempts to live within it, to confront it, and to selectively reject and appropriate aspects of its structures and dynamics.

Community gardening initiatives add another dimension to the interweaving of visions of the past and the future. According to Williams, fictions of the pastoral situated in an imaginary past are characterized by a distortion or removal of the realities of rural life in favor of an idealized image, while fictions of the cities of the future involve a perceived set of overwhelming and insoluble problems such as destruction of the environment and alienation (Williams 1973: 277). For community gardeners, both rural and urban worlds are affected and damaged by the same set of dynamics; consequently, escape is not an option. Instead they choose to challenge their own world in the vacant lot next door, on the block, and in the neighborhood. In that process they draw on a broad range of concepts and ideas as inspiration and guidance, from anthropology and its descriptions of alternative forms of community to the utopian thought of Charles Fourier, Marxist critiques of capitalism, and the poetry of Wendell Berry. Wilson makes reference to the image of the world created and enforced by global capitalism:

> "Finally there no longer exists an "outside" of the Image [sic], since everything is now inside it. Just as human relations can no longer be envisioned outside the universality of exchange, so too no imaginal activity can now be situated outside the universal Image. The line between wild and tame has finally been erased. No Exit—or, as Benjamin put it: one-way street" (Wilson 1999: 23).

Community gardeners contest that image on its own turf. They fight for the gardens, because there is no other place to go.

Introduction

Spirituality

The eclecticism that characterizes the assemblage of conceptual ideas in conjunction with community garden initiatives is particularly pronounced in the realm of spirituality—here used in the broadest sense of the term. Community gardens are notable for containing a vast range of spiritual concepts and ideas, in part reflecting the diversity of the population involved and in part the eclecticism frequently encountered in environmental activism. Community gardeners appropriate diverse symbols, beliefs, spirits, beings, and gods from religions from all over the world, blending these together in a creative fashion. One encounters Buddhism, Christianity, pre-Christian imagery, ancient Celtic beliefs, Native American beliefs, and astrology, among others.

In May 2000, the Cherry Tree Association, together with two other organizations, the More Gardens! Coalition and Time's Up, extended an invitation to the Cherry Tree Garden at 136th Street and Cypress Avenue to celebrate and encourage "Healing and Gardening all over the World." In its invitation the Cherry Tree Association described itself as "creating the Mott Haven Green Zone, Free of Violence and Free of Pollution, a 21st-century model of community empowerment and self-sustainable development." The purpose was to "collaborate with community residents, city-wide activists and naturalists from around the world as we revitalize open space for harmonious purposes of local autonomy and long-term sustainability." The invitation made reference to Beltane, an ancient Celtic fertility festival, and also to the notion of a realignment of the planets.[8]

A central figure that presides over much of this spirituality is Gaia (alternately spelled Gaea), often referred to simply as "the Goddess." In ancient Greek mythology Gaia is the Earth Mother, credited with having created everything—the universe, deities, and humans; an "all-producing and all-nourishing" goddess. Gaia was born as the daughter of Chaos, and appropriately so—the frequent invocation of her name reflects a central tenet of this brand of spirituality. Nature is not perceived as an idyllic space; rather, it is filled with tension and involves cycles of birth and death, pain and suffering, as well as growth, beauty, and vitality. By contrast, in earlier notions of the environment the dominant concept was a static equilibrium, while any disruption or change involved interference by human agency. "And the literature of pagan feminist spirituality reiterates these concepts of a powerful dark goddess who is destructive, instinctual, chaotic, and yet the source of feminine creativity and wisdom" (Luhrmann 1993: 228).[9] Gaia embodies the notion of a dynamic environment, which must be nurtured and protected as well as celebrated in its own right.

James Lovelock is known as the originator of the so-called Gaia theory, according to which earth and all beings on it are seen as a single complex organism (Lovelock 1979). Lovelock tried to suggest ways in which human beings might live in harmony with Gaia. Milton (1996) draws attention to the ambiguity in the Gaia concept with regard to the location of power. Gaia as a living organism is vulnerable, yet at the same time Lovelock appears to suggest that Gaia is able to survive without human input. "[The Gaia theory's] implications are such that environmentalists have felt unable or unwilling to ignore it, but suggest neither that Gaia is totally in control of her own destiny, nor that her future is fully in our hands" (Milton 1996: 133). However, the interesting element is not so much the ambiguity about the locus of power, but rather the notion that responsibility for keeping the planet in good order as it were is shared by all human beings. According to Lovelock, if Gaia is another way of referring to the earth, "we may find ourselves and all other living things to be parts and partners of a vast being who in her entirety has the power to maintain our planet as a fit and comfortable habitat for life" (Lovelock 1979: 1). Hence, individuals are responsible and, further, cooperation

Introduction

among them is required to make their actions effective.

Subscribers to the goddess movement include not only eco-feminists but also environmental activists and intellectuals with specialties outside environmental issues. It has been questioned at many levels, among others for implying an "innate" and "natural" relationship of women to the environment, valorizing women's nurturing capacity, and anthropomorphizing the environment as "Mother Nature" and "Mother Earth." While such reservations are valid, they cannot detract from the fact that in community garden initiatives this brand of eco-feminist spirituality with Gaia as a focal point has provided a compelling set of symbols around which activism and events in support of the gardens have been organized.

Luhrmann points out that for its subscribers this spirituality is not necessarily uniquely feminine. Rather it is perceived as expressing an essential aspect of human existence, the presence of despair and suffering in connection with ongoing struggle and hope (Luhrmann 1993: 229). At the same time it is perceived as inseparable from women's experience of cycles of pain and pleasure within their own bodies. Much of the imagery associated with Gaia embodies notions of death, pain, anger, and transformation. Through the medium of this imagery, personal and individual experience is transformed and raised to the level of a political struggle of a group. Further, Gaia and the spirituality framed around the goddess reflects not merely a striving for an existence in harmony with nature but also a means of becoming more fully human in the form of a conscious embrace of the existential condition of life, suffering, and death. In this striving nature is the medium, providing a space for immediacy of experiences.

This eco-feminist spirituality has provided ways to bridge symbolically and conceptually the various components and themes in community garden initiatives: resistance to economic, political, and cultural aspects of society, construction of community, individual expression and creativity, and a search for meaning. More concretely this spirituality helps to link the realm of garden work, situated at the threshold of the domestic and the public arenas, with the realms of food production, environmental activism, art and aesthetics, individual life cycles and life experiences, and political struggle and community organization.

THE POWER AND USES OF THE MEDIA AND NEW FORMS OF NEGOTIATING THE CITY

A critical component in the history of community gardens in New York City is the media. Initiatives on the Lower East Side and other areas of New York City in support of community gardens take their struggle into the public realm and into the streets. They consciously draw on the media as an organizing tool and a means to convey their message. At the same time garden activists have carefully monitored the media, immediately reacting and responding to any actions by the media that have the effect of marginalizing and trivializing community gardeners and their struggle.

In the 20th century new patterns and dynamics of relationships among individuals and groups have emerged. In this connection one might point to Castells' analysis of the informational society and new possibilities for individuals and groups to create their own images and assert their identities through the use of the computer and other elements of communications technology (Castells 1989). One might also refer to Mitchell's description of a new infrastructure that includes virtual places, electronically interconnected within the global world (Mitchell 1999).

The extent to which these developments will profoundly change the forms of interaction and life in cities has yet to be fully

Introduction

explored. However, the need for the development of new kinds of communication, already foreseen by Williams (1973), is indisputable. Community gardeners seek to control and manipulate new forms of communication while simultaneously resisting what Williams describes as the appropriation and exploitation of the same media for capitalist purposes (Williams 1973: 295). In this process they have developed a shared consciousness that extends beyond a set of techniques to an identification with other gardens and other neighborhoods and even other cities and struggles in the country. The use of modern means of communication is paralleled by efforts to recreate spaces and opportunities for directly discoverable and unmediated experiences. This self-conscious awareness and indeed manipulation of two levels of existence—direct and unmediated experiences and mediated, constructed, secondhand experiences—is central to shifting conceptualizations of individuality and the role of individuals within community.

SHIFTING CONCEPTUALIZATIONS OF INDIVIDUALITY AND INDIVIDUALS IN SOCIETY

The tension between the attraction of the city with its elements of fascination, splendor, anonymity, and an immense wealth of possibilities on the one hand and the search for "knowable communities" in the context of isolation and alienation on the other is central to the way in which individuals experience urban life (Williams 1973: 16). According to Williams, urban life has forced the development of new notions of "community." "Community, to survive, had then to change its terms" (Williams 1973: 107). Engaged in the paradoxical effort to construct immediacy and authenticity of experience at the individual and community level within the context of fragmenting, alienating, and also exhilarating experiences of life in the city, community garden initiatives represent a concrete and tangible link between these two levels of experience.

Community gardens, in themselves endlessly diverse, further exacerbated by equally endless variation between neighborhoods and cities, with tenuous links and fragile coalitions among each other, reflect and embody a particular aspect of the modern experience, that is, the fragmented nature of experience. The fragmented nature of experience in modernity is a potential source of wealth, providing a conceptual and concrete space for individuality. At the same time it can also splinter communities. Efforts to address this conflict can be traced in the writings of philosophers and social scientists from the 17th century to the present.

For instance, one could consider Gianbattista Vico, who saw individual knowledge as located in "shared moments within a flow of social activity which afford common reference" (Hirsch 1995: 17). In Vico's discourse on knowledge formation, learning, based on experience, was seen as a creative process and a state of being (Vico 1965). In this conceptualization, individual knowledge, and by extension individual experience, is contingent on the social context.

The 19th century philosopher Johann Gottfried Herder adds to Vico's conception of the learning process the importance of an intense awareness of existence. In this conception of learning, experience and knowledge are not gained for the sake of passing them on, but are in themselves valuable to the one who lives through them at a particular moment (von Hassell 1981; Herder 1881). Herder sought for ways to bridge constructed mediated experience and immediacy of experience, or reason and emotion, arguing that such a split was an artificial construct of modern civilization. He found such a possibility most strongly in poetry, which he considered to be at once reflective and immediate.

Concerned with the relationship of experience, individuality,

Introduction

and community, Herder outlined essential characteristics for a model community. These involved the realization that it was futile to attempt to transcend inherent limitations in life; the essence of life involved cycles of being and non-being or life and death. Thus, Herder saw a basic vitality in the process of continual growth, collapse, and reemergence as an inherent and necessary contradiction of human life. Herder's model community was not to have a single focus of power, and politics was to be a fluid medium of exchange and arbitration rather than an abstract separate polity. Further, such a model community had to contain spaces for immediacy of experience or a "poetry for living" (Herder 1881).

One of the most compelling discussions of the relationship between individual experience and community in modern life is offered by Gellner. Rejecting both the theory of atomistic individualism, which in the end is solitary, and the theory of romantic organicism in community, which subsumes the notion of individuality, Gellner holds forth the promise of transcendence. "Cultures are not terminal. The possibility of cultural transcendence is a fact; it is the single most important fact about human life" (Gellner 1998:187). In a discussion about Wittgenstein and Malinowski,[10] he defines the shifting nature of community and reminds us that we are not self-sufficient individuals or even self-contained communities but instead part of a wider community. He rejects any form of absolutizing the polarities of individualism and communalism (Gellner 1998: 188).

These polarities are negotiated in community gardens on a daily basis. Community gardeners self-consciously embrace a "direct" relation to the land, aware that they exist in the context of and are shaped by the market economy. Within the parameters of city life they try to construct settings for unmediated experiences. To use Herder's phrase, community gardeners seek to reinject a kind of "poetry for living" into their day-to-day activities. The fragmented nature of experiences in modern existence is reflected in community gardens in the realms of internal organization, aesthetics, pageants, and political activism on behalf of the gardens. At the same time, gardeners claim that fragmentation and turn it into a source of strength and vitality that bridges disparate individual elements and experiences and offers a shared identification with the struggle on behalf of the gardens. In the annual pageants celebrating the gardens, the fragmentation reappears personified as Gaia, the daughter of Chaos, and is celebrated in the context of an affirmation of community, however fragile, tenuous, and imaginary.

In the history of community gardens in New York City, a central symbol and a strategic device is the notion of a map. Maps tell stories by what they include as much as by what they exclude. City administration maps do not show community gardens, regardless of the length of time any given garden has been in existence. Official maps show vacant lots where there are active gardens. A community gardener from a garden called La Plaza Cultural on 9th Street told me about a map project on the Lower East Side. He and other gardeners from different gardens were creating a map that was to show all the gardens in the neighborhood. This gardener was also involved in plans for a summer camp for children from the gardens at La Plaza Cultural. Each group of children was supposed to help on the production of a gift to the garden, a giant banner with a map of the area. At the time of this conversation, this gardener was working on a 26" × 36" fold-up map that was to contain every detail, all sidewalks, buildings, structures, and open spaces in the neighborhood.

In cooperation with Green Map, the New York City Council on the Environment is active in a city-wide mapping project, seeking to identify and represent all community gardens in all boroughs. The Brooklyn Alliance of Neighborhood Gardens has been working on a mapping project with the Neighborhood Open

Introduction

Space Coalition, hoping ultimately to create a guide to community gardens in New York City. During an annual pageant on the Lower East Side, the so-called Rites of Spring Pageant, a hand-painted map of the area is carried from one garden to the next, and every garden is formally entered into the map with a green marker, proudly attesting to its existence.

This interest in maps is indicative of key elements of urban community garden initiatives. It reflects individual gardening communities' need to affirm their existence and to stake a claim. It also reflects and reinforces a sense of identification, however vague, with other gardens in other areas of the city. The concept of a map, containing individual sites that form part of a whole, provides a starting point for understanding the history of urban community gardens in America in the last three decades of the 20th century. There are as many histories as there are gardens; shared themes and struggles link these histories.

FIELDWORK

When beginning to write up my research results, I happened to read the science section of the *New York Times* and was uncomfortably reminded of the physics experiment involving that unfortunate creature known as Schrödinger's cat.[11] The fate of this hypothetical cat in a box depended on what chain of reactions would take place. Furthermore, in accordance with quantum theory, which holds that a particle does not have a definite position until it is observed, the chain of reactions and consequently the cat were in limbo until the observer opened the box to look inside.

Schrödinger's cat, suspended between life and death, with the observer in the role of unwitting executioner or life giver, haunted me, as I thought about my involvement with community gardens and the entirely correct accusation by an anonymous reviewer about a piece of writing I had submitted for publication. This reviewer pointed out that I was too partisan in my portrayal of the gardens. This partisanship involved two dimensions, one at the level of my immediate personal and emotional experience of individual gardens and garden communities and the other at the broader conceptual level of urban community gardening.

Admittedly, by some standards not all gardens are successful. However, beauty is in the eye of the beholder. I saw beauty in community gardens because I had come to love them. My involvement made me perceive the intent behind the effort, for all that this was perhaps not always immediately visible, in individual gardens and in coalitions extending beyond the garden and the neighborhood. As I researched the subject, I also found the "project," that is, the themes and concepts that tie the many diverse initiatives together, to be one of the most compelling grassroots-based initiatives of the late 20th century. Consequently, I profess partisanship; at the same time I seek to offer as comprehensive a portrayal as possible in order to tell a story of community gardens—vivid, complex urban spaces carved out by people in their own neighborhoods, many of which may no longer exist in a few years—and to provide a better base for an understanding of community gardens' potential for contributing to cities of the future.

As a result of other research on the Lower East Side, I had been aware of the gardens from the late 1980s on.[12] I began active research in 1995. This research involved informal observation and conversations, formal interviews with gardeners, activists, members of the city administration and various greening organizations, and observation of events such as pageants and political activism. Throughout those years I also served as a volunteer in community gardens in different parts of the city. Like community gardeners, I came to the gardens when I had time off from my job. My experience of the gardens and of community

Introduction

gardeners was fragmented, and yet the gardens appeared to represent entities complete in themselves, miniature communities with distinct lives and souls all their own. Living in midtown Manhattan, the experience of working in these gardens had become essential to me, a vital counterweight to my personal sense of anomie and my growing difficulties in negotiating life in the city. My fieldwork and research activities had become inextricably enmeshed in my personal search for dimensions of life that the gardens appeared to offer. At the same time I also had become increasingly aware of the active playing to the observer that represented one of the central strategies of gardeners and activists in their struggle to protect the gardens. Thus, observer and observed were caught in a slow dance—detached observation gave way to a perception that was clouded or illuminated by fascination and affection; I found community gardeners' self-conscious display to coexist with its opposite, and partisan portrayal spilled over into social science analysis.

In 1998, when I had been researching the gardens for several years, I had a conversation with a gardener and activist that helped me to refocus and regain my sense of balance. This conversation took place during preparation for an annual pageant on the Lower East Side in celebration of the gardens. Every year this gardener played the role of "Compost" in the procession. He was working on his costume, aptly consisting of potato sacking covered with kitchen cuttings, dirt, and leaves. I told him about my work and my quandary with regard to participating in the pageant by carrying one of the puppets or helping to push a float throughout the seven-hour procession through the Lower East Side, while at the same time observing the pageant and doing fieldwork. He said bluntly: "Don't do any of the pageant work, don't get drawn in, do your work!" I said I might help in the afternoon, when people get tired. He said: "No, not even then, just do your work." He also came up with an analogy for the element of time, saying that it takes time to get to know an area and that one can begin to say anything or write about it only after a long time. "Too many people just come in and claim some knowledge after a short time." His analogy was gardening, which provides concrete experiences of the growth year, plants, and the life cycle. In part he was kidding and laughing at me, as he was decorating his potato sacking with earth to show that vegetable peels, twigs, and flowers all turn to compost; but he was also serious.

It was odd and comforting to find myself listening to a lecture on anthropological fieldwork and to be thus firmly instructed to do my work. It also helped to reconcile me to the paradox of Schrödinger's cat, reminding me once again that observer and observed are linked inextricably. My writing reflects my own experiences, and the portrayal of urban community garden initiatives is simultaneously a portrayal of my own world and my hopes and fears for that world.

CONCLUSION

New York City's community gardens are contested terrain, subject to erasure overnight, as bulldozers come to reclaim these spaces on behalf of the city administration. Gardens disappear, and the visions associated with them are consigned to memory. In the same vein Knox points out that "the great bulk of the urban fabric symbolizes the impotence of the majority of its inhabitants" (Knox 1982: 293). The history of urban community gardens in New York City illustrates Jacobs' point that mere "readings" of the existing built environment are inadequate if not actively distorting, "ignoring those less powerful visions which did not win out and get built" (Jacobs 1993: 833). Other studies also are concerned with the erasure of the work of ordinary people, leaving "an urban landscape that provides no 'place memories' for women, immigrants, and other minorities" (Low 1996: 391; also see Boyer 1994; Hayden 1995). But, of course, while many community gardens are now gone, the crucial point is that they were "built"—by community gardeners with their own hands. Vacant lots have been transformed into places invested with memories and histories. These gardens existed and many continue to exist, life-filled, complex and full of contradictions like other human communities, and their effects have radiated outward beyond the confines of individual gardens into the neighborhood and occasionally further.

Voltaire's *Candide* tells us: "We must cultivate our garden."

Voltaire for one saw no point in naively railing against the heavens. Towards the end of Candide's journey, Candide and Pangloss encounter a Dervish. Candide complains to him about the evil that he has found in the world. Pangloss joins in and asks what they should do. The Dervish's terse response is: "Shut up."[13] When Pangloss, dense philosopher that he is, continues to remonstrate, the Dervish in frustration simply shuts the door in their faces. Candide's—and Voltaire's—decision to go home and to cultivate his garden is by no means a withdrawal from the world. Instead it can be seen as a directive to engage in one's community, to go to work, and to apply oneself to what is (Voltaire 1970: 126–127).

During one of many confrontations with the garden community in New York City, Mayor Giuliani derided the gardeners for "living in an unrealistic world" (Chivers 2000). This is arguable; definitions of reality and beauty alike are subjective exercises at best. Looking at community gardeners through another lens might reveal not so much a group of people engaged in the pursuit of unrealistic dreams, but rather people squarely confronting critical problems and dilemmas of their time and doing so in their own neighborhoods and cities. In the context of the world being transformed into a predominantly urban environment, community garden initiatives are often perceived as marginal. Yet, the issues addressed by community gardeners are vital and relevant to the future of all cities. Concerned about the Pandora's box of biotechnology, the destruction of the environment, urban sprawl and development, the degradation of individual and community life, food security, and social economic injustices, community gardeners try to enact change in the place where they are with the means at their disposal, from bare hands to cyberspace to increasingly sophisticated organized activism.

A community gardener and activist reminded me of the term used by the Koch administration in conjunction with the so-called Artist Homeownership Program, which was to bring artists into the Lower East Side during the early 1980s. The city planned to allocate $3 million in public funds for rehabilitation of vacant tenements for use by artists; the city was forced to abandon this plan in view of effectively voiced protest on the part of community organizations (Deutsche and Ryan 1984). The city referred to the program as "seeding" the neighborhood, preparing the ground for later redevelopment and gentrification.

However, by that time another set of seeds had already taken hold in the neighborhood. The Green Guerillas, a non-profit greening organization founded in 1973 by Liz Christy and other gardeners of the Liz Christy Garden at the Bowery and Houston Street, made a name for themselves by popularizing the now famous seed grenades—old Christmas tree ornaments or water balloons filled with pelletized time-release fertilizer and wildflower seeds. These seed grenades were then tossed over fences into vacant lots to start a literal grassroots revolution on "acres of opportunity," as they were called by one Green Guerilla member. It is a strategy still used on occasion, more for its powerful symbolic component than for the actual chance of success; seeds do not necessary do well in rubble and debris.

Since the 1970s undoubtedly many of these balloons, actual and conceptual, landed on stony ground. However, just as many

Introduction

have given rise to a new generation of "seeds"—community gardens and related initiatives and coalitions at diverse levels in New York City and in other cities in the United States. The Artist Homeownership Program met with such resistance on the Lower East Side, in part because by the early 1980s the neighborhood already was the setting for community-based housing initiatives, other community initiatives, and community gardens. People had staked claims and seeds had begun to sprout.

NOTES

1. Original words by Ralph Chaplin in support of the Industrial Workers of the World (I.W.W.), known as Wobblies, who were involved in a labor dispute between copper mining companies and their workers in the second decade of the 20th century. The text was adapted for the struggle for community gardens by the artists Lisa Van Guard, a member of the Bronx-based Cherry Tree Association, Inc., an organization working on behalf of community gardens. The Cherry Tree Association is one of a range of organizations under the umbrella of La Casa del Sol, a Bronx-based cultural center that began as a housing and garden cooperative. The Cherry Tree Association together with La Casa de Sol was instrumental in founding the More Gardens! Coalition. Members proceeded to write other songs, which were used at demonstrations, public hearings and meetings and assembled in a collection, More Gardens! Coalition Songbook.
2. Accordingly, between 1993 and 1997, the city lost 113,000 of its most affordable apartments ($500 or less). City-wide rents increased by 18.4 percent (1981–1993 total increase $100, 1993–1996 another $100). At the same time real incomes declined by 2.3 percent between 1993 and 1996, and one third of all renters (40,000 more than in 1993) were below the poverty line. In 1997

the proportion of income New Yorkers use for rent increased from 30.8 percent to 32.8 percent; the poorest tenants pay nearly three-quarters of their income on rent. The city's In Rem policy has created a "permanent underclass" of over 10,000 deteriorating buildings in poor neighborhoods; the number of buildings in tax arrears has hovered at around 14,000 for several years. From 1994 on, New York City put a stop to the use of federal and city funds for building maintenance and renovation. The Department of Housing Preservation and Development's [HPD] anti-abandonment program, which would have transferred many of these buildings to responsible third-party landlords or non-profit groups, has foundered for lack of planning and funding. Congress and the Clinton administration eliminated the proposed increase in the number of Section 8 rent vouchers, so that tenants eligible in theory have to wait for current voucher holders to die; in New York City 236,000 families are on a waiting list for Section 8 assistance. Congress cut funding for poor tenants from $24.9 billion in 1992 to $15.7 billion in 1997 (Thrush 1997).

3. In 1990, the median household income in Community District 3 was $20,007 compared to $30,000 for New York City. The per capita median income in 1990 was $11,309. In 1989, 27.2 percent of the population in Community District 3 received some form of income support, while in New York City 17.2 percent received such support (New York City Department of City Planning 1992). The median household income for Puerto Ricans in New York City was $21,000. In 1990, the poverty rate for Puerto Ricans in New York City was 40.6 percent (U.S. Census 1990). The 1998 Community District Needs report is based on the 1990 Census figures and estimates from the following years; essentially it reiterates previous reports (New York City Department of City Planning 1998).

4. Carmen Pabón chose the name Bello Amanecer Borencano (Beautiful Dawn of Borinquen); she told me that she thought of it

when she came into the garden one early morning and saw the sun rise. Borinquen is the indigenous Taíno name for the island of Puerto Rico.

5. *Casitas* are airy wooden structures for outdoor socializing, which originated in rural Puerto Rico (also see Chapter 4).

6. Also see Daniel Coleman for a discussion of green politics. He calls for "a movement and a society that value the earth, empowering all people to participate actively in the realization of their own well-being and fulfillment. Grassroots democracy is antithetical to the identification of people merely as passive consumers. It entails an active citizenship that transforms the character of the citizen through the process of participation in the public life of the community" (Coleman 1994:116).

7. For instance, some housing activists on the Lower East Side trace the notion of community ownership of land in the development of the concept of community land trusts to the Middle Ages (von Hassell 1996: 26–27).

8. Beltane, an ancient Celtic fertility festival, also known as May Day, May Eve or Walpurgis Night, officially begins at moonrise on May Day Eve (April 30), and marks the beginning of the second half of the year.

9. Also see James Lovelock on the so-called Gaia theory, according to which earth and all beings on it are seen as a single complex organism; "we may find ourselves and all other living things to be parts and partners of a vast being who in her entirety has the power to maintain our planet as a fit and comfortable habitat for life" (Lovelock 1979: 1). Lovelock tried to suggest ways in which human beings might live in harmony with Gaia. Milton draws attention to the ambiguity in the Gaia concept with regard to the location of power. Gaia as a living organism is vulnerable, yet at the same time Lovelock appears to suggest that Gaia is able to survive without human input. "[The Gaia theory's] implications are such that environmentalists have felt unable or unwilling to ignore it, but suggest neither that Gaia is totally in

control of her own destiny, nor that her future is fully in our hands" (Milton 1996: 133). However, the interesting element is not so much the ambiguity about the locus of power, but rather the fact that responsibility for keeping the planet in good order as it were is shared by all human beings.

10. Bronislaw Malinowski (1884–1942), British social anthropologist, and Ludwig Wittgenstein (1889–1951), Austrian philosopher.

11. The Austrian theoretical physicist Erwin Schrödinger (1887–1961), known for his work in quantum physics, had devised a thought experiment, involving a cat in a box and a chain of possible reactions. These reactions are initiated by particles of light or photons that are fired at a half-silvered mirror; there is a 50–50 chance that the mirror reflects the particles or lets them pass through. If a particle passes through the mirror, it strikes a photoelectric detector acting as a tripping device and breaking a vial of poison, thus killing the cat. If the mirror reflects the particle, the cat lives. However, according to quantum physics, when in pure isolation, sealed off from the influence of their surroundings, particles remain in a state of what is known as quantum superposition, a suspension between various states. The act of observation—the opening of the box—forces the particle to choose one state or another. Taking Schrödinger's thought experiment to its logical conclusion, the photon in the box "would linger in a superposition of the two possible paths it could take, leaving the cat in the uncomfortable position of being simultaneously dead and alive" (Johnson 2000).

12. See von Hassell 1996.

13. "Mais, mon révérend père, dit Candide, il y a horriblement du mal sur la terre.—Qu'importe, dit le dervishe, qu'il y ait du mal ou du bien? Quand Sa Hautesse envoie un vaisseau en Égypte, s'embarasse-t-elle si les souris qui sont dans le vaisseau sont à leur aise ou non?—Que faut-il donc faire? demande Pangloss.—Te taire, dit le dervishe" (Voltaire 1970: 126).

History of Urban Community Gardening

"We cleared out six feet of debris. There were needles, rats, a refrigerator, empty bottles, glass, you name it."[1]

INTRODUCTION

Community gardeners tell the history of their gardens in vivid narratives.

They talk of enormous hardship and struggle in frequently inclement conditions, with the threat of eviction from the site a constant presence and a reminder of the political context. Sitting under a lovingly constructed arbor or in front of a goldfish pond or standing between plots filled with tomatoes and zucchini and marigolds, gardeners talk of the immensity of the task of clearing debris-filled abandoned lots, the effort of carrying buckets of water into a garden for first scraggly plantings, and the search for a barrel to hold rainwater, plywood to build a tool shed, or discarded dock pilings to line a walkway. Photographs are pulled out to show the transformation. The shards and fragments of past urban existences retrieved from mountains of debris lend color to these narratives and are transformed into mosaics of the past, just as glass and pottery fragments reappear glued to lamp post bases at street corners on the Lower East Side. Gardeners' narratives are shaped and defined by the ongoing struggle over the gardens. At the same time gardeners search for connections to the past. They look for signs of previous urban existences, which they have appropriated as part of their own personal history. Digging for debris, removing syringes, carrying out polluted soil, and digging for roots become metaphors for digging for one's own past and thereby claiming the future. Community gardeners' historical consciousness and their visions for the future turn the narratives into a rallying cry on behalf of the gardens.

On a sunny mild February morning in 1998, a group of college students toured community gardens on the Lower East Side in New York City. Bemused and puzzled, they walked past plywood barriers erected along the street fronts of recently bulldozed gardens, staring at posters of protest about the ravaging of community spaces. Some gardens were open, but it was a weekday, and many gardens were empty of life, awaiting their resurrection. The students peered through wire fences at gardens, filled with remnants from another season, weeds overflowing out of wood-encased plots, miscellaneous sculptures constructed out of the detritus of urban life, hints of man-made ponds and waterfalls, and vivid murals that stood out starkly in the pale winter sun.

The students asked why the gardens were so unkempt. They asked why the gardens were not more organized and cleaner looking. They saw only the desolation of an urban midwinter spring in a poor neighborhood and could not envision the coming season. Their experiences did not include an understanding of the dead of winter as a prelude to growth. Their imagination did not extend to tires as planters or salvaged pink flamingos perched amid dried tomato vines equally valid as carefully clipped and pruned suburban privet hedges.

The last stop of the walking tour, when the sense of disassociation and cultural distance had stretched to the breaking point, was a community garden on Avenue B and 6th Street. This is one of the oldest gardens on the Lower East Side. It boasts a thriving program of community activities. It contains individual member plots alongside common areas, a children's area, and a stage. In the late summer laden fruit trees lean over the fence, and a riotous combination of flowers and vegetables blurs the borders between individual plots and spikes the air with scents of basil and roses. The students assembled on the gravel area in front of the stage with its mural of plants and animals as a backdrop and listened to a garden member describe the garden, its current organizational structure, its activities, and some of its history.

Like most community gardens in New York City, this garden at one time had been a debris-filled vacant lot between tenement buildings. In the mid-1970s it was claimed by residents in the surrounding buildings. In a backbreaking and slow process they cleared the land and began to plant it. The garden member went on to describe a project that the gardeners had recently started. "We are planning to dig up parts of the garden as an archaeological project. We know that some portions always were open backyards. That is where we plan to dig." For a brief while, students were captured and interested, able to enter into this project of hope, resilience, and imagination in the face of urban alienation.

A fascination with the long-term history of community garden sites is apparent in many narratives of community gardeners. In some instances these narratives are formalized and placed on record in the form of brochures describing individual gardens. For instance, the Liz Christy Garden on the corner of Houston Street and the Bowery makes a brochure available to visitors, in which the garden's history is described: "During the 17th century our site was then the corner of Bouwerie and North Street, the southern tip of a large farm owned by Peter Stuyvesant, the last Dutch Governor of New Amsterdam. In the centuries following, this bouwerie (which is Dutch for farm) changed radically. It was in complete decline in the 1970s when many buildings were abandoned and torn down." The brochure goes on to describe the founding members' early struggle to gain control of the site; in 1974, the Department of Housing Preservation and Development (HPD) agreed to lease it to the gardeners for $1 a month. They started with sixty raised beds planted with vegetables. Twenty years later the garden had turned into an exquisite horticultural jewel. Unlike many other gardens it has succeeded in attaining a modicum of protection under the umbrella of the Cooper Square Committee, the local development group, which in 1990 pledged to preserve the garden.[2] The garden has become a source of inspiration and education for many other garden projects in New York City.

In different ways gardeners again and again consciously situate their gardens and consequently their own work in them within the context of the long-term history of the urban environment. The "creation myths" of community gardens, recounted with enthusiasm by garden members, are narratives of struggle inspired by the goal of salvaging and reclaiming urban spaces. Notions of the need to retrieve something valuable that was lost and buried are joined to the perception of a long-time destruction of the environment, infesting the soil and the air. Perception of destruction in the immediate present is acute, as gardeners watch gardens that they have worked on for decades being erased by bulldozers in a matter of minutes. Many gardens have passed out of history, known now only to those who tended them, never recorded in any documents or city maps other than as vacant lots. Gardeners' narratives reflect a sense of fragility and impermanence, both in terms of political experience and in terms of a philosophy of living that finds concrete expression in the cycle of death and rebirth of plants. Together they are transformed into a vision for a life in cities of the future, which embraces urban existence rather than seeking to escape from it, all the while rejecting certain components of the present.

An article in *City Limits* echoed this sense of fragility (McGowan 1998). It described the precarious foundations of many buildings on the Lower East Side. The Lower East Side is situated on land that used to be predominantly swamp land, with a lot of underground streams crisscrossing the area. In the 17th century, at Canal Street "tidal marshes and ponds stretched from river to river and were covered with sea-water at high tide" (King 1893: 10). Tenements built at the end of the 19th century and in the early 20th century were built on what is literally shifting ground or filled-in swamp land. Many of these buildings shore each other up, and any major excavation and construction work near them may lead to their collapse and the collapse of other buildings (McGowan 1998).

Gardeners on the Lower East Side have seen buildings collapse and have witnessed the transformation from a densely built-up tenement area into an area filled with burned-out buildings and vacant lots. They have witnessed gardens being created within the space of a season in a vacant lot, and they have witnessed thriving gardens being bulldozed and fenced in with plywood in the space of a morning. Time and change and the effects of politics and economics are concretely visible in the neighborhood on a daily basis. Community gardeners repeatedly point out how the experience of working in and for their community gardens has sharpened their historical consciousness and made them more interested in the history of the contested sites and by extension the history of their communities.

In the spring of 1998 an exhibit on community gardens was housed in the lobby of a building on Times Square. The exhibit focused almost entirely on the Lower East Side. Community gardeners had contributed a diversity of representations of their gardens. In one exhibit gentle watercolors of a garden were contrasted with a series of black and white photographs of vacant lots, crumbling pavement areas, stark fences, and plywood walls, with words slashed across these images: "Destroyed," "Burnt," "Empty," "Scored," "Vacant." These words evoke the language of the drug wars and of urban desolation. Some exhibits were decorated with newspaper articles that pointed to the ongoing destruction of community gardens; for instance, an article headline read: "Gardeners' harvest may be their last." Others showed children engaging in various activities such as pumpkin carving and performing plays. A particularly memorable display was a giant fragrant wall painting of a bucket excavator, decorated with dried flowers and smelling like a bowl of potpourri; in front of the living wall there was a bucket of debris. In another exhibit a colorful patchwork quilt was contrasted with photos of the 1997 destruction of the Chico Mendez Mural Garden on 11th Street on the Lower East Side. One garden had produced an elaborate collage of the history of the garden, situated in a panorama of New York City's history from 1639 to 2000.

Another narrative of the history of community gardens is offered by the Theater for the New City, a professional theater located on the Lower East Side. In 1999, the theater produced and performed an open-air musical depicting the history of and struggle over community gardens in New York City. The musical *Survivors*, written by Crystal Field, a long-time resident of the Lower East Side, was performed in all boroughs in the late summer of 1999. In a colorful mix of slapdash theater, salsa, hip-hop, and improvisation, the musical presented a history of community gardens that emphasized their creation at the hands of local residents with little or no help from the authorities. Local residents were shown struggling with poverty, inadequate and deteriorating housing conditions, dangerous settings for children in streets and debris-filled lots, and police oppression, while retaining their creativity and humanity. The musical described local people taking over gardens and developing a sense of community in and around these gardens. While its principal focus in terms of historical portrayal was on the Lower East Side, the musical identified with community gardens all over the city. Developers were outsiders without any comprehension of the destruction they were trying to wreak. City officials were depicted as initially caught up in self-deception in their belief that they were doing a generous deed by providing community gardens with temporary leases, before becoming more culpable by consciously joining with the exploitative and ruthless developers. The musical echoed narratives of individual gardeners in its representation of community gardeners as a unified front with a set of shared values and ideals. At the same time it emphasized the diversity of urban community gardeners as a source of strength. The musical portrayed community gardens as central elements in an entire way of life, contributing to education, social life, entertainment, and community activism.

The history of community gardens is constructed through the medium of storytelling in theater, art, and personal narratives. It appears on garden leaflets and bulletin boards, and it is told and retold in annual pageants on the Lower East Side. As such it is a living component of the struggle, a justification and plea for the continued existence of these gardens.

A HISTORY OF COMMUNITY GARDENING

The concept of community gardening as it is currently understood is fundamentally different from any notions of urban gardening prior to the 1970s. Yet some of the conceptual roots of community gardens of the present day reach back to the 19th century and to earlier times. A historical overview of urban community gardening necessitates a consideration of definitions. One could consider community gardens as a form of "urban agriculture," an umbrella term for referring to productive cultivation within city limits. One also could consider them a form of community-based open space management.

"Community gardens are neighborhood open spaces managed by and for members of the community" (American Community Gardening Association n.d.).

The Struggle for Eden

A definition of urban community gardens as a form of urban agriculture is narrow; community gardens involve many other dimensions, while there are forms of urban agriculture that are not found in community gardens. The American Community Gardening Association definition is too broad; many open space initiatives would logically fit that definition, while people involved in them would not describe them as community gardens.

For instance, in the mid-1980s in the middle-class community of Laurelton, Queens, a group of concerned residents started a hugely successful initiative to take care of neglected open spaces in their neighborhood; it has inspired adjoining neighborhoods to try to follow suit. Reflecting the demographics of the neighborhood, founding members and the current membership of 132 families of the Garden Club of Laurelton are predominantly African American, while also including several other population groups. The goal is beautification of the neighborhood, for instance by planting the medians or so-called malls and tree pits along the neighborhood streets and boulevards, adopting highways, and taking care of neglected green strips along public facilities such as the Long Island Railroad parking lot. The Garden Club of Laurelton has engaged in extensive fund raising; the Borough of Queens, various state and city agencies, and the Trust for Public Land, among others, have been supportive. Some motives that inspire these urban gardeners are the same as those that inspire community gardeners on the Lower East Side—taking care of vacant land, so that it does not turn into a dump or a staging area for crime and violence, creating beauty in one's neighborhood, and taking control of and assuming responsibility for what is around one, because there is no other place to go. Laurelton residents refer to the importance of the process of creating a garden and by extension a community. They perceive this process as ongoing and as important as if not more important than a finished product. The motto that appears on the newsletter of the Garden Club of Laurelton, "Working for a Better Community and a Happier Planet," reflects sentiments that many community gardeners would share.

However, despite the parallels and shared themes with initiatives such as the Garden Club of Laurelton, a community garden on the Lower East Side is different. The key is the term "community." Each community garden represents a community, within which private and public lives meet—reflected in the existence of individual member plots next to common or shared areas within gardens, in the use of the gardens for family and community activities and often for growing and also consuming food. The principal goal is not so much the creation of a beautiful area that one can enjoy while walking or driving alongside; instead, community gardens represent places within which life occurs.

In a consideration of the historical background of late-20th-century urban community gardens, urban agriculture and community-based open space management are both relevant dimensions. The concept of community gardening as urban agriculture goes back to the very beginning of cities and to the provisioning of cities. Certainly, with the onset of specialization and the development of an administrative class and an incipient bureaucracy alongside with class stratification, increasing portions of the population became dependent on the labor of others to ensure their food supply. Some of this food was brought to cities from the surrounding countryside; some of this food was produced within the city limits. The history of ancient civilizations abounds with examples of urban agricultural systems to feed city residents (Mougeot 1994; Smit et al. 1996). As examples one might consider China, India, or Peru. Aztec, Mayan, and Incan cities were self-reliant in perishable fruits and vegetables. In Tenochtitlan, Spanish invaders in the 15th century encountered the so-called *chinampas*, a form of aqua-terra farming, with intricate and sophisticated methods of soil improvement, involving among others the recycling of city wastewater for irrigation.

Provisioning of cities has historically represented a social and political problem for city administrations and rulers. A description of urban life and the state in the early modern era in Edo (later Tokyo) and Paris indicates the degree to which food supply and provisioning was defined by political expediency (McClain et al. 1994). Edo and Paris administrations were frequently caught unprepared to meet the needs of a rapidly growing population; rice riots and bread riots forced administrations to address the issue. However, once a crisis had passed, food had been distributed to provide relief, and regular food supplies started to flow back into the city, administrations returned to acting in accordance with the interests of a ruling class or a merchant class, as the case may be, involved in and economically benefitting from provisioning the urban center. By the same token, support by various city administrations of community gardening in any form has always been subject to economic and political expediency.

In several cities in Europe some form of urban agriculture survived from earliest times into the 19th century or was reintroduced at some point in time. Thus, provisioning of cities was not based solely on the exploitation of agricultural surplus from the countryside, but also on food produced within the city environs. Cities in Germany in the 17th century relied on farming inside and outside city walls for their food supply (Saalman 1968). In 18th-century England the enclosures and the attendant loss of means of survival available to an increasingly impoverished rural population pushed people into the cities in search of labor and food. At that time in a combination of philanthropic leanings, notions of encouraging "self-help" and strategic attempts to control and appease the landless poor in order to stave off violence and rebellion, patches of land and open spaces were lent or made available to the urban poor for food cultivation. These plots were cultivated like kitchen gardens. In the early 19th century, following the example of the British example, Germany along with other European countries established so-called *Armengärten* or gardens for the poor on land within the immediate vicinity of cities (Meyer-Renschhausen and Holl eds. 2000: 162). However, the land used for such food cultivation always remained vulnerable and subject to sale, as cities grew and space became increasingly valuable real estate (Warner 1987).

Nineteenth-century Paris boasted an urban agro-ecosystem, the Marais, a form of highly intensive urban farming, which continued until World War I. It involved the use of glass-covered frames and bell-shaped glass cloches as protection during severe weather conditions. Stable manure produced by horses that provided the power for the city's transport system was recycled as fertilizer for the production of high-value, year-round salad and vegetable crops, with three to six harvests a year (Smit et al. 1996: 28–32).

In the mid-19th century the *Schrebergärten* movement in Germany and Austria resulted in the creation of allotment gardens that in principle were modeled on the earlier "Armengärten" or "gardens for the poor." However, in contrast to previous urban agriculture efforts, the Schrebergärten movement emphasized another conceptual element, the notion of the "healthfulness" of gardening allied with notions of aesthetic and moral improvement. Its originator was Dr. Daniel Gottlieb Moritz Schreber, a doctor from Leipzig. For Schreber the activity of gardening and the associated physical exercise represented one of the routes toward creating healthy minds and bodies and by implication a healthier society, hence strengthening the German people and enabling them to gain ascendancy over other nations. This nationalistic ideal was taken to its extreme by Nazi ideology; it is difficult in retrospect to consider the Schrebergärten movement in Germany of the present day as something separate and distinct from this ideology.

It is important to acknowledge this set of ideological strains underlying "back to nature" notions in community gardening. At the same time, it is equally important to refrain from reducing all these strains to their later reincarnation as part of an ultra-nationalist and racialist agenda. Rather, one must recognize the equally powerful and compelling elements of communitarian thought and notions of sustainable communities, allied to a fundamental critique of society, which have been inspiring community gardening initiatives in the latter half of the 20th century.

The first garden based on the ideas of Schreber started as a playground on an open meadow in Leipzig. By 1870 there were over 100 garden plots on the site, worked on by children and their parents. There already was an organizational charter, a chairman, and a central committee (Rotenberg 1993: 23–24). The Schrebergärten movement spread throughout Germany and Northern Europe as well as to Austria at the turn of the century. The focus was on the working class, providing members of the working class with an opportunity to cultivate gardens, generally marginal pieces of land, without the burden of ownership.

Rotenberg demonstrates how notions of environmental degradation and healthfulness of spaces are linked to urban residents' shifting perceptions of city life. Such concepts of the need for healthful environments first began to dominate the language of urban residents in the 19th century. The Schrebergärten movement is an expression of this. Gardening was perceived as beneficial to gardeners, improving their physical and psychological well-being while living in urban environments (Rotenberg 1993).

"Environmental degradation certainly ranks among the more obvious outcomes of the process of urbanization. The information people share with each other for recognizing and evaluating the urban environment is locally constituted" (Rotenberg 1993: 17).

History of Urban Community Gardening

Rotenberg points out that this has been an issue of concern since cities were first constructed; he refers to a first-century Roman architect, Marcus Vitruvius Pollio. Pollio called for the need to plan and construct cities that were wholesome, airy, and dry. Hence, the 19th century "back to nature" movement was hardly a new concept. These themes also resonate in the environmental movement of the 1960s onward, taken up by community garden activists in the 1970s. The difference in the community garden movement lies in the element of participation and initiative on the part of gardeners and their conceptual linkage of this theme with themes of urban agriculture and the social and economic reorganization of urban life.

The Schrebergärten movement and its later incarnations reflect a shift in the conceptualization of the activity of gardening. Initially conceived as an activity suitable and beneficial for members of the working class, providing access to subsistence farming and kitchen garden produce, the emphasis shifted to notions of beautification, both of the soul and its environment, combined with healthfulness as bulwarks in a stressful industrial city. Gardening for food production was no longer the sole or principal goal. Meanwhile, the current fee structure determined in accordance with German allotment garden law distinguishes between productive and non-productive uses. Gardeners lease individual plots in allotment garden "colonies" from the city of Berlin, and the amount of their annual payment depends on whether they are growing vegetables or flowers. There is a higher fee attached to cultivation of flowers and other decorative plants. The distinction between "decorative gardens" and "use gardens" (*Ziergärten* versus *Nutzgärten*) in urban environs reflects the distinction in rural areas, where land in agricultural production is subject to a lower tax rate.

In urban garden initiatives in the United States over the last decades of the 20th century, the emphasis has shifted to a renewed concern with food production, paralleled by a growing concern with organic food production and the perceived need to reinject the experience of food production into daily lives. This is supported by nationwide associations that are seeking to develop sustainable communities and to establish food security in urban areas. In the current community garden movement, utilitarian concerns and aesthetic concerns are most closely allied in the environmental movement, where food production, in particular organic food production, and greening or beautification of the environment are part and parcel of the same effort. Together, such concerns also lend impetus to initiatives of social reconstruction of neighborhoods.

Whether one is talking about urban agriculture in ancient times or in Europe in the 19th century, the burgeoning urban agriculture movement in the developing world, or the community garden movement in the United States in the last three decades of the 20th century, the history of different forms of urban agriculture must be considered in the context of the history of urbanization, land scarcity, and the politics of space. Another component is the extremely rapid transformation of the relationship between production and cities over the last two centuries. This component has proven to be a powerful emotionally galvanizing factor in the present-day community gardening movement. Societies in the Western Hemisphere have been transformed from societies where food production was an essential component of the psychological base of existence to societies in which a majority of the population is largely alienated from any processes associated with food production and where production is essentially something that happens elsewhere, even in other countries. The community gardening movement meanwhile is increasingly allied with diverse organizations involved in restructuring food production and food supply in urban areas in the United States and elsewhere. The language employed in efforts to promote and protect community gardens from encroaching city administrations and development interests reflects efforts to emphasize relevance in terms of notions of concrete, even marketable "productiveness" such as food production and tangible benefits to the environment, along with unquantifiable social, cultural, and aesthetic benefits.

HISTORY OF COMMUNITY GARDENS IN AMERICA

In a protest effort to protect a garden on the Lower East Side in New York City from being bulldozed, an interesting creature made an appearance in the late fall of 1999. In the Jardín de Esperanza on 7th Street between Avenue B and C, the gardeners created a giant steel and canvas sculpture of a *coqui*, a Puerto Rican tree frog, with clear domes for its eyes peeking over the fence. The sculpture housed a sleeping platform, and garden members and other supporters kept nightly vigils on top of the platform in order to be on site in the event of the arrival of bulldozers. Supporters visited the garden to bring food and blankets and take turns at keeping watch. As the coqui is a Puerto Rican national symbol and an indicator species, it was particularly appropriate as a watchdog for the garden, the proverbial canary in the mine.

By the same token community gardens have been a kind of canary indicating economic and political fluctuations in the country. Federal, state, and municipal support for community gardens in America has waxed and waned over the past century, driven by shifts in real estate markets, labor markets, immigration, as well as economic depressions and wars. Policy shifts as much as actions by gardeners have been sustained by ideologies and counter ideologies that replicate other social and political struggles in the country. Major ideological strains include paternalism and notions of moral betterment and improvement, education, and beautification as well as notions of returning back to nature, environmental struggles, efforts to overcome individual alienation in urban environments, and a critique of and resistance to capitalist society.

Economic rationale has been the predominant factor in determining administrative policies regarding community gardens and urban open space planning. Open space has been turned into a commodity that can be traded just as air rights over buildings in New York City and pollution credits. For instance, Fox draws attention to the growing number of developers that trade favors for the creation of open space, a development paralleled by a simultaneous shrinkage of city government funding for open space planning efforts and an increasing trend toward privatization in the management of urban open spaces (Fox 1990). The Central Park Conservancy in New York City is an example for such a private effort. This in turn is paralleled by neglect by local administrations of low-income neighborhoods, in particular, with regard to open space planning and parks management in such areas, and increasing grassroots activism.

From the mid-19th century on, municipal governments were interested in open space as an organizing element in new real estate development (Fox 1990: 6). He points to the greenbelt towns and garden cities as cases in point, as well as to more recent efforts to reclaim waterfronts or redevelop industrial wastelands. Fox in his report seeks to put a dollar value on the relationship between open space and real estate. While clear-cut figures may be hard to establish, there is little doubt that developers and urban planners have long been aware of the relationship. Studies have illustrated the linkage between urban property values and the relative proximity to open space, parks, and gardens (Malakoff 1995). In response to the bulldozing of a garden on the Lower East Side, Gretchen

History of Urban Community Gardening

Dykstra, former president of the Times Square Business Improvement District, wrote to the *New York Times*: "Green spaces make cities livable, and housing and open space should not be seen as competitive. Enhanced public spaces increase the economic stability and property values of a neighborhood" (Dykstra 2000). A study written under the auspices of the Trust for Public Land further demonstrates the long-term economic benefits to society of land conservation, open space planning, and locally based open space initiatives such as community gardens (Lerner and Poole 1999). According to this study, community gardens as well as urban parks and recreational open space stimulate commercial growth and promote inner-city revitalization. However, very few cities in the United States can boast a comprehensive approach to urban development and open space planning.

Bassett identified seven distinct periods, in some instances overlapping, in the history of urban gardening in the United States (Bassett 1979). He describes the Potato Patch Gardens (1894–1917), School Gardens (1900–1920), Garden City Plots (1905–1920), Liberty Gardens (1917–1920), Relief Gardens (1930–1939), Victory Gardens (1941–1945), and Community Gardens (1970–present). Bassett maintains that the primary function of urban community gardening in America has been to act as a buffering mechanism, a "supportive institution" that has helped people to cope during periods of social and economic stress (Bassett 1979: 2).

"In short, community gardening has successfully served as a supportive institution during seven critical periods by its uncanny replication of an ideal society, based on the cultivation of small holdings and rooted in the tradition of Jeffersonian democracy—notwithstanding the evolution of a very different social and economic system, and the contradiction that the myth of the garden is acted out on someone else's land" (Bassett 1979: 181–182).

The various periods identified by Bassett are characterized by a range of themes, practical and ideological in content, replicated over and over again in differing degrees of intensity. Until the 1970s—the beginning of the last period named by Bassett, which was characterized by a major shift in the ideological thrust of governmental paternalism—federal and local governments were instrumental in initiating community gardening. A principal purpose of such community gardening was to provide poor relief. During the early years of the Depression, it was the only form of poor relief that some local and state agencies were able to provide—in the form of vegetables and fruits produced (Bassett 1979: 76). Community gardening was also expected to enhance food supply with homegrown and fresh produce. At the same time community gardening was associated with notions of moral improvement. It was to provide moral uplift and encourage self-reliance and hard work, while helping to dispel social tensions and curb disorder. Another theme was the notion of beatification and enhancement of the neighborhood. In addition, during the two world wars community gardening was actively encouraged and indeed marketed as a way to make a direct contribution to the war effort.

The period of Potato Patch Gardens (1894–1917) echoes themes about the healthfulness of gardening circulating in Europe at that time. Cities were increasingly perceived as unhealthy; the term "lung blocks" was coined at that time. In Detroit in 1894 Mayor Hazen S. Pingtree envisioned a poor-relief scheme that involved vacant lot cultivation, in which 975 families were encouraged to cultivate about 455 acres of city-owned and privately donated land. These families grew potatoes, beans, and turnips. In one year they reaped $27,792 worth of produce, while there had been an investment of

$5,000 in site preparation, supervision, seeds, and tools.

Other cities such as Omaha, Baltimore, Chicago, Philadelphia, and New York followed suit. The ideological underpinning was the belief that traditional values of self-reliance and independence needed to be fostered; allotment gardening would not only help to tide poor people over bad periods, but would also help them to transcend the degradation and waste of human energy associated with made-work relief. The dignity and freedom attained from tilling the land was mingled with the Jeffersonian agrarian ideal, for all that the social economic parameters were rather different. The work was thought to be healthful in both physical and moral terms, even transforming confirmed drunkards into sober and industrious citizens (see Bassett 1979: 10–15). Warner pointed out that this embrace of the Potato Patch Garden scheme was paradoxical, in that both city officials and private charity officers accepted that the American city was first and foremost a real estate proposition based on rents and sales, a notion not easily reconcilable with donating land for kitchen garden cultivation, whatever the supposed qualitative and quantitative benefits (Warner 1987).

Other garden schemes at the time were similarly paternalistic. For instance, in 1897 the National Cash Register Company in Dayton, Ohio supported a garden on company grounds for the express purpose of fostering the physical, mental, and moral development of sons of employees. In a holistic vision of the "company as home," the garden was part of a range of offerings including a library, education, social activities, and hygiene instruction. Children were to be taught to work and to be better workers by being taught to know and respect nature (Bassett 1979: 24).

In the School Gardens of the early 20th century, the emphasis was on the notion of "cultivating children" and the values of self-reliance, patience, and perseverance. Children were to be taught to "acknowledge a systematic operation and its components—individual responsibility, cooperation, interchangeability, a steady, uninterrupted flow of movement and production, efficiency and progress" (Bassett 1979: 35).

Throughout this period a reigning theme was beautification, the elimination of "civic blemishes," and the notion that garden design affected moral character, while a "gardenesque style" was thought to enhance physiological well-being and contentment. Beauty was to inspire love for higher ideals (Bassett 1979: 42). This was especially pronounced in the Garden City Plots in the first two decades of the 20th century.

The Liberty Gardens during World War I are remarkable for having resulted from a successful large-scale campaign involving the use of media, cartoons, and posters in order to increase the food supply available for domestic consumption and to free American farm supplies for shipment overseas to allied countries. The aim was to "arouse the patriots of America" to work every available bit of land. In 1917 the War Garden Commission reported that 3,500,000 war gardens produced $350,000,000 worth of produce; in 1918, 5,285,000 gardens produced as much as $525,000,000 worth of produce. Approximately 5 percent of the American population were engaged in war gardening and produced approximately 8 percent of the nation's gross value in agricultural commodities (Bassett 1979: 63–70). The campaign was based on skillful and compelling analogies of gardens as trenches or munitions plants, produce as "bread bullets," and gardeners as a "mighty army" and as "soldiers of the soil" (Bassett 1979: 54–55).

The Relief Gardens (1930–1939) emerged in the context of the Depression. "Like a play within a play, the development of relief gardening in some ways paralleled the expansion and contraction of assistance programs between 1930 and 1939"

(Bassett 1979: 72). Traditionally public welfare had been a local responsibility and not a federal one. Local and state governments were overwhelmed by the need for food, shelter, and clothing and had little other than archaic relief plans at their immediate disposal to deal with the crisis. In 1932 at least 23 states embarked on garden programs as a way to provide relief. The sudden popularity of this mode of assistance was due to the fact that its cost was minimal, land was available, the popularity of the program during the war years was still remembered, food would be produced, and values and the work ethic would be restored. It was infinitely attractive in economic and ideological terms. In the early years of the Depression, relief gardens were the only form of relief that some local and state agencies could afford (Bassett 1979: 76).

During the Depression years corporate-style strategies of paternalistic management of labor are reflected in "industrial plan" gardens on large tracts of land as opposed to other types of gardens involving more individualized organizational structures. In various work relief projects during the 1930s, laid-off workers were trucked or bused to land tracts outside cities in order to cultivate that land in what was termed as "industrial garden operations." "It was believed that men who were more accustomed to performing the same task in the company of others rather than in overseeing the process of production from beginning to end would be more productive in an industrial garden operation than under the allotment plan" (Bassett 1979: 89). These gardens were characterized by notably regimented routines, an imposed discipline of piecework, and assembly-line production.

Until 1935, the Federal Emergency Relief Administration (FERA) provided money for relief programs. FERA had appropriated as much as $500 million for all states, and was reimbursing cities for 40 percent of all their expenditures (Bassett 1979: 95). However, after FERA's demise in 1935, there was a fundamental shift in relief programs, and relief funds declined.

The Struggle for Eden

After 1937, relief gardens were mostly abandoned. The Works Project Administration abandoned the relief program and instead initiated a food stamps program for surplus farm products. The Federal Surplus Relief Corporation began to distribute agricultural surplus, in part helping to mollify farmers, who had been considering urban gardeners as the root of all evil, in particular as the reason for overproduction. Thus, many municipal administrations decided to abandon gardening programs, since food was coming in free from the government (Bassett 1979: 78, 99–101).

The Victory Gardens during World War II, just like the Liberty Gardens in World War I, resulted from a national campaign to deal with a looming national food crisis. In 1941, Franklin Delano Roosevelt initiated a conference to address the problem, the "National Nutrition Conference of Defense," for strategy planning in a "civil war against the greatest domestic enemy, malnutrition" (Bassett 1979: 109). Half of the country's commercially canned vegetables and many other foodstuffs were shipped overseas. The Victory Garden propaganda once again skillfully linked compelling symbols of warfare with gardening. Slogans such as "Vegetables for Vitality, for Victory," "Food for Freedom," and "Food is no less a weapon than tanks, guns and planes" were allied with an "orchestrated effort that included the U.S. Department of Agriculture (USDA) and its extension agents, horticultural groups, business, landowners, cities, Civilian Defense Volunteers, school teachers, [and] the media" (Bassett 1979: 143). At the peak of production in 1944, 20 million Victory Gardens, which included community gardens, backyards, city parks, and even town commons, yielded 42 percent of the fresh vegetables in the United States (Goodman 2000).

The most interesting element that emerged during this period of gardening is the growing conceptualization of gardening as part of an entire way of life, an activity to be combined with regular work. Employers and various federal and municipal supporting agencies and neighborhood committees began to consider the need to provide individuals with access to land near their work sites, with support to complete rough labor such as plowing and harrowing, and with other forms of support. Gardening was increasingly perceived as something to be incorporated into daily life. This period saw the first beginnings of a qualitative change from gardening managed from above, imposed by federal or local agencies as a form of relief or for the beautification of neighborhoods, to gardening as an activity that involved community input. This period also saw a rise in the number of women involved in garden work. Women had been taking over jobs in industry and agriculture vacated by men serving overseas. Consequently, in light of the fact that their role in the domestic realm continued as before, they were suffering from more time constraints than men, who had previously been involved in urban gardening projects. At this time, garden work became increasingly characterized by cooperation at the level of the community (Bassett 1979: 138–142). There were the beginnings of on-site communication and information exchange and cooperation, as people were working in gardens after work and on weekends. This qualitative shift in conjunction with a shift in gender roles and distribution of labor, is echoed by the dynamics of grassroots activism and community gardening from the 1970s onward, in which women have played a pivotal role.

A few Victory Gardens have survived into the present, most notably the Fenway Gardens in Boston, the Dowling School Garden in Minneapolis, the Cornell Oasis in Chicago, the Warren/St. Mark's Garden in New York City, and several gardens in Cleveland. However, most gardens were abandoned. From the end of World War II into the late 1960s, community garden programs and open space planning in cities were placed on the back burner of administrations' concerns.

The 1960s and 1970s have provided much of the ideological impetus behind the community garden movement in the latter part of the 20th century. The civil rights movement spawned a generation of pioneer community organizers. From civil rights the focus turned to poverty, housing, labor, and the environment. The multi-level approach to community revitalization that emerged in the 1980s can be traced back to these years. At the grassroots level the growing awareness of a threatened environment gave rise to a multitude of efforts ranging from organic gardening to "back to nature" initiatives. These efforts were informed by idealized concepts of "Mother Earth," a perception of human beings as destructive, as proverbial snakes in paradise, and a notion of a biotic community in which human beings had to relearn to find their proper place. Simultaneously the shift from an industrial age to a service industry was becoming more apparent; it was reflected in changing labor markets and increasing disenfranchisement of large portions of the population. This was conjoined to a growing realization of the effects of a global market economy and population shifts. In many communities across the United States these processes resulted in various kinds of retrenchment and siege mentalities at the local level from utopian communities to gated communities. At the level of community activism, it was reflected in a return to the micro context; locally based efforts presented themselves as a form of concrete resistance and action in the face of an overwhelming, alienating, and opaque environment in both real and symbolic terms.

These years were also marked by a renaissance of city planning and urban development that tried to take the environment into consideration. Some reports and writings from the 1960s leave one with a bemused impression of

History of Urban Community Gardening

tremendous optimism and naivety, in the face of the enormity and complexity of the current struggles over open space in urban areas. Mumford with great assurance called for landscape design planning to address regions in their entirety (see Seymour 1969). Mumford envisioned the creation of "balanced communities" as opposed to bedroom cities or "residential dormitories." In Mumford's cities of the future, "ribbons of green must run through every quarter, forming a continuous web of garden and mall, widening at the edge of the city into protective greenbelts, so that landscape and garden will become an integral part of urban no less than rural life, both for weekday and holiday uses" (Seymour 1969: 19).

In 1967 Boulder became the first American city to set aside money for the purchase, management, and care of open space. Boulder incorporated farm land outside the city into its open space planning. The policy was founded on the recognition that property values were affected by their relative proximity to open space and on the increasing compelling need to protect the mountain backdrop that made Boulder attractive to begin with (Fox 1990).

The city of Philadelphia has been called the grande dame of urban community gardens. Philadelphia has benefitted from the concerted efforts of the Pennsylvania Horticultural Society, which inaugurated a comprehensive community gardening program for Philadelphia in 1974. This program, "Philadelphia Green," has thrived in conjunction with its emphasis on a cooperative approach to neighborhood redevelopment and involving local residents as active participants in the design, construction, programming, and maintenance of projects. Asner (1969) describes the Philadelphia Neighborhood Park Program of the early 1960s as the earliest and most advanced municipal effort. It was unique and innovative in its focus on low-income residential areas, particularly the focus on the need to deal with abandoned buildings and vacant lots. The program also developed guidelines for design and community development that emphasized the need to have any projects suit the particular needs of each neighborhood and the involvement of residents in design, planning, and maintenance of urban public spaces.

The USDA's Urban Gardening Program, which emerged in the mid-1970s,[3] represents an attempt by the government to support urban gardening initiatives, albeit hardly on the scale of the Liberty Gardens and Victory Gardens programs during the two world wars. At that time, the Cooperative Extension Service was established as the educational arm of the USDA. In 1977 Congress appropriated funds to establish gardening programs to be administered through the Extension Services. These gardening programs initially were located in six cities. Another ten cities were added in 1978, creating the 16–Cities Urban Gardening Program (Brown 1980). The Urban Gardening Program eventually supported gardening programs in 23 of the nation's largest cities. The goal was to develop and support urban gardening for food production.

Despite indications of the positive potential of the Urban Gardening Program, federal spending on the program was frozen at $3.5 million in 1985, eventually resulting in cuts of 50 percent to 80 percent in many of the 23 cities' programs. The lack of funding, however, was not the only reason for less success than initially anticipated. Urban gardening initiatives as well as other community initiatives—USDA supported or others—that have continued despite the disappearance of funding did so because they were driven by other factors, that is, active involvement on part of intended beneficiaries in the organization, setting of goals, and daily running of such initiatives as well as in the struggle to secure tenure.

Bassett, constrained by the timing of his research in the late 1970s, did not fully appreciate the profound difference between the various community gardening episodes from the turn of the century to World War II and the last one that he recognizes as having started in 1970. Beginning in the 1970s, there was a shift from a theme of orchestration of gardening from above, initiated by federal, state, and municipal governments and institutions for the benefit of society and gardeners in particular, to a theme of empowerment at the local level. In fact the language of the USDA report about the Urban Gardening Program reflects this shift:

"A gardening program and its logical spinoffs will not solve a community's problems. The implication of such a program is, however, that people, no matter how poor, can take a responsibility for part of their own well-being. With this humble start, some inroads into the cycle of dependency can perhaps be made, with far reaching consequences" (Brown 1980: 3).

The concept of empowerment, which acquired such political capital in government initiatives in the 1970s and 1980s to ameliorate the effects of poverty, has been subject to criticism as a manipulative form of social control and a code word for abandonment by government agencies.[4] However, in the history of community gardens from the 1970s on, the defining element was not the role of federal or local governments and attempts to impose ideologically driven notions of self-help from above. Heretofore allotment gardening and other urban gardening initiatives had emerged on the basis of federal and local government support and organizational input. From the 1970s on, community gardens in the United States emerged as local grassroots-based initiatives, if not in resistance to governments, but certainly in the face of a very fragmented support base (also see Ferguson 1999a). Community gardeners and activists appropriated the concept of empowerment and allied it with themes of political, economic, social, and cultural resistance and concepts of reclaiming community spaces. The increase in the number of urban community gardens across the country since the mid-1970s is the result of a range of factors and agents, not reducible to the waxing and waning support extended by the USDA and local administrations.

According to a 1994 national survey, 30 percent of US families were gardeners; 80 percent of these lived in urban areas (Gallup Organization 1994). There were more than 80 American cities with community gardening programs. In the 1990s, cities with thriving community gardening programs supported by municipal administrations included Boston, Seattle, San Francisco, Boulder, Philadelphia, Denver, Washington, D.C., and St. Louis. According to a national survey in 1996, to which a total of 38 cities responded, there were 6,018 gardens (American Community Gardening Association 1998). The most prominent type was the neighborhood or community garden, which accounted for 67.4 percent of the total. Site permanency was an issue for most of the respondents.[5] Only 92 of all these gardens were in permanent ownership or a land trust with 32.3 percent of the gardens being over ten years old. Only 15 cities reported significant open space initiatives such as spending of funds for garden development or maintenance, formation of coalitions with other groups for advocacy of open space and garden preservation, and inclusion of community gardens in a city's overall plan.

Despite the evident popularity and increase in the number of community gardens across the country, by 1994 many federally funded urban gardening programs were in trouble or disappearing altogether. Ironically, many programs survived the Reagan and Bush presidencies only to fall victim to the budget cuts during the Clinton administration. However, the 1996 Farm Bill, which incorporated and passed into law the Community Food Security Act of 1995, was an effort to provide a new basis for a comprehensive approach to food security, urban agriculture, sustainable communities, and community gardening. The effects of this legislation are filtering down to regional and local levels only gradually; nonetheless they have helped to put community gardening initiatives across the country on a different footing.

THE GREENING OF NEW YORK CITY

The history of community gardens in New York City as in other cities in the United States is inseparable from the history of economic fluctuations, changing labor markets, immigration, and the transformation from an industrial city to a services-based city. These developments are reflected in processes of inner-city deterioration, housing abandonment, poverty, and gentrification. The real estate market is the decisive factor in the fate of contested public spaces. In a city where air rights above church courtyards are sold to the highest bidder, community gardens, situated for the most part on city-owned land with insecure tenure at best, have been and continue to be subject to the forces of the market as much as to shifting political and ideological pressures.[6]

In New York City, in the 17th century, when Petrus Stuyvesant was Director General of New Netherland and New Amsterdam, every house had a garden and pasture for livestock (King 1893: 242). In the 19th century, urban policy makers for economic reasons abandoned any notion of the need to protect common land or open space. The gridiron street plan of the present is the legacy of a 1807 commission. This commission argued that it was economical and prudent to let go of open space; land was too costly to be frittered away as open space, and the sea around New York City provided enough fresh air for health purposes. The conditions on the Lower East Side at the end of the 19th century were one result of such attitudes.

"Tenement houses are as a rule great towering buildings,

many of them squalid and in bad repair, and devoid of any but the rudest arrangements for existence. They are packed with human beings. In a single block between Avenue B and Avenue C and 2nd and 3rd Streets there are over 3,500 residents, and a smaller block on Houston Street contains 3,000 people, which is at the rate of 1,000,000 to the square mile" (King 1893: 244).

However, in the second half of the 19th century attitudes shifted toward the realization that there was a need for open space planning as well as a need to create spaces for the rapidly growing poor and working-class people of the city. The creation of Coney Island was one such result, with its manifest purpose of providing affordable entertainment cleverly disguising notions of manipulating, socializing, and controlling an extremely diverse immigrant population. The allotment garden movement in New York City was another.

From the late 19th century until World War I, factories, schools, orphanages, and public parks all played a role in establishing allotment and school gardens all over New York City, including Corlears Hook Park on the Lower East Side. These gardens emphasized the notions of healthful exercise and education, or more specifically moral and social training. When World War I started, it was relatively easy to translate these educational initiatives into growing food for the war effort.

Gardens for the unemployed were part of a statewide relief project in New York from 1932 on (Bassett 1979: 90). New York depended on government grants for its relief work. Until 1935, the Federal Emergency Relief Administration (FERA) had been providing such money. In 1935, there were approximately 80,000 gardens under cultivation in New York, 60,000 of these of the municipal allotment type. In 1936, the Work Projects Administration (WPA) still sponsored at least 5,000 relief gardens on vacant plots and in parks throughout the city, including Tompkins Square Park. After 1937, relief gardens in New York

History of Urban Community Gardening

City were mostly abandoned.

During World War II once again all available city-owned land was released for gardening in Victory Gardens. The close of the war and the end of food rationing led to the abandonment of most Victory Gardens in New York City for the next decades. One Victory Garden, the Warren/St. Mark's Garden in Brooklyn, has survived into the present.

In New York City, the 1960s were the era of so-called vest pocket parks and other small urban spaces, mostly developed with funds from municipal, state, and federal governments. The Park Association of New York City in 1963 pointed to the need for such spaces, referring to Lewis Mumford's emphasis on the need for open space planning. In contrast Robert Moses argued that such vest pocket parks would be little more than nuisances. Vest pocket parks were created in different parts of the city. A well-known and popular vest pocket park is Paley Park at 53rd Street, built and maintained by the Paley family in honor of the father of the founder of CBS, William S. Paley. It is used mostly by employees of corporations in the area. Perhaps this space has been so successful because of the factor of personal control and input, albeit at a corporate level, while many other vest-pocket parks and public spaces, dependent on top-down management and the availability of funding, have remained sterile and lifeless. Some community gardens began as vest pocket parks, for instance, the Rev. Linnette C. Williamson Gardens and Unity Park at 128th and 129th Street in East Harlem. The site on 128th Street had been opened in 1965 as the nation's first vest pocket park, but over the years had fallen into disuse. In the 1980s, community members with the assistance of the municipally run community gardening program GreenThumb worked to revitalize the garden. However, with a few such exceptions, vest pocket parks are fundamentally different from community gardens in terms of the level of involvement of users in the design, maintenance, organization, and uses made of such spaces.

In a discussion of vest pocket parks Shiffman refers to the need for community participation. "Community participation has become crucial in the growing trend toward interaction between low-income communities and government, private industry and philanthropy. In this context, community participation can no longer be defined by its old affluent, 'middle class' orientation if it is to become meaningful and effective" (Shiffman 1969: 149). Looking at the last decade of relations between intensely active community garden groups and the New York City administration, the image of the sorcerer's apprentice comes to mind, that hapless individual who called forth the spirits to help him with his housework and then found the spirits would not return to their various cabinets and cupboards.

In the 1960s, the Pratt Center for Community Improvement, with its emphasis on hands-on involvement in neighborhoods, had a more nuanced understanding of the complexity of the task involved in the construction of parks and green spaces in low-income communities. The history of Lefferts Place Park and Quincy Park in Brooklyn demonstrated that community participation was critical, if parks were to be used fully and positively. In 1965, four sites in Bedford Stuyvesant were cleaned, surfaced, fenced, and leased by the city to community groups, with special emphasis on projects involving children in the design, creation work, and maintenance of the sites. The labor force employed for this preparatory work consisted of local unemployed males, who were paid wages that approximated the prevailing scale for that type of labor (Seymour 1969: 152–153).

In 1963, the New York City Housing Authority initiated a program to encourage tenants' groups in low-rent housing projects to plan and care for flower gardens. The program was formalized and involved a monitored application process, education, contests, and guidelines, such as the restriction to flower growing. For several years this program was extremely successful. Growing from 1,000 active participants in 1963 to 4,600 in 1969, the program was granted an award by the Horticultural Society of New York. In New York City, as opposed to a similar program in Chicago at that time, total responsibility was given to groups of residents. This program also falls under the category of programs for the "beautification of the city" (Bassett 1979: 42). The emphasis on community participation foreshadows a critical element of the vibrant community gardening movement of the 1970s and thereafter (Robbins 1969).

In New York City the 1965 Housing Act, which included the Urban Beautification Act, led among others to the creation of the playground at the Jacob Riis Houses and the playground at La Guardia Houses, public housing on the Lower East Side. The Henry Street Settlement took an active role in the creation of the La Guardia Houses playground. Neighborhood children designed and executed the concrete play sculpture (Seymour 1969). However, many of these playground initiatives failed to actively involve the residents who were to benefit from such improvement, and the playgrounds eventually were inadequately maintained and not fully utilized.

The first community gardens in New York City as we know them today date back to the early 1970s. In the 1970s and 1980s, there was a proverbial flowering of gardens; in all boroughs, neighborhood people claimed and remade abandoned lots. The mushrooming of these green spaces is inseparable from the history of inner-city deterioration; in all boroughs, but especially in neighborhoods such as the Lower East Side, Harlem, parts of the Bronx, and Brooklyn, buildings were neglected, burned, and eventually demolished. This process gripped many neighborhoods in the 1960s and continued unabated for decades, leaving yawning garbage-filled spaces in its wake. In 1965, the Pratt Center, in cooperation with the Central Brooklyn Coordinating Council, conducted a survey of vacant lots and abandoned and burned-out buildings throughout Bedford Stuyvesant. It found 378 vacant lots, mostly city-owned, and 346 abandoned buildings (Seymour 1969). A decade later the acceleration of large-scale building abandonment, deterioration, and arson had produced a vast numbers of vacant lots all over New York City, as many as an estimated 11,000 by 1999, and an estimated 20,000 abandoned buildings (Neighborhood Open Space Coalition 2000).

By early 1998, there were 1,906 community gardens in New York City (American Community Gardening Association 1998). In 1999 there were an estimated 14,000 community gardeners in the city (Neighborhood Open Space Coalition 2000). Ninety-eight percent of the gardens have been initiated by gardeners themselves rather than by an outside agency or group. This figure includes 869 community or neighborhood gardens, 834 public housing gardens, and miscellaneous school gardens, senior housing gardens, and other types; 700 of these gardens were more than 10 years old. Some 335 gardens were lost over the preceding five years, with most of the losses in so-called neighborhood gardens that had been under the auspices of GreenThumb. According to GreenThumb, 40 gardens were discontinued in 1998. Most of the gardens added over the past five years were New York City Housing Authority gardens or public housing gardens. Only four gardens were on lots owned by one or another community group and hence protected. Many gardens had no legal status whatsoever: 70 gardens were permanent ("permanent" defined as having a 10-year lease, owned by a land trust, or having another legal agreement that assures more than ten years of protection such transfer to the Department of Parks and Recreation), and 5.65 percent of all gardens were situated on private land (American Community Gardening Association 1998). From the 1970s on, while rubble-filled lots all over New York City were transformed into gardens, several organizations emerged that have acted in support of gardens from

History of Urban Community Gardening

various perspectives. These organizations focused on urban ecology, notions of public ownership of land, waste management, and community revitalization. They included GreenThumb, the Green Guerillas, the Council on the Environment of New York City, the Bronx Green-Up Program, the Cornell Cooperative Extension Urban Horticultural Program, the Environmental Action Coalition, and the Trust for Public Land, and the Neighborhood Open Space Coalition, as well as numerous grassroots coalitions at neighborhood and city-wide levels.

The municipal organization Operation Green Thumb, now called GreenThumb, was formed in 1978 without a budget and with one part-time staff person. By the mid-1990s, funded by federal Community Development Block Grants, with a staff of eight, it had become the largest municipally run community gardening program in the United States. At that time it was leasing over 1,000 different lots comprising approximately 125 acres of vacant city-owned property to over 700 community groups in 40 of New York's 59 community districts.

The Green Guerillas were founded in 1973 by a group of urban gardeners who had started the Liz Christy Garden on the Lower East Side. The founders were witnesses to a neighborhood falling apart; it was literally going up in flames as building after building fell victim to neglect and arson. Involved in housing struggles and other community-based initiatives, the founders were inspired by the notion of sustainable communities through community farming. Their efforts coincided with the appearance of permaculture experiments, Buckminster Fuller domes, greenhouses on rooftops, windmills, and the solar wall at the Quanda Building on the Lower East Side. Through donations from local nurseries and support by people in the neighborhood and increasingly from other boroughs, the founders were able to start a membership organization; fast growth and incorporation by 1976 were the result. The Green Guerillas were the first of the greening groups to engage in "direct action," by making extensive use of the "seed grenades" or balloons filled with pelletized time-release fertilizer and wildflower seeds. Today Green Guerillas is a nonprofit, member-supported organization that provides plant materials and garden supplies, design assistance, community organizing help, and horticultural consultations and has been active in advocacy on the behalf of the gardens, food security initiatives, and community organization.

The Council on the Environment of New York City was formed in 1970. A privately funded citizens' organization, it has promoted environmental awareness and works at developing solutions to environmental problems. Its main areas of emphasis are environmental education, waste prevention and recycling, the Open Space Greening Program, and the Greenmarket Program, a program to support regional food producers and bring fresh produce and other farm products to weekly markets all over New York City. The Council and the Environmental Action Coalition (EAC) both emerged in conjunction with the first Earth Day in 1970. The EAC has been focusing on street trees and the issue of waste management. The Trust for Public Land is a national non-profit land conservation organization that offers technical assistance in establishing community gardens. Its focus is on the establishment of community land trusts as a way to safeguard such properties in perpetuity. The Trust for Public Land and the New York Restoration Project together acquired 112 gardens in a last-minute rescue operation before a scheduled city-wide auction in May 1999.

The Neighborhood Open Space Coalition (NOSC) was founded in 1980 as the result of a meeting called by authors of a study about New York community open spaces (Francis et al. 1984). NOSC grew to include 61 organizations. In 1983 NOSC succeeded in convincing the city administration to accept a public/private open space task force to coordinate funding and policy to support local greening efforts. In recent years NOSC has acted as an arbiter of sorts in the city-wide community of garden supporters. NOSC publishes a newsletter and also runs a list serve for open space and community garden issues. This has been a vital resource, a bulletin board, a forum for exchange—at times heated—and a device for calling people to action. NOSC further has been instrumental in drafting a proposal for community garden legislation as a basis for a city-wide policy for preservation of existing gardens and creation of new ones. This proposal was submitted to the city council in 2000.

These and other organizations have played an important role in the community gardening movement. They also are linked to national groups such as the National Gardening Association and groups with a global focus like the organization Reclaiming the Streets, which started in England. This growing network of supporting organizations across neighborhoods, borough lines, and cities is particularly relevant in light of the fact that local governing bodies, such as the community boards in various districts, are by no means unanimously supportive of so-called neighborhood or community gardens.[7]

Examples for community gardening affecting entire neighborhoods can be found in Manhattan, on the Lower East Side, in Brooklyn, and in the Bronx. For instance, Brownsville in eastern Brooklyn, like other New York City neighborhoods, suffered a dramatic decline during the 1960s and 1970s as the result of landlord negligence, housing abandonment, and arson, with attendant environmental degradation and increase in health threats and crime. The neighborhood has been making a gradual recovery over the last few decades. Housing stock is being rebuilt and renovated. Starting in the 1970s, community gardens sprang up all over the neighborhood, with a total of 21 in Brownsville. There is a great deal of diversity. One garden features an African hut, fruit trees, and a duck pond. Another is graced by a mural created with the assistance of the Green Guerillas Youth Mural Project. The Jes Good Rewards Children's Garden boasts a composting project and a thriving wildlife habitat area with plants that attract birds and butterflies. Even more important, there is an active coalition of fourteen Brownsville gardens called the Brownsville Garden Coalition. This coalition is involved in educating residents and promoting cooperation among gardeners from various gardens. The coalition has reinforced gardeners' increasing involvement in economic and political issues relevant to the gardens and the neighborhood as a whole.

Another example of a successful community garden initiative is the Clinton Community Garden on the West Side of Manhattan in a neighborhood known as Hell's Kitchen, which has been subject to extremely uneven processes of gentrification over the last decades of the 20th century. The garden was created in 1977 on a 150" × 100" lot originally filled with abandoned cars and trash. It is cleverly landscaped to give the impression of space. Its 108 members work individual plots, and a group of approximately 30 volunteers work on flower beds and other plantings in the common area. Managed by a steering committee of 18 to 20 people, the garden's orientation is to serve to the immediate and extended community. This is reflected in the fact that as many as 2,000 individuals from an area extending from 53rd Street to 34th Street have access keys and also is apparent in city-wide events such as a summer solstice celebration in June 2000.

The garden members, predominantly middle class, became politically active on behalf of their garden earlier than most other community gardens in New York City. In 1984 they succeeded in obtaining the transfer of the land to the New York City Department of Parks, consequently obtaining permanent site status for their garden at a time when real estate pressures had not yet escalated to such an extent. They also engaged in successful fund-raising for the garden, for instance, by selling square inches of the garden in an advertisement in the *New York Times* as a money-raising ploy. The garden boasts an elegant gate donated by the Astor Foundation. From the beginning gardeners were aware of the problem of soil contamination; they plant all vegetables in raised beds and concentrate on vegetables that do not absorb as much lead from the soil as root vegetables and leafy greens. Vegetable scraps from all over the neighborhood are recycled in composting drums donated by the Queens Botanical Garden. Among other innovative ideas, the garden includes an individual member plot designed for someone working out of a wheelchair, an "enabled garden."

An equally noteworthy instance is the story of the Greening of Harlem Coalition, started by Bernadette Cozart in 1989. A gardener working for the New York City Parks Department, Cozart began by working with children and went on to create a coalition of key community institutions in Harlem to create community gardens and restore parks and playgrounds (Hynes 1996). Hynes describes the Greening of Harlem Coalition as "a circular chain of individuals and institutions in which each link is unique, relies on the others, but also works from its own center of strength" (Hynes 1996: 37). Cozart's vision extends from a fight against drugs, crime, violence, malnutrition, and other attendant ills of poverty to the creation of gardens, small farms, and playgrounds and the conversion of vacant buildings into spaces for woodworking, carpentry, and other trades. Among the achievements of the Greening of Harlem Coalition are the restoration of Charles Young Park, the creation of the tree-pit garden program, and the reclaiming of Jackie Robinson Park and Marcus Garvey Park, brought about by neighborhood involvement and the work of volunteers.

The Struggle for Eden

RECENT HISTORY

At this writing, the number of community gardens is in the process of being reduced radically. Meanwhile, the city owns vacant lots, as well as abandoned buildings, in all five boroughs that do not contain gardens and would conceivably be available for development. In 1999 estimates of vacant lots ranged from 11,000 to 15,000, and there were about 1300 vacant buildings in the city's inventory. City officials argue that there are no other suitable sites for the construction of housing. Fran Reiter, the Deputy Mayor for Economic Development and Planning, said bluntly: "The bottom line is, we're going build wherever we can, whenever we can. Do we sacrifice gardens to build housing? You're damn right we do" (Raver 1997).

In 1994, Mayor Giuliani's administration ordered a survey of the city's holdings of vacant lots to determine possible uses, as parking lots, staging areas for the Sanitation Department, and sites for housing development, to name a few. HPD chose about 3,000 lots suitable for housing. About 300 of these lots contained gardens that were holding GreenThumb leases. According to projections made in 1997, GreenThumb, a municipally run community gardening program then under the auspices of the New York City Department of Parks, expected to close about 300 of its 750 gardens over the next few years as the city developed the land or auctioned it (Raver 1997).

The first New York City gardens to be bulldozed were in Brooklyn; the Puerto Rican Community Center of Brownsville and Satellite en Orbita, also in Brownsville, both were bulldozed in 1984. Between 1984 and 2000 a total of 91 gardens have been destroyed. On the Lower East Side one of the first gardens to be eliminated was the Garden of Eden on Forsyth Street between Stanton and Rivington Streets. It was bulldozed on January 8, 1986, a historical event solemnly commemorated in an annual

History of Urban Community Gardening

pageant through the neighborhood.[8] Since then many other gardens have suffered a similar demise, with an escalation during the mid-1990s. Since the early 1990s gardeners have become increasingly organized, creating coalitions throughout the city and working with organizations such as the Trust for Public Land and the Council on the Environment in order to defend these spaces.

In 1995, GreenThumb was transferred from the Department of General Services, which manages vacant land inventory, to the Department of Parks and Recreation. This transfer was welcomed by community gardeners and activists, since it seemed to provide more opportunities for long-term protection of gardens. However, in April 1998, Mayor Giuliani moved to transfer all gardens administered by GreenThumb to HPD, with the mandate that they be developed in the future. This eliminated any form of long-term protection other than permanent transfer to the Parks Department. The mayor's action galvanized an already existing and increasingly sophisticated and organized set of coalitions across New York City into a full-scale campaign on behalf of community gardens. The campaign peaked in the spring of 1999, when the city administration scheduled an auction of city-owned lots, including 112 gardens throughout New York City. Much pressure was exerted in the form of media blitzes, demonstrations, and acts of civil disobedience, as well as efforts to line up the support of politicians and lawsuits.

At the proverbial last minute before the May 1999 auction, the Trust for Public Land and the New York Restoration Project headed by the entertainer Bette Midler stepped in and successfully negotiated with the city for acquisition of these gardens for a total of $4.2 million. In December 1999, this deal was finalized, and 112 gardens were placed in permanent land trusts. The Trust for Public Land has been going forward with setting up land trusts for the ongoing administration of those gardens. At the end of 1999, there were 90 gardens under the jurisdiction or hold of the Department of Parks and Recreation, 22 of these transferred to the Department of Parks that year. A handful of gardens were under the jurisdiction of other agencies such as the Department of Environmental Protection and the Department of Transportation. Approximately 366 sites remained under the jurisdiction from HPD, with development plans pending for the majority of these gardens.

Since the dramatic May 1999 rescue, the city administration has shifted its strategy to a more piecemeal approach. Four gardens were removed from the bill of sale to the relatively young organization New York Restoration Project and the Trust for Public Land by city council members who felt that their communities had greater needs than open space. These gardens are now returned to the list of sites that will be developed at some point. Eleven gardens have been bulldozed in 1999, and two on the Lower East Side were bulldozed in February 2000; many more received eviction letters by HPD. Ten gardens in Community Board 3 in the Bronx, including Peachtree and Sunset Gardens, both founded more than twenty years ago, have received orders to vacate. Various coalitions working on behalf of the gardens are currently struggling to develop a strategy that is effective in the face of this piecemeal approach of the city administration. Meanwhile, on July 25, 2001, the Brooklyn Supreme Court upheld a temporary restraining order, imposed in response to a lawsuit filed by Attorney General Eliot Spitzer on behalf of the community gardens in New York City. As of this writing, this injunction effectively blocks any bulldozing of community gardens until the final decision of the lawsuit or a change in the city administration's policy, possibly as a result of the November 2001 mayoral elections.

History of Urban Community Gardening

THE HISTORY OF COMMUNITY GARDENS ON THE LOWER EAST SIDE

The Lower East Side in many respects is a microcosm of urban history. The effects of shifts in labor markets and housing markets over the last century have repeatedly scored the neighborhood with deep scars. A history of the Lower East Side provides a concentrated perspective on immigration to America; immigrants from all over the world, especially from Eastern Europe, Asia, Puerto Rico, and most recently Asia again, have been coming to the neighborhood. Some of this history of the "teeming millions" has found its way into the writings of Charles Dickens and the photography of Jacob Riis, to name just a few artists and writers profoundly affected by the area. The Lower East Side has been subject to the effects of rapid industrialization and deindustrialization over the past 100 years; this is evidenced by deterioration of the housing stock, large-scale housing abandonment, and gentrification and the socioeconomic profile of a neighborhood marked by unemployment, underemployment, and poverty.

A densely built-up neighborhood of tenements in the early 1900s, the Lower East Side had been transformed into a virtual urban wasteland by the early 1970s, with abandoned and crumbling buildings and vacant lots given it the appearance of a blackened slab of Swiss cheese.[9] Generations of New York City administrations have coveted the Lower East Side as a potentially exploitable area, by virtue of its closeness to the financial district and its relatively un-developed state in comparison to any other neighborhoods in Manhattan; at the same time they viewed it as a thorn in their side by virtue of its history of contention and intense political activism. A long tradition of activism and grassroots movements has provided a dynamic counterweight to the forces of the economy.

The Struggle for Eden

Many community efforts developed and flourished from the early 1970s on. Diverse coalitions of residents, block associations, local housing and community service agencies, activists, and churches spearheaded anti-arson and anti-drug struggles, efforts centering on housing rehabilitation and construction, and the reclamation of abandoned lots for community gardens. However, it is difficult to disentangle to what extent some of these efforts were allowed to flourish since they served the interests of the administration and to what extent they flourished despite these interests. The various cultural cross-currents of bohemian culture, counterculture, ecological movements, and social activist and radical movements that have given the neighborhood its complex character are inseparable from and indeed the outgrowth of these concrete market forces and the perception of the neighborhood as a marketable commodity.

It is necessary to contextualize the community garden movement in terms of this history. More specifically one might consider the construction of affordable artist housing by the Koch administration in the 1970s by way of attracting more galleries into the neighborhood as an envisioned vanguard of future gentrification, the encouragement by the city administration of grassroots housing initiatives in the 1980s as a cheap method to upgrade the neighborhood, and the encouragement of developers in conjunction with increased efforts to evict squatters in the 1990s in order to make way for market-rate housing development as part of the same set of dynamics that has produced the increased focus on gardens occupying potentially exploitable real estate (see Chapter 3 for a definition and discussion of the term "squatter").

The control of public space, the increased marginalization of powerless low-income and poor people by social and geographic displacement, and the escalation of efforts at "taming" and "disciplining" the populace, in particular street vendors, community gardeners, and artists, are all part and parcel of a systematic and instrumental set of processes to control and claim the neighborhood as a multi-faceted economic commodity.[10] Sharff implies that these gardens themselves were instrumental in the process of gentrification of the area: "When the rabble was finally cleared out from big swaths of the Lower East Side and the neighborhood became safer for "urban pioneers," the gardens with their little *casitas* were left behind" (Sharff 1998: 85). At the same time, the history of community gardens, the politics in and over these gardens, and the neighborhood and city-wide struggle on their behalf contain a set of transformative elements with an impact on the city that is not reducible to community gardens as a mere reflection of the forces of the market.

The composition, internal organization, and culture of community gardens, as well as neighborhood and city-wide coalitions of gardens, reflect these contradictions and disparate strains. Community gardens are characterized by great diversity of membership, echoing various generations of immigrants into the neighborhood from different cultural, class, and ethnic backgrounds, and by a range of activist traditions in the gardens, sometimes overlapping and just as often opposed to each other. The ecological counter-culture movement, the squatter movement, Puerto Rican pride initiatives, artists' involvement, public housing advocacy, food cooperatives, environmental justice initiatives, and efforts at community organization for the purpose of gaining control over issues of housing, education, and the physical environment are represented to differing degrees in community gardens on the Lower East Side. The Lower East Side has spearheaded several garden coalitions and a city-wide effort to save the gardens.

Some of the oldest community gardens in New York City are on the Lower East Side; for instance, the Liz Christy Garden was founded in 1972. In 1973 Liz Christy and other gardeners and landscape professionals founded the Green Guerillas, a gardening organization that has been instrumental in helping other gardens get started, in educating gardeners and neighborhood activists, and in advocacy work on behalf of the gardens. In the 1990s, another woman, Felicia Young, started a tradition of annual pageants in celebration of community gardens. These pageants, which involve hundreds of participants from the Lower East Side and other neighborhoods of New York City, have lent color and inspiration to the political effort.

In the 1990s, Community Board 3, reflecting political divisions within the Lower East Side, repeatedly has voted in favor of releasing gardens for development, despite strenuous lobbying efforts by members of the community. The 1998 HPD list for proposed housing sites included several of the oldest and most successful community gardens in this area. Dramatically and unforgettably, the Chico Mendez Mural Garden on 11th Street between Avenues A and B was bulldozed, together with three other gardens on December 30, 1997. In 1998 there were approximately 45 community gardens on the Lower East Side. The 1999 May auction list included eight gardens from the Lower East Side. Among these were the All Peoples Garden, established in 1979, and Parque de Tranquilidad, established in 1980. Both of these gardens had been approved by the community board for transfer to the Parks Department.

Since the dramatic rescue by the Trust for Public Land and the New York Restoration project, many other gardens have been threatened and/or bulldozed, including the Jardín de Esperanza on 7th Street. The history of community gardening on the Lower East Side provides insights on the notion of the construction of "community," that is, community in the sense of a conflict-ridden, dynamic, and constantly changing construct. The Lower East Side also has been the locus for efforts to extend the struggle on behalf of community gardens to a city-wide level.

CONCLUSION

The end of 1999 was marked by the continuing 24-hour vigil at the Jardín de Esperanza; community activists and gardeners had prepared lockdown devices, steel tripods, and other barricades to stop the trucks and bulldozers that were parked outside the garden and had already demolished the back wall of the garden. The call for participation in this effort went out to the entire gardening community in New York City via the Internet. On February 15, 2000, this garden was bulldozed, two hours before the State Supreme Court issued a restraining order to the city to desist from bulldozing other gardens until the case could be argued in court on March 1; 31 protesters were arrested and held overnight. Devastated, exhausted, and in mourning over the loss of the 22-year-old garden and this particular battle, gardeners and activists were if anything even more determined to fight on behalf of the remaining gardens. The struggle for Esperanza (hope), presided over by the giant coqui, represents a memorable and telling milestone in the history of community gardening. Beginning in the late 19th century as a form of paternalistic charity and moral and physical improvement of the poor and working class imposed by federal, state, and municipal authorities, community gardening initiatives have evolved into vibrant locally based grassroots movements that also are increasingly allying themselves with nationwide and global concerns.

Community gardens in New York City and on the Lower East Side in particular have emerged under the shadow of the seesaw of housing abandonment and gentrification. Contradictory trends and dynamics of urban history are played out in these spaces. Analyses of individual gardens provide micro histories of urban life in America, revealing not only the shifting forces of the market but also histories of different population groups as active agents. Community gardens become repositories of various ideological strains and historical perceptions and as such have been the locus of and transformative agent for a new urban politics.

NOTES

1. A community gardener talking about the history of her garden.
2. The garden will be preserved as a component of a $230 million mixed-use development project covering four sites in the Cooper Square Urban Renewal Area, construction of which was scheduled for the spring of 2001. The project will include a recreation center, retail space, and 618 residential units; 155 units will be set aside as low-income housing units. In 2001 the developer tried to renege on the promise to the gardeners to preserve the garden in its entirety, proposing to cut a path through the middle of the already small space as an access to the retail space. However, an extensive lobbying effort and letter-writing campaign was successful, and the garden will be preserved.
3. A report prepared under the auspices of the USDA in 1980 describes the first beginnings of such urban gardening initiatives (Brown 1980). Based on the responses from a questionnaire and a series of informal interviews conducted in 1980, the report indicates that there is a great deal of variety in urban gardening programs in the different cities involved and that many of the questions cannot be properly addressed within the parameters of such a short survey. However, it also implies that urban gardening programs have a positive impact on a community's economic and social cultural well-being.
4. Marcuse has been one of the sharpest critics of this concept, arguing that self-help efforts and other forms of citizen participation provide the state or local administration with tools for social control, while not effectively altering the distribution power,

resources, or services in a neighborhood. Meanwhile, feelings of self-confidence and empowerment that develop through self-help efforts obscure the fact that the power of central political leadership is unabated (see von Hassell 1996: 174; Marcuse 1987).

5. The American Community Gardening Association as well as GreenThumb use the term "community garden" to refer to the so-called neighborhood gardens and as an umbrella term to describe all urban gardens that involve a certain degree of community involvement, such as public housing gardens, senior gardens, and other types. I am concerned with the so-called neighborhood gardens, and I generally use the term "community garden" to refer to them, since that is also the term used by the gardeners themselves.

6. Garden site tenure represented a problem from the beginning. For instance, in 1980 urban gardening programs in various cities reported that the first sites that a developer likes to consider are those that have been cleaned up by gardeners (Brown 1980: 11).

7. For a discussion of the very limited power of community boards, see Marcuse 1987. Set up in the late 1970s, community boards were designed to reflect the voices of the community and to provide a forum for discussion. Their role is essentially advisory, and any of their proposals or decisions can be overruled by various bodies in the city administration.

8. Two other New York City gardens bear that name, the Garden of Eden at 927 Faile Street in the Bronx and the Garden of Eden in South Jamaica, Queens. The garden in Jamaica was featured in a *National Geographic* article (Graham 1995). Both gardens were included in the list of GreenThumb gardens to be auctioned off in the May 1999 auction.

9. For a more detailed history of immigration to the Lower East Side, see Abu-Lughod 1994.

10. David Maynard suggested these terms in the course of a conversation about developments in New York City in the mid-1990s.

The Struggle for Eden

The Frog and the Rooster: Urban Community Gardening and Community-Based Grassroots Initiatives

"If you live in an unrealistic world, then you can say everything should be a community garden."[1]

"Dear Mr. Giuliani, our community is being destroyed. I would like to ask you for a favor. I am not asking for a lot. All I want you to do is stop destroying the gardens and stop cutting the trees. My name is Santa, and I'm thirteen years old. I live in Harlem, and five years ago our community was beautiful. Now my community is just awful, the trees are gone. There is a big hole where they were. The trees left on the edge are dead. All the flowers are dead, because they were hit by the bulldozer. If this letter gets to your hands, please do me the favor: help our trees and gardens. Our community is being destroyed. [Enclosure: samples of leaves, one "live," one dried out.] Dear Mr. Giuliani, just look at the difference! Thank you. Santa."[2]

INTRODUCTION: THE FIGHT FOR THE JARDÍN DE ESPERANZA

"The rooster lives!" This message appeared in my e-mail two days after the Jardín de Esperanza on 7th Street was bulldozed on February 15, 2000.

Feeling cut off from the action while writing about community gardens in my home on Long Island, I had not witnessed this event. I had been in the garden the previous day and had observed the garden rooster clucking peacefully amid the piles of Christmas trees set up as a temporary wall against the already bulldozed lot behind the garden, while gardeners were standing around a fire in the middle of the garden discussing the protective measures taken against the imminent destruction. When I was following the news the next day, the rooster's fate was unclear. I envisioned him crushed and buried under the remnants of the garden. A friend assured me that the rooster had been placed into the basement of the adjoining building shortly before the bulldozers began to roll. In the strategy meetings taking place in that basement after the loss of the garden, the rooster could be heard crowing in the background. Symptomatic for the nature of the change taking place, this rooster and his brothers in kind have been gradually vanishing from the Lower East Side, as lot after lot are developed and colorful gardens and *casitas* make way for sleek new housing with fenced-in hidden backyards.

The story of the Jardín de Esperanza contains many of the elements characterizing the history of community gardens in New York City—a medley of lies, confusion, and betrayal involving political power and corruption running up against fragmented opposition as well as tremendous resilience, occasional group cohesion, and creativity. Founded by a group consisting predominantly of Puerto Ricans, supported by the community board and individual politicians on the Lower East Side and also eventually abandoned by these same parties, defended by an extremely diverse group of gardeners, activists, and supporters from different parts of New York City and also exploited by some groups for their own ends, Esperanza mirrors the social, cultural, and political contradictions inherent in the struggle for all community gardens in New York City.

On the day of its demise the garden was 22 years old; it was created in 978 on the site of a building that had burned down. Its founder Alicia Torres and many other members of the garden live in the tenant-managed building next to the garden on 7th Street between Avenues B and C. Esperanza had been a relatively small garden, with a little *casita*, an arbor, a grapevine that reached over the fence, huge rosebushes, vegetable plots in the back, and a common area lined with stones. On one side of the garden a gardener had begun an elaborate project of arranging bricks in a geometric pattern. Stone dogs and other sculptures inhabited the garden together with the rooster and the American flag on a pole next to the *casita*.

The garden had a lease from GreenThumb. For decades, the garden represented one of the most stable elements on the block. Three times Community Board 3 approved the garden for transfer to the New York City Department of Parks; however, the city administration did not act on the recommendation of Community Board 3. In the 1980s, East 7th Street between Avenues C and B had a certain notoriety; one of the more well-known drug dealers was doing business out of a basement space across from the Esperanza garden. The block contained a soup kitchen, an abandoned synagogue, a neighborhood recycling center, a building occupied by squatters, and a building rehabilitated through a program known as urban homesteading.[3]

In the 1980s and early 1990s the Lower East Side was buzzing with community-based housing rehabilitation efforts and community garden initiatives. By the 1990s many drug dealers either had been arrested or had disappeared. Today the block is altered almost beyond recognition, featuring most astoundingly an apartment building with a doorman, built in the late 1990s on the site of another former garden. Efforts by people in the neighborhood to reclaim the street are subsumed by gentrification; meanwhile, these same efforts—sweat-equity building rehabilitation, tenant management of buildings, block associations to combat drugs and related crime, and community gardens—together have created an area increasingly attractive to outside developers and to people able to afford market rate rents.

The beginning of the end of Esperanza occurred in the summer

The Struggle for Eden

of 1999. At that time the city approved a plan to sell the East 7th Street lot to BFC Partners. One of its principals is Donald Capoccia, dubbed "Serial Garden Killer" in connection with the bulldozing of the Chico Mendez Mural Garden, the Angel's Garden, the Jardín de la 10th Street, also known as "Little Puerto Rico," and Maria's Garden on December 31, 1997. The Esperanza deal was brokered by Councilwoman Margarita Lopez; as a result of the deal a famous mural with the text *La Lucha Continua* (The Struggle Continues) and a small portion of a garden known as Carmen's Garden, the Jardín Bello Amanecer Borencano, on Avenue C and 8th Street would be preserved. Gardeners were surprised by the action of Councilwoman Lopez; they felt betrayed by someone whom they had helped to elect and whom they considered one of their own.[4]

    The gardeners, supported by activists, went into action to defend the garden. While a portion of these efforts centered on fighting the garden's destruction in the courts, a prominent and much publicized effort revolved around direct action. Gardeners and activists set up elaborate structures in order to prevent the bulldozers from entering the property and as a form of protest. Lockdown devices were scattered throughout the garden; so-called "sleeping dragons" were buried in the back of the garden—concrete sunk into the ground with devices to which demonstrators could anchor themselves. The most prominent lockdown device was a steel pillar crowned by a sunflower. The petals of the huge sunflower towering above Esperanza were inscribed with the following words: Esperanza/Hope, Lindo/Beauty, Communidad/Community, Oxygeno/Oxygen, Comida/Food. A steel and canvas structure, shaped and painted to look like a giant coqui, a Puerto Rican frog, perched on top of the fence and doubled as a shelter. Throughout the winter nights until February 15, people held vigil on the coqui's hidden platform and in the three pup tents in the garden, armed with cell phones in order to be able to alert the "Bulldozer Hotline" and the media when the bulldozers came. The gardeners were trying to buy time for the garden in the hopes that other concurrent efforts in the courts and in the state and city legislature would bear fruit. At the same time this ingenious and creative makeshift encampment was a media campaign and an opportunity to marshal more support for the gardens.

In May 1999 State Attorney General Eliot Spitzer sued the city to halt the auction of community gardens on the grounds that putting up the lots for sale violated state environmental laws. Spitzer also argued that many community gardens may qualify as dedicated parklands and cannot be sold without approval from the state legislature. Despite the fact that this case had not yet been decided by the court, the city administration decided to act. On February 14, alerted to the impending action, lawyers acting for Esperanza unsuccessfully tried to obtain an injunction from the State Appellate Division Court, which would have stopped the transfer of title from the city to BFC Partners and allowed Esperanza gardeners to go to court to fight for their garden.

The bulldozers arrived the next morning. About 80 garden protesters quickly assembled at the site. One of the garden defenders had locked himself to the platform on the top of the sunflower pillar. Another defender, incidentally someone who had come all the way from Mineola, Long Island, chained his hand to one of the "sleeping dragons," with his arm stuck in the ground all the way to his shoulder. One protester had chained her neck to a pole with a large bicycle lock. The police used emergency rescue equipment to cut through these devices. It took the city construction crew less than an hour to level the garden. Thirty-one protesters, 16 men and 15 women were arrested and charged with criminal trespass, obstruction of government process, and resisting arrest; the garden community referred to them with pride and affection as the "Esperanza 31" or the "Esperanza warriors."

Meanwhile, lawyers were arguing the state attorney general's case at a Brooklyn Supreme Court hearing that same day. A judge ordered the city to temporarily halt the destruction of any GreenThumb gardens. The temporary restraining order was handed down two hours after Esperanza was bulldozed. Esperanza was excluded from that injunction on the grounds that its lawyers had tried to obtain one the previous day and had failed. On March 15, 2000, despite an appeal by the city administration, Judge Richard Huttner of the State Supreme Court in Brooklyn indefinitely extended the temporary restraining order, leaving it in place until the city administration had conducted the necessary environmental analysis of the loss of gardens.

In the days after the bulldozing several facts emerged. The Esperanza gardeners made public a letter they had received from Capoccia, in which Capoccia explicitly promised that the Esperanza garden would be maintained as a GreenThumb garden in perpetuity and that only the lot directly adjoining the garden in the back would be developed. Various newspapers reported that BFC Partners and the Gethsemane Garden Baptist Church had obtained the property from the city without competitive bidding after having approached the Department of Housing Preservation and Development (HPD) with a proposal to develop the site. The deal was described as proper by the mayor's office and by HPD spokespersons. Campaign finance records showed that three principals of BFC and a BFC consultant had given $46,800 in donations to committees created by Mayor Giuliani to finance his 1997 mayoral race and his 2000 senate race.

Barraged with letters and phone calls from the garden community, the press also reported in greater detail precisely what type of housing would be constructed on the site. Initial reports had referred to planned construction of low-income housing. Later reports pointed out that the actual development plan involved a so-called 80/20 formula of the Cross-Subsidy Program, created in 1987. Accordingly, 80 percent are to be rented at full market value and the other 20 percent are reserved for low-income tenants; after 10 years those spaces will also be rented at full market value. Less well-known is the fact that a developer agreeing to such development terms receives subsidies, tax-exempt bonds, and loans from the city.

For weeks the plywood wall enclosing the former garden was covered with protest letters, newspaper articles, and graffiti denouncing Capoccia, while candles and vases with flowers were arrayed on the ground in front of the wall. Sustained by a supportive and outraged garden community, the Esperanza gardeners continued to fight for their garden, determined to appeal the court's decision. One of the arguments was that in 1977 the city administration had designated a portion of the entire area acquired by Donald Capoccia for "community facility use only." Such a zoning designation means that whether or not there is a building on the lot, that area may only be used for recognized "community" uses such as an open space play area or a building used as a non-profit cultural center.

That lot had housed the first neighborhood recycling center, established by residents with the assistance of the community organization Charas in the 1970s. In order for Capoccia's project to proceed, the city would have to lift this zoning restriction. If the zoning restriction were lifted, Capoccia would have to pay a $152,000 penalty to the city administration to go through with his proposed project. Meanwhile the gardeners were hoping that the city officials would deny his request. In that case Capoccia would have to alter his plan, either stopping the whole project, re-designing the building at enormous cost (also potentially stopping the building because of the cost), or, at the least, would be forced to provide a community center for the neighborhood instead of a retail establishment and market-rate housing.

At a public hearing on June 21, 2000 gardeners asked that the zoning restriction not be lifted; someone who attended the meeting sadly pointed out that the statements made by the gardeners were lovely as eulogies for Esperanza, but less compelling in terms of legal logic or concrete reasons for the city to desist from lifting the restriction. In October 2000, upon intensive discussions with their lawyers the Esperanza gardeners decided to refrain from pursuing their case further, recognizing that the garden was effectively lost.

THE STRUGGLE FOR COMMUNITY GARDENS AS A SOCIAL MOVEMENT

The community gardening movement, in particular the struggle for gardens in New York City, in some respects fits the pattern of new social movements of the late 20th century. It involves participation of diverse groups; is characterized by fluid boundaries in terms of membership, strategies, and objectives; incorporates diverse traditions, themes, and religious concepts; links notions of cultural and social change with change of physical surroundings; and comprehends a focus on global factors and dynamics. Generally it is possible to discern four stages in the life of a typical social movement—emergence, coalescence, bureaucratization, and decline. New social movements have also been characterized by non-economic agendas and usually attract predominantly members of the middle class.[5] However, the standard components and course of development of a social movement are applicable in this context only to a limited degree.

The community garden movement, if one wants to use such a term to describe a multitude of initiatives that have developed over the last thirty years of the 20th century, is characterized by a unique composition of actors. There are individual gardens or individual micro communities with their respective histories, often characterized by internal diversity and fragmentation, a great deal of diversity among these gardens, loose coalitions that cut across these micro communities, diverse greening and food security organizations, and individual activists, lawyers, and other supporters. The community garden movement with its eclectic set of agendas cuts across economic and non-economic interests. Community gardeners come from a range of class backgrounds, with the majority being low-income and poor people—and furthermore, low-income and poor people of color. The diversity in terms of race, class, and cultural backgrounds is evident within and among individual gardens and in coalitions, and it is tested repeatedly, on an almost daily basis in the gardens and in the struggle on their behalf.

The community garden movement has grown steadily over the last decades, but has retained much of its ad hoc character. The nature of the praxis of gardening, particularly within the confines of an urban community garden, involves a continuous reworking and revitalization of activism on the ground. The generally flexible organizational patterns within gardens are mirrored in the organizational patterns of coalitions. The tenuous nature of relationships among community gardeners, bound by nothing other than individual commitment, that is, the very frailty of these micro-communities, has proven to be a strength. Individual commitment combined with the need for ongoing reworking and renewal of relationships and organizational flexibility has contributed to the continued existence of community gardens over the years.

Social and economic conditions, particularly housing, are inseparable from the debate over community gardens. It is necessary to evaluate competing claims and arguments for and against such use of open space in urban areas.

Further, it is necessary to consider the history and organization of individual gardens. An understanding of patterns and dynamics within individual gardens provides a basis for an analysis of the organizational patterns and dynamics of activism on behalf of community gardens.

THE SOCIAL, POLITICAL, AND ECONOMIC CONTEXT OF ARGUMENTS FOR AND AGAINST COMMUNITY GARDENS

Two sets of arguments have been at the forefront of the struggle for community gardens. The argument advanced by the city administration is the need for housing. The other revolves around the notion of environmental justice advanced by community garden activists and greening groups. Other arguments are generally not publicly stated or acknowledged, but represent a powerful subtext in the battle. These arguments revolve around cultural factors as much as a struggle for political power. They surface occasionally in ad hominem attacks by the various parties involved, for instance in name calling ("communists," "hippies," "fascists"). However, such strategies are mostly abandoned again; the obvious ideological component makes them less suitable in a battle that is often defined as a matter of rational and pragmatic considerations, for all that interpretations of what is rational and pragmatic are in themselves ideologically driven.

The central argument advanced by the city administration as rationalization for actions vis-à-vis community gardens is the need for housing. The media has largely echoed this argument, equating the existence of gardens with the dearth of affordable housing. Speaking about the Lower East Side, a journalist refers to lots planted with rows of corn. "In the middle of America's most densely populated city, during a severe housing shortage, prime residential real estate has been converted to . . . [sic] farmland" (Tierney 1997).

Activists argue that generally the city administration's efforts to release lots for development have nothing to do with making up for a lack of affordable housing. Instead, these efforts facilitate the construction of market-rate apartments. Accordingly the "housing versus garden" argument is fallacious, based on a misrepresentation of facts with regard to housing, sites available for construction of housing, and the type of housing construction that has taken place on sites that formerly had contained community gardens. Activists further argue that such a justification is advanced without consideration of the context— both in terms of environmental justice and in terms of the social and economic factors in the neighborhoods most affected by the elimination of community gardens. Activists argue that the city administration's portrayal of the matter as a question of either housing or gardens is misleading and that housing development plans could and should incorporate the need for community-controlled green spaces and gardens.

At the center of arguments to demonstrate that community gardens are not in the way of housing construction, activists point out that in 2000 there were over 11,000 vacant lots and 20,000 abandoned buildings in New York City; the number of gardens threatened was around 500. In 1990, a report prepared under the auspices of the Green Guerillas and the Lower East Side Technical Assistance Group, with assistance and input from the Trust for Public Land, Cornell University Cooperative Extension, and the Urban Homesteading Assistance Board among others, demonstrated how many of the gardens on the Lower East Side slated for destruction could be saved while other vacant lots could be utilized for development (Kwartler 1990). Gardeners and activists were further incensed by the fact that many of the sites released for development and auctioned, including former gardens, have remained unutilized for years and returned to a derelict state. Brooklyn Borough President Howard Golden, a vocal supporter of community gardens, published a study which demonstrated that of 440 lots sold by the city between 1990 and 1995, 423 remained undeveloped; 148 of them were used for vehicle storage and 240 were filled with litter (Golden 1999). The Coalition for the Homeless is another supporter of community gardens. The Coalition released the following statement to the press on August 1, 2001, after remarks by Major Giuliani about the number of homeless families in New York City shelters and the need for housing overriding any calls for community gardens.

The Coalition for the Homeless objects, in the strongest terms, to Mayor Giuliani's recent statements implying that the construction of affordable housing in New York City must come at the expense of community gardens. Over the past many years, the non-profit sector of the city has developed myriad models of cost-effective, mixed-income housing. Given that the City has other parcels of land at its disposal, it is simply not necessary to encroach on the precious few remaining green spaces for new development of affordable housing. The technology, community commitment and manpower exists to deliver significant numbers of newly constructed homes. What has been lacking over the past few years is the fiscal commitment by the local government (Coalition for the Homeless 2001).

Activists have argued that not only is the action of taking away community gardens for contested forms of development objectionable, but that also the manner in which the city administration has proceeded is unacceptable. That is, many garden sites are sold without gardeners having been notified of such a possibility, thus without having had an opportunity to get involved in the process, regardless of the number of years that they had worked on a site. Activists argue that this is depriving gardeners of a basic right as residents. Furthermore, since community gardens are not identified on city maps, politicians voting on releasing lots for sale frequently were not aware of the fact that particular sites, identified only by tax lot number, contained community gardens. The city administration in turn reiterates that community gardens have always operated only on the principle of one-year leases that can be canceled at 24-hour notice, that they have always known that they were working on borrowed time, and that essentially gardeners are squatters who have been temporarily tolerated but have no legal standing.

Garden activists have also advanced an environmental justice argument. The proposed legislation on community gardens to create a city-wide garden preservation policy draws attention to the fact that in the year 2000 New York City did not have a cohesive open space policy. New York City had one of the lowest open space standards for its citizens of any metropolitan area in the country, only 2.5 acres per 1,000 residents. Thirty-three of New York City's 59 community planning districts or 56 percent did not meet this standard. Forty-nine percent of New York City community planning districts had less than 1.5 acres of open space per 1,000 people, while 29 had less than 1.5 acres of open space per 1,000 residents; 19 of these were community districts in which non-white population groups exceed 65 percent.[6] The Lower East Side had only .7 acres per 1,000 people (Ferguson 1999a: 73; New York City Environmental Justice Alliance 1998). In areas like the Lower East Side or the South Bronx, with only 0.2 acres of parkland for every 1,000 residents, the loss of any green space is painful, especially when such green space is intimately linked to the daily life, patterns of socialization, and free time of people in the neighborhood.

For many years activists have argued that community gardens contribute to the physiological and psychological health of gardeners and hence to that of the respective neighborhoods. Their contentions are supported by a growing body of literature and reports in the media.[7]

For instance, in 1999 the results of a research report by a team at the Center for Children's Health and the Environment at Mount Sinai about hospitalization rates in connection with asthma attacks were made public. The study provides strong evidence of the degree to which economic and social factors determine when and at what ages people are most likely to be afflicted with the disease and reports marked differences in hospitalization rates of poor and richer neighborhoods for all age groups. Further, a distribution map indicates that communities with the highest incidence of asthma also have the least green space per capita. While more study would be required to establish a definite causal link, the study implies that there is a connection between asthma and environmental conditions (Noble 1999).

Other arguments involve social and cultural benefits of community gardens, which are less easily quantifiable. Garden supporters point out that gardens provide safe places for children, are educational, contribute to the ecological enrichment of urban environments, contribute to food production, offer a range of cultural and educational events and programs, help to reduce crime in the neighborhood, and sustain community life. The proposed legislation cited some figures along these lines. For instance, in 1999 75 percent of GreenThumb gardens were managed by community and block associations interested in improving their neighborhood; nearly 90 percent of GreenThumb gardens offered public programming aimed at improving the quality of life for gardeners of all ages.

The city administration and developers have ignored these points and avoided discussing them. Supposedly pragmatic and measurable aspects such as the dollar value of development and the need for affordable housing are cited and contrasted with attempts to marginalize these spaces as dingy backyards for extended families. Further, the city administration has argued that community gardens were based on temporary leases and that gardeners always were aware that the license agreements were never intended to be permanent.

INDIVIDUAL GARDENS: IN SEARCH OF TRANQUILITY AND HOPE AMID THE RUBBLE

I chose four gardens for a more detailed analysis. Very different from each other in terms of their histories, internal organization, legal status, and composition of members, together they represent some of the key aspects and problems confronting community gardens in the entire city. These gardens are or were located in the Lower East Side neighborhood called Loisaida between 14th Street and Houston Street and Avenues A and D. They are Parque de Tranquilidad, La Plaza Cultural, and Jardín del Paraíso; the fourth, A BC Garden, is no longer in existence.[8]

The Parque de Tranquilidad is located the south side of 4th Street between Avenues C and D. Its founding members, a group of predominantly white middle-class people, lived in an adjoining building, which they had rehabilitated through sweat-equity labor in the mid-1970s. The current membership of the garden reflects the diversity of the neighborhood. In 1979, building members began to clear the rubble-filled site. Operation Green Thumb and the Council on the Environment of New York City have supported their efforts. The garden is comparatively small, accommodating at most one or two townhouse slices, and has only 25 members. It is not broken down into individual member plots with vegetables and flowers; rather, it is a single landscaped entity with sitting areas, plantings, and sculptures by local artists. Its cast iron fence serves to accentuate the beautifully maintained plantings.

In the 1990s the purpose and form of utilization of Tranquilidad was contested repeatedly. Some members envisioned the garden as a peaceful setting with an emphasis on its horticultural and aesthetic appeal. Others were interested in the garden as a setting for lectures, musical performances, and programs for children. For others again, the garden was important not as an end in itself but rather as a rallying point and forum for community issues far beyond gardening. Acrimony among members involved differences of an ideological nature as much as personality conflicts, at times deteriorating to the level of mudslinging. In the course of these conflicts, many members have withdrawn from active involvement, leaving a small core group of five people to manage and run the garden. The garden has weathered these tensions and attained a degree of stability as a small, visually stunning sanctuary on the block, occasionally participating in community events. The garden regularly hosts the Rites of Spring Pageant. One of the key scenes of the pageant is enacted inside the garden; children as harbingers of growth and renewal are dressed up as butterflies and perform a dance on its tiny lawn area in the back of the garden (also see Chapter 4).

Gardeners felt that the legal status of Tranquilidad was relatively secure; given the size of the lot, it was thought unlikely to be of interest to any major developer. However, this sense of security proved to be an illusion. Tranquilidad along with 112 other gardens was on the list of gardens to be auctioned in the May 1999 auction. Had it not been saved by the last-minute rescue acquisition by the Trust for Public Land, neither its status as one of the oldest gardens on the Lower East Side nor its beauty would have protected it.

The history of La Plaza Cultural on 9th Street and Avenue C goes back to the 1970s and the beginnings of an all-embracing activism that focused on youth problems, housing, drugs, arson, culture, and environmental issues. In the early 1970s, the site was filled with garbage, abandoned cars, and debris. In 1976 Chino Garcia and Armando Perez, leading members of the community organization Charas, together with people on the block and in the neighborhood began to clear the large corner lot. Members of Charas in cooperation with a local artist, Gordon La Matta Clark, also persuaded Buckminster Fuller to construct a geodesic dome in the center of the lot.[9] Trees were planted, large murals painted on the building walls surrounding the site, and an amphitheater constructed around a tarmac surface, doubling as a stage and a playing surface for children. By 2000 La Plaza contained three six-story willow trees, 15 fruit trees, and a fish pond among other attractions.

Over the years, La Plaza Cultural has hosted many musical and theatrical performances, festivals, weddings, and memorials. In the late 1990s there were about twenty members; their diversity reflects the demographics of the neighborhood. Some of the members have been actively involved since the garden's founding.

In the late 1980s, portions of La Plaza Cultural were occupied by a soup kitchen and a tent city. Supporters of the soup kitchen emphasized images of sharing limited resources, ingenuity, and survival skills on the part of a small group of people. Neighborhood people, in particular members of the block association, emphasized other elements such as drug use, disrespect for property, and occupation of the site to the exclusion of anyone else. Ensuing conflicts involved the individuals operating the soup kitchen, squatters in the area, peddlers who wanted to use the space for marketing their wares, Community Board 3 and the city administration, both interested in the site for the construction of a senior citizen housing project, and neighborhood people who wanted the site to remain a park. The existing park did not remain unscathed; portions of it were destroyed in the course of the conflicts, and abuse was heaped on, among others, the members of the block association as "yuppies and gentrifiers." Several development plans for the site have been derailed over the years. One reason may have been vigorous and increasingly well-organized protest by the members of the garden.

Further, the site is situated on top of several underground streams, which would complicate any construction project.

On June 6, 1995, HPD awarded a one-year lease to the 9th Street B/C Block Association for the entire site including the adjoining community garden. Plans for the renovation of the park are underway. Volunteers from all over the city, in particular from New York Cares, a volunteer organization, have been involved in some of this work over the past two years. The plans are based on the founding members' concept of La Plaza Cultural as a community place that welcomes cultural events, school programs, and day care centers, and contains space for plantings as well as paintings and sculptures by local artists. The derailed senior citizen housing project has been moved to a site on the next block, the A BC Garden described below.

However, since 1996, despite all this ongoing activity, La Plaza Cultural has been on the list of sites targeted for development by HPD. The proposed 7-story market-rate housing project is supposed to contain 64 units for luxury housing and 16 units for low-income housing and office space for the Lower East Side Girls Club. Supporters of La Plaza have accused this group of having sold out to the city administration for the sake of some promised space in the new building. The members of La Plaza Cultural have been expecting the arrival of bulldozers at any time; as of August 2001 the garden was still in existence.

The A BC Garden was located between Avenues B and C on 8th Street. Short lived, it was created in 1992 and bulldozed in January 1996. In those four years it flourished as a garden and gave rise to a vocal and organized group of gardeners. Most of the members lived in buildings around the site and could see the garden from their windows. About 40 percent were Puerto Rican. The garden had 70 member plots. The governing structure fluctuated, as one gardener put it, with a president, two co-treasurers, a vice president, and a secretary. The principal purpose of the garden was to provide a place for gardening rather than a site for community events. People helped each other with some of the work, for instance, taking turns at watering garden plots. Some people raised only vegetables; most had some flowers as well as vegetables and herbs on their plots. In the short time of its existence the garden flourished; it even included several small trees. One was a six-foot fir tree that a member had planted in memory of her grandmother. There was a sandbox, and a common area with a table and benches had been set up where gardeners and their families congregated.

Until the early 1980s the site contained several apartment buildings; they were abandoned and eventually demolished. Adjoining buildings in the back and on one side of the site were renovated as homesteading projects. Buildings on the other side were occupied by squatters. In the summer and fall of 1991, homeless people who had been evicted from nearby Tompkins Square Park occupied the site. The lot had the appearance of a little city, with distinct neighborhoods of squatters, divided by occupational specializations and ethnicity. With some ingenuity the occupants of the site rigged a shower at the fire hydrant on the sidewalk. Neighbors were concerned about this development. Homesteaders working on an adjoining building renovation project spoke of their fears of arson and vandalism (von Hassell 1996). At that point, residents on the block and in buildings in the back of the site received support from the city administration and Operation Green Thumb to start a garden. This support was extended despite existing plans for the construction of the Casa Victoria, a senior citizen home, on the site. City agents proceeded to evict the homeless people from the site and erected a high fence around it. Gardeners began to work on the garden with the understanding that eventually they would have to leave.

In 1994, a film crew wanted to use the garden for a scene. Most gardeners were opposed to allowing the film crew into the garden, since it would further cut back the already limited time left to the garden. The city supported the film crew. In ensuing protests, squatters from nearby buildings supported the gardeners, arguing that the gardeners were being pushed around by the city just as squatters are pushed around. Ironically, members of the city administration, having previously used the gardeners in efforts to keep homeless people out of the lot, described the gardeners as "squatters" with no rights to the site. Eventually, the film crew successfully approached another garden in the neighborhood. That garden, Orchard Alley, was then in its early stages of development; gardeners accepted plants and materials in turn for allowing the film crew to proceed. Orchard Alley was on the site of a former squatter area known as Bushville.[10]

Garden members and other neighborhood people were in disagreement over the impending demolition of the garden for the new senior citizen home. For some the Casa Victoria represented future housing for their parents and aunts and uncles. Several gardeners also felt bound by the original agreement with the city, when the garden was initiated. For others it represented yet another arbitrary decision by the city administration to bulldoze the labor of their hands—a "precious" and "productive green space"—while truly vacant lots remain unused.

On October 22, 1995, the A BC Garden hosted a harvest festival. During the festival, adults and children painted large panels as a living memory wall in honor of this garden and as a way to draw attention to its scheduled destruction. According to some gardeners, the purpose of the harvest festival was to call attention to the importance of all gardens on the Lower East Side and to the dangers of unchecked development, not to fight the senior citizen housing project on the A BC Garden site. Yet, in this struggle as in others over gardens, individuals and groups are forced into specific roles, and motivations and actions are reduced and reified. Thus, gardeners are alternately depicted as the

The Frog and the Rooster

"deserving poor," trying to plant a few beans on land that nobody wants, as illegal squatters on city-owned land that block efforts to construct much needed housing, and as "gentrifiers," willing to push out the elderly or low-income housing projects in order to plant hollyhock and roses (Tierney 1997). The garden was bulldozed on January 22, 1996. The new building was completed in 1997. Some of the gardeners have migrated to other gardens. A small group founded a new garden in a smaller lot across the street, the De Colores Community Yard and Garden.

The Jardín del Paraíso on 4th Street between Avenues C and D is arguably the most complex and ambitious garden project on the Lower East Side, striving to realize a vision of a public-private venture, in which portions of the garden or park have semi-private status and other portions are treated and used as public parkland. The entire area, consisting of five building lots, has been transferred to the New York City Department of Parks, assuring the site a modicum of protection for the years to come. The five lots are the Jardín del Paraíso Park, two private lots, Jardín Flowers and Vegetables, and Jardín de los Niños (Children's Garden), the latter two bordering on the public school and the school yard.

The garden was started in the early 1980s. Founding members had been instrumental in the housing movement, including a few leading activists in the neighborhood. The founding members were white; one man and three women did most of the work in the early years. One woman expressed frustration with the difficulty of involving other people in the neighborhood. She described the early days of her working on the garden, often the only one and a woman; she would get upset with the people across the street watching her and not willing to get involved and to help. She also pointed out that she did not reach out to them and say: "Hey, do you want to get involved?" She did not feel that was right or necessary. Eventually the founding members decided to recruit members more actively by holding a barbecue. The current membership of 35 people reflects the neighborhood's demographics, in that the majority are Puerto Rican. Throughout the garden's history, tensions between Puerto Rican members and white founding members surfaced, and charges of racism were bandied about when there were conflicts over particular matters. In 1986 garden members attempted to provide a means of conflict resolution by shifting the organizational structure of the garden to depend less on individual leadership and better reflect the demographics of the membership. The current charter stipulates that five officers must be elected on an annual basis, and two must be bilingual.

Operation Green Thumb supported the Jardín del Paraíso from the beginning; in fact the garden received a lease, although its organizational structure was still informal. The Trust for Public Land also has been supportive of the gardeners' efforts. In the early 1980s, founding members of the garden started a campaign to obtain a designation for the entire site as a city park. The original idea had been to include all the properties, including the lot behind the church and the one paved as schoolyard. The two smaller private lots represented the biggest obstacle to the plan. After years of effort and waiting, while the matter was digested by the bureaucratic juggernaut of the city administration, in 1993 the city administration allocated money for purchasing these lots for the garden. While other hurdles still need to be cleared, it appears that the vision for the site will become a reality. The property has been placed under the jurisdiction of the New York City Department of Parks.

How and by whom the park area of the site will be administered and who is to determine its design is yet to be decided. The site might become the flagship experimental model for a new type of community garden with common land, community participation, private flower and vegetable plots, and possibilities for an educational focus in cooperation with the school. Other experimental concepts may also be utilized to support the project; for instance, the Council on the Environment of New York City is interested in supporting environmental pockets in urban areas where bees and butterflies can thrive. Consequently, one portion might be designated a bees and butterflies garden.

PROBLEMS ENDEMIC TO ALL GARDENS

Certain problems plague all community gardens to different degrees. These problems mostly revolve around issues of control, ownership, and organization. Such conflicts are then played out in the domains of racial and ethnic divisions and gender role conflicts. They become further exacerbated when individual gardens have to compete against others in the same neighborhood for the support of the community board, for all that such support has been shown to be relatively meaningless in the face of concrete interest on part of a developer.

A key issue is access. For smaller gardens this issue is not such a problem; generally these spaces are open, as long as members are in it. Many gardens post regular opening hours. Gardens such as La Plaza Cultural or the Jardín del Paraíso, which try to combine semi-private community gardens with public park areas, have greater difficulties in working out acceptable models of managing access. Questions about access also involve the extension of the right of usage to diverse groups, whether these are operators of soup kitchens, musicians who feel they have established a right to a space by virtue of having spent a lot of time in it, or people who have constructed *casitas*. In other gardens members and an extended group of individuals in the community have keys, while the gardens remain closed to people on the street.

The Struggle for Eden

Another central problem is organization, which is worked out differently by the various gardens. Organization involves definition of membership rights and obligations, rights to pass plots on to family members as if they represented a form of private property, dues, membership participation, and conflict resolution. This also includes the search for supplies and donations, handling matters such as insurance coverage for the gardeners, work with greening groups such as the Green Guerillas, and planning of community events. Levels of member involvement shift in most gardens; in some instances, only a few individuals do a large portion of the organizational work, with a resulting top-heaviness of leadership. Each garden works out different governing structures; some structures are highly formalized, with elections of a president, treasurer, and secretary. Other gardens try to de-emphasize individual leadership and make a point of involving the community by broadening the decision-making body.

A gardener described the tendency of some individuals to "hog lots," that is, to accumulate garden plots in different gardens on behalf of fictive family members. Some people hang onto their plots by asking someone else to do the work, so eventually a few people are doing the gardening for a number of others. A related aspect is the notion of separatism, or in a gardener's words, an attitude of "this is my space, that is your space," which operates as a divisive factor within and among gardens. It contributes to an attitude of suspicion toward outsiders.

By the same token, gardeners repeatedly pointed out that gardening has presented them with a key to the neighborhood. One gardener, a single mother, told me: "I got to know people all over the neighborhood." Garden events also reach out to people in the neighborhood who are not themselves gardeners. By attending workshops organized by GreenThumb or the Green Guerillas, gardeners get to know gardeners in different neighborhoods of the city. Thus, gardening is a way to become part of an extended community.

The perception of an extended community is reflected in identification with struggles by people in other contexts, other neighborhoods, and other countries, symbolized by the names assigned to gardens. For instance, the Mendez Mural Garden was named in honor of the Brazilian rain forest activist Chico Mendez. Campos Plaza Residence Garden is named in honor of Pedro Albizú Campos (1891–1965), a Puerto Rican fighter for the nationalist cause. One encounters similarly creative names when looking at buildings rehabilitated by people in the neighborhood (von Hassell 1998).

Community gardens in New York City and on the Lower East Side are extremely diverse in organizational structure, membership, objectives, legal status, and levels of participation and acceptance by people in the neighborhood. Many gardens reflect tensions in purpose and organization, striving to answer to all needs—small backyard spaces for family and friends, semi-private gardens, spaces for individual creativity, welcoming community places, and political rallying grounds. Squatters, peddlers, homeless people, residents in sweat-equity buildings and in other buildings, activists, politicians, and gardeners, all speak of "community." The complexities are apparent in something as seemingly straightforward as the garden names Tranquilidad or Jardín del Paraíso, chosen in order to reflect the predominantly Puerto Rican membership—over 60 percent of gardeners on the Lower East Side are Puerto Ricans. The subtext involves founding members and major actors in these particular gardens who are predominantly white.

Different interest groups in the neighborhood and within individual gardens come into conflict over immediate and long-term uses of these spaces. A member of one garden has been lobbying for middle-income housing in the garden space. Another example is the lobbying by a respected poet and resident on the

Lower East Side, Miguel Algarín, for a housing development for retired artists on the site of the Peachtree Garden.

Community gardens provide arenas for the refashioning of normative gender roles. At the most immediate level, the gardens, by controlling access, provide safe and relatively healthy places for activity and socialization. Women can bring their children and feel comfortable in the company of neighbors with whom they are working in the garden. At another level, women are empowered by their work and roles in these gardens. In most gardens women are the principal contacts and spokespersons, while women outnumber men in terms of membership only slightly (60 percent to 40 percent). A similar distribution is reflected in local politics, community organizations, and housing initiatives (von Hassell 1996). In many gardens, founding members and women in particular had been involved in housing struggles of the 1970s and 1980s.

The distribution of labor along gender lines in community gardens to a degree reflects the ethnic, cultural, and class origins of the gardeners as well as their individual generational affiliations, varying from garden to garden. It is defined by class and race dynamics and the economic context, in particular the labor market, in the specific neighborhood as well as the composition of members in each individual garden. It is also subject to the individual garden's orientation on decorative plants, food production, or a mix of these. A critical component is the distinction between food production for subsistence as opposed to food production for the market and for income production, in conjunction with the value placed by the government and the society on such activities. In the United States as well as in other countries, where there are urban community gardens, the more value is placed on such activities by respective governments as much as by gardeners themselves—either as a source of income or as a component of political activism—the more men tend to be actively involved (Bellows 2000; also see Chapter 6). However, it is important to qualify such generalizations by pointing to the individual nature of each community garden and, more important, to the transformative character of community garden activities, which cut across race, class, and gender lines within both private and public domains.

Community gardens provide settings for the reproduction of culture and family life and for the production of food and power. Here power is understood to refer to the tools of power, that is, support in organizing coalitions on the local level, the possibility for labor exchange and mutual assistance, improvement of communication, and political education, among others. In the context of poverty, unemployment, underemployment, and scarcity of housing affecting Puerto Ricans on the Lower East Side, and women and women with children in particular, community gardens provide "place memories" (Low 1996) and play a critical role in the transformation of the neighborhood. In community gardens action, initiative, work, and creativity are rewarded in tangible ways in the creation of semi-public spaces for family and community life.

Community gardens have served as arenas for the development of resistance and community mobilization against drugs, arson, and displacement and around environmental issues and cultural themes. At times the city administration, when engaged in efforts to contain and eradicate squatter settlements, has supported the gardens. As part of a "gentler, kinder" method of keeping vacant lots free of squatters, the city administration has repeatedly encouraged the granting of GreenThumb leases to gardeners, only to revoke these leases when development of a particular lot became imminent.[11]

The Struggle for Eden

COMMUNITY-WIDE EFFORTS ON BEHALF OF THE GARDENS

The language of resistance developed by gardeners and activists has its roots in community initiatives in the 1970s. In the last two decades it has been gradually shaped into more cohesive images for the neighborhood and visions for new urban communities. In particular, one might consider a 1979 film about the Lower East Side and Charas, a Lower East Side organization founded in the 1970s. The themes and concepts from those periods are recapitulated and developed in the present garden preservation efforts.

A film produced in the late 1970s reflects some of the early language and themes that in the 1990s have been developed into a more comprehensive image of "community." Produced by Matias Bienvenida and Marci Reaven, *The Heart of Loisaida (El Corazón de Loisaida)* covers a period of years in the late 1970s on the Lower East Side (Bienvenida and Reaven 1979). In those years, residents in the neighborhood began to organize themselves into tenant associations in order to repair and renovate their decayed and landlord-abandoned tenements and to provide services to their buildings. The film shows residents describing their reasons for getting involved and what the tenant associations and related efforts mean to them and to their neighborhood.

The film emphasizes themes of decay and revitalization, with reference made to children playing in rubble-filled lots and the high number of abandoned buildings. Tenants talk about their buildings, the lack of services, inadequate heat and hot water, and rats and holes in the walls. Tenants describe the process of organizing buildings and starting rent strikes. One man said that he initially was not interested; he thought it was just talk, "until I fell in love with this movement." Repeatedly, one hears phrases such as: "Now we are united." "If something breaks we fix it." "You have a stronger sense of accomplishment when you do something yourself than when the landlord does it." "People are so used to having other people do stuff." Tenants refer to "the idea of being part of something" as a central factor in their involvement. One man said: "I never had confidence in myself, thought I was not needed." Tenants talked about "fixing the neighborhood, fixing ourselves."

The film uses the image of the "*milagro de Loisaida*" or miracle of Loisaida. According to tenants this effort gave rise to a sense of community that reached out to other buildings, other problem areas, and gardening in vacant lots. The camera moves over the Lower East Side, showing scenes of people clearing debris out of an empty lot, people planting in a garden, children playing and helping in a garden, people making music, and people caring for a tree on the sidewalk. A song plays in the background, "Cuando tengo el tierra. . ." (When I have the land . . .). The film leaves the viewer with compelling images of struggle and renewal; adults and children are shown carrying buckets of debris, turning the soil, sowing seeds, and watering their gardens.

This film reflects the 1970s language of individual and community empowerment, before it was revealed as mere words, however attractive and compelling. Nonetheless, it resonates in the language of community garden initiatives, transmuted into a more sophisticated and complex vision of the city and neighborhoods within it and combined with themes from the environmental justice movement of the mid-1980s.

Another source for the images that have lent strength and a sense of cohesiveness to the struggle over community gardens was the alternative technology movement on the Lower East Side (Chodorkoff 1980; Mottel 1973). Alternative technologies included ecologically sound organic gardening techniques and the goal of reintroducing food production into urban living, developing low-cost ways to use solar energy, experimenting with waste recycling, exploitation of wind mills, solar space heaters, greenhouses on rooftops, even experimental fishponds in basements of buildings on the Lower East Side. A goal of the movement was the development of a "reconstructive utopian tradition." The reconstruction of "community" through the use of alternative technologies was understood in the concrete sense of reconstruction of buildings and places and in the conceptual sense of providing individuals in the neighborhood with tools and themes on which to rebuild their lives.

Such a reconstruction was inspired by the perceived need to heed the Puerto Rican cultural values of self-reliance and mutual aid within a network of family and friends, derived from the rural *jíbaro* tradition (Chodorkoff 1980). In Puerto Rico, the *jíbaro* rural way of life fed on family and community life outdoors and in informal public settings (Santiago 1993).[12]

For Puerto Ricans in New York City, recreation in comparable informal settings has been central to the reproduction of their culture. A Puerto Rican woman in a garden on Avenue C told me: "I grew up on a farm. Everyone needs space to breathe. I need this for my soul."

The concept of a reconstruction of community was critical to the central ideological framework of a community organization called Charas/El Bohio Cultural and Community Center, still in existence today. Founded by Chino Garcia and five others in the late 1960s, Charas was active in vacant lot reclamation and youth organization and played a critical role in the flowering of Puerto Rican culture on the Lower East Side.[13] In its various projects Charas placed a premium on participation and learning processes. As an organization it defined leadership in non-hierarchical terms, shifting from individual to individual in relation to activities being undertaken. Charas emphasized concepts of self-management, collectivity, and decentralization of power and authority (Mottel 1973). These themes resonate in the language of various Lower

East Side community organizations and initiatives in conjunction with housing issues as well as community gardens (von Hassell 1996).

ORGANIZATIONS AND COALITIONS IN SUPPORT OF GARDENS

Gardeners and activists sometimes asked me with a certain quizzical expression of forbearance: "Have you attended any of the garden meetings? Then you know what that's like." I was frequently reminded of the Orpheus Orchestra, a successful and respected orchestra that works without a conductor. The Orpheus Orchestra operates on the principle of flat organization; no one individual or set of individuals is in charge over a longer period of time, and all decisions are made on a consensus basis. Rehearsals can be chaotic, to say the least. In some respects this description can be applied to community garden coalitions.

The history of activism and struggle on behalf of community gardens in New York City has been characterized by a constantly shifting playing field of actors and allegiances. In part this is a reflection of dynamics internal to such coalitions and power struggles among them; in part the shifts reflect successes that bring other actors on board. Finally such shifts occur in the context of political and economic developments in the city administration and also at a wider level.

The extended community of gardeners has acquired increasingly concrete shape over the past decade of strenuous efforts to save gardens from destruction. City-wide greening and open space groups such as the Neighborhood Open Space Coalition and the Trust for Public Land had been trying to move the city administration to institute a comprehensive review process for community garden preservation from the mid-1990s on. But ultimately, it took grassroots activism to bring the issue to the attention of politicians and the public. On the Lower East Side and in other New York City neighborhoods numerous community garden groups and coalitions have emerged. These coalitions and "players" include, among others, Earth Celebrations, the Lower East Side Garden Preservation Association, New York City Community Garden Coalition, Lower East Side Collective, More Gardens! Coalition, Cherry Tree Association, Inc., BANG (Brooklyn Alliance of Neighborhood Gardens), East New York Gardens Coalition, BUG (Bronx United Gardeners), and Project Harmony. There is an overlap among these various groups; certainly they have cooperated to the point that the contributions of each cannot be easily sorted out. While it is impossible to do justice to the range of coalitions, initiatives, and efforts by groups and individuals, the following description of some of these groups gives a flavor of their diversity.

A central impetus behind community-wide organization of gardens has been a small organization called Earth Celebrations. Earth Celebrations was started by Felicia Young on the Lower East Side as a one-woman initiative on behalf of the gardens, with a predominant focus on processions and pageants. Over the past seven years it has blossomed into an organization with support from foundations, private corporations, and individuals. It operates on the basis of a broad network of volunteers, including gardeners, activists, environmentalists, schools, other community organizations, members of various churches, artists, actors, and individuals from all walks of life and all areas of New York City. Earth Celebrations has chaired countless meetings of gardeners, made extensive use of the media, and initiated letter-writing campaigns on behalf of the gardens. In 1994 Earth Celebrations initiated the Lower East Side Garden Preservation Coalition, a precursor of which had been started by the Green Guerillas in 1984 in response to the threat of development of the 6th Street and B Community Garden.

Earth Celebrations and the Lower East Side Garden Preservation Coalition explored the possibility of forming a garden land trust and other garden preservation options, for instance through permanent site status granted under the auspices of the New York City Department of Parks. These efforts gave rise to the New York City Coalition for the Preservation of Gardens, which was formed in 1996 in response to the bulldozing of gardens throughout New York City. It is an umbrella coalition of garden coalitions all over New York City, including the Bedford-Stuyvesant Garden Coalition, Bronx Garden Coalition, Bronx United Gardeners (BUG), Brooklyn Alliance of Neighborhood Gardens (BANG), Brownsville Garden Coalition, Bushwick Garden Coalition, East New York Garden Coalition, La Familia Verde, Manhattan United Gardeners (MUG), and Lower East Side Garden Preservation Coalition. This coalition has been instrumental in initiating city-wide action on behalf of the gardens, reaching out to gardens in all boroughs, inviting members from gardens that were previously destroyed to share their experiences with other gardeners, encouraging community attendance at meetings of community boards, canvassing elected officials, supporting marches to City Hall, and taking the battle into the courts. Several web sites and list serves on the Internet disseminate information, provide updates on developments, and issue regular calls for action.

The Lower East Side Collective is another organization involved in the struggle to preserve community gardens. It has worked to educate gardeners and the public about the struggle by designing bilingual posters and leaflets. The Lower East Side Collective also has helped to orchestrate direct action campaigns to protest city policy and to draw the attention of the media and the public. While this group has emerged on the Lower East Side, the focus of their efforts has been city-wide. After five garden activists plus "John Doe 1 through 10" were sued by Donald Capoccia for defamation, harassment, and tortious interference with contract in 1998, the Lower East Side Collective gave birth to Jayne Doe, styled "Subcommandante, Garden Diva, Protectress of Activists, Propagandist par Excellence and Occasional Gender Illusionist," who has also presided over a city-wide garden action web site. The suit was dropped after the lawyer threatened a full-scale examination of the developer's finances. Jayne Doe was quoted as saying "Throughout the entire campaign, we will look stylish, feel fabulous, and refuse to be intimidated or discouraged. We take our inspiration from the final words of Joe Hill, the Wobbly agitator who was executed in 1915: 'Don't waste time in mourning. Organize.' "[14] The Lower East Side Collective has come into conflict with other garden preservation organizations over strategy and ideology. Nonetheless, Jayne Doe and her cohort have lent tremendous style and color to the proceedings throughout the struggle for the gardens.

In the last two years of the 20th century, the More Gardens! Coalition, originating in the Bronx, has emerged as one of the more vocal groups. "We have mobilized an army of dedicated volunteers to reach out to every gardener in the city, to make them aware of the impending doom" (More Gardens! Coalition 1999). They were actively involved in every protest action and individual efforts to defend gardens, most notably the defense of the Esperanza garden. Associated with the More Gardens! Coalition, the Cherry Tree Association, Inc. in Mott Haven, the Bronx, has spoken out on behalf of community gardens. For the Cherry Tree Association the overarching goal is the creation of environmental health; it has also been engaged in efforts to shut down a medical waste incinerator in the Bronx and in working for park and recreation space along the inaccessible waterfront of Mott Haven and Port Morris and has lobbied for bike lanes and art and cultural events. The Cherry Tree

Association is one of a range of organizations under the umbrella of La Casa del Sol, a Bronx-based cultural center that began as a housing and garden cooperative. The Cherry Tree Association together with La Casa del Sol was instrumental in founding the More Gardens! Coalition.

Project Harmony is a Harlem neighborhood group that has initiated a number of community gardens; most of these gardens have been bulldozed in the late 1990s. Project Harmony has a comprehensive orientation. Community gardens are a central component in community revitalization, cutting across education, experiences of children, urban agriculture, social dynamics in a neighborhood, and the environment. Its founders Cynthia and Haja Worley look beyond their specific neighborhood toward the significance of such initiatives in urban areas across the country and think in terms of linkages to environmental as well as social issues at a global level.

At a city-wide meeting of garden coalitions and greening groups in July 1999, Haja Worley, who had just seen a number of gardens in his neighborhood eliminated, spoke about the need to work in grassroots community development. He reiterated that the problem at hand is much larger than just a few gardens; the health and life of a community, urban life, the future of young people, and the environment are at stake. He further spoke about the need to help young people make the move from garden lessons to reclamation in the wider sense and the need to provide services to the community, beginning with block watchers and safety and extending to education. He advised his audience to stay connected and to share information—not only within New York City but across the country: "It is all connected; it is all relative."

The Struggle for Eden

FRAGMENTATION AND COHESION

These organizations and coalitions have been engaged in local turf wars, which occasionally acquired an acrimonious character and involved individual personality conflicts as much as conflicts over ideology, strategy, and competition for funding. Motivations of individuals and organizations have been called into question. As one gardener put it: "People are in this for all sorts of reasons." Over the years some of these groups have retreated or have been forced into the background, while others have become more prominent. There are differing narratives about the roles played by the respective organizations in the struggle for garden preservations. Like other groups and organizations engaged in the struggle for a cause, participants at times have been beleaguered by tiredness, disillusion, and disorganization.

One example for disagreements over strategies and objectives is the debate about garden rules and guidelines. While some suggested that it would be good strategy to establish certain standards for community gardens as a way to deflect attacks of these spaces as misused or aesthetically questionable and consequently "unworthy" of being saved, others objected to any such general rules as unnecessarily restrictive, if not elitist. Another conflict involved the degree to which aggressive strategies ought to be employed. Here the fault lines divided the more established greening groups from some of the grassroots garden coalitions.

Another debate involved the concept of a community land trust. Several years before the Trust for Public Land together with the New York Restoration Project acquired 112 gardens with the intention to establish community land trusts for their preservation, gardeners engaged in heated discussions about such a notion as a possible means to save the gardens. In various boroughs garden coalitions have been exploring the land trust concept; for instance, the Brooklyn Alliance of Gardens (BANG) has been working on establishing a land trust for gardens in Brooklyn. On the Lower East Side these discussion were inspired by ideas that first emerged in connection with housing rehabilitation. In the 1970s and 1980s housing activists had considered the community land trust concept as a vehicle for retaining community control over low-income housing (von Hassell 1996).

In garden coalition meetings the community land trust concept incited fears about privatization and control issues. At the time, the idea did not take hold; however, it remains a remarkable instance of an effort to apply this concept, which runs counter to normative concepts of property ownership to semi-public outdoor spaces. Further complicating this issue is the argument advanced by some activists that organizations such as the Trust for Public Land, ostensibly defenders of community gardens, are pursuing an agenda of privatization of these spaces and a restriction of community input.

In a few instances gardens have obtained separate agreements with the city administration or were able to acquire site control by purchase. Consequently their motivation to participate in the struggle was understandably lessened; however, for the most part such gardens have continued to remain involved and supportive. Other gardens have pursued individual courses of action in the legal system, for instance, the J.D. Wilson Memorial Garden in Harlem or the Jardín de Esperanza. However, the city-wide garden community has supported these gardens in their efforts. Of course, this raises the continually debated question of whether it is more effective to fight as a group than to pursue individual courses of action, never mind how promising. Unquestionably, the largest crowds and greatest outpouring of efforts revolved around the possibility of 112 gardens being auctioned at a single time. Nonetheless, as different gardens or groups of gardens were threatened over the years, the various coalitions went into action accordingly. The most lasting impression after observation of the struggle over the past decade is the degree to which all these various groups again and again have rallied and marshalled extraordinary efforts, with at times memorable and impressive results.

STRATEGIES

Strategies employed in the struggle for community gardens are as diverse as the gardens themselves. Principally there are legal efforts, legislative efforts, public outreach and media campaigns, and direct action. Many of these efforts have overlapped and reinforced each other.

Legal efforts include class action lawsuits and lawsuits brought by individual gardens. For instance, the Esperanza garden sued the city, arguing that the city has not provided the gardeners with an adequate opportunity to be heard. One judge ruled against the Esperanza gardeners on the grounds that they had no standing and no legal right to sue. The gardeners planned to appeal this decision, arguing that their twenty-year involvement with the garden and the fact that many of the plaintiffs are owners of the adjoining building gave them such legal standing. According to a lawyer involved in this case, there is a leeway of interpretation of what is defined as "legal standing"; in cases of doubt the tendency on the part of local courts has been to rule against the gardeners. However, in October 2000 the gardeners decided against filing an appeal. Another individual lawsuit involves a Project Harmony garden in Harlem; in this case the gardeners are proceeding against the private owner of the lot. The gardeners have been trying to buy the lot from the owner, without success to date.

One of the first suits was brought in 1997 by two Lower East Side gardens, the Chico Mendez Memorial Garden and the Jardín de la 10th Street, together with nine Harlem gardens against the city administration and the New York City Housing Partnership (Ferguson 1999b). The State Supreme Court ruled against the gardeners, arguing that they could not challenge the city's plans since they did not own the lots or hold long-term leases. Other suits followed.

The most prominent lawsuit is the one brought by District Attorney General Eliot Spitzer. In addition to arguing that many community gardens should be declared parks, the Spitzer lawsuit also contends that the gardens cannot be treated on a case-by-case basis, but rather that a proper environmental review process must consider all of the gardens in a comprehensive fashion. A court decision supporting the attorney general's argument would effectively prevent any additional individual community gardens from being razed before being subject to such review. New York City appealed the Temporary Restraining Order handed down by Judge Huttner of the State Supreme Court in Brooklyn on March 15, 2000; however, in a September 2000 decision Judge Huttner upheld the injunction, which prohibits any sales of gardens, pending a decision on the case filed by the attorney general.

Two other groups, the Natural Resources Defense Council (NRDC) and the Puerto Rican Legal Defense Fund (PRLDF) have filed federal lawsuits. In 1999 the NRDC together with the Green Guerillas filed a lawsuit against the city for failure to conduct environmental and land use reviews of gardens to be auctioned in May 1999.[15] About the same time the PRLDF together with the New York City Environmental Justice Alliance (NYEJA) filed a class action lawsuit on the grounds of an environmental justice argument and environmental discrimination against people of color. Activists considered the acquisition of these gardens by the Trust for Public Land and the New York Restoration Project a bittersweet victory. While 112 gardens were saved, the NRDC lawsuit and the one brought by the PRLDF were effectively scuttled as a result.

Since May 1999 the city administration has chosen to target smaller groups of gardens or individual gardens at a time. Another negative effect has been a loss of interest by the public, which was generally under the impression that the dramatic rescue acquisition represented the successful conclusion of the struggle on behalf of the gardens. In an attempt to correct that misperception and to keep up the pressure, the Green Guerillas together with eight community gardeners from Brooklyn and the Bronx as co-plaintiffs filed a lawsuit against New York City in the State Supreme Court in September 2000. The lawsuit charges that the city ignored the positive impact of community gardens and that it must abide by the Uniform Land Use Review Process (ULURP), including public hearings, before selling or disposing of community gardens on public land. As of summer 2001 the case was still in court pending a judge's decision.

Other efforts have focused on the city and state legislature. One is a state bill introduced by state senators Montgomery and Sampson, which operates roughly parallel to the injunction sought by the state attorney general. It declares New York City's community gardens to be parkland, which cannot be sold without an extensive review process. This would force the city administration to look more closely at other lots, in particular the estimated 11,000 lots described as truly vacant by the garden community.

Senator Sampson also endorsed the Nemore report, a study about community gardens in New York City prepared by Carole Nemore of the New York State Senate Minority Program Office (Nemore 1998). Sampson said that the report strengthen his resolve to work for a comprehensive policy to preserve community gardens. The report refers to New York State's Open Space Plan, the official document that was to guide the State's permanent open space goals and strategies (New York State 1995).

New York State's Open Space Plan unequivocally supports the use of open space for community gardens, particularly in urban areas chronically and severely underserved by open space, and recommends community gardens for open space acquisition in New York City as a way to redress an existing imbalance among different neighborhoods. The Nemore report, based on a survey of 229 community gardeners, states that destruction of community gardens "will rip the heart out of the community" (Nemore 1998: ii). More importantly the report emphasizes that the debate has been improperly skewed as one of a choice of housing over gardens. Rather, the report argues that these spaces can be preserved, while other spaces can be utilized for development in addition to rehabilitation of existing buildings.

In 2000, New York State Senator Tom K. Duane, representing the 27th Senatorial District and a former member of the New York City Council, introduced a legislation that would amend the New York City charter. This legislation, if passed, would require the mayor's office to notify the City Council of any GreenThumb garden that has been approved for sale or disposition and for which disposition has not been completed within a ten-year period. The City Council could then rescind their approval of the disposition.

On the city level a coalition of community gardeners and their supporters are seeking city council sponsorship for a legislation that would create a process for preserving gardens. The legislation asks for a moratorium on developing or disponing of existing community gardens while this legislation is being considered. Once the legislation would be in effect, each garden would have to go through what is known as the Uniform Land Use Review Process (ULURP) process before it can be taken away. The accelerated-approval process called UDAAP (Urban Development Action Area Program) process used for the Esperanza garden would no longer be valid.[16]

By request of Brooklyn Borough President Howard Golden,

The Struggle for Eden

Councilman Ken Fisher introduced a legislative proposal to the city council in February 1999 to amend the New York City charter to impose a moratorium on the sale of gardens; the proposal required disposition of GreenThumb gardens to be approved by the city council. Another legislative proposal by Councilman Adolfo Carrion at the request of the Bronx borough president called for an amendment of the charter to the effect that no GreenThumb garden be sold auctioned, exchanged, leased, or otherwise alienated. A third piece of legislation was introduced by Carrion and Fisher to call upon the State of New York to limit the power of the mayor with regard to such land disposition. By July 2000, 22 city council members had co-signed the proposed garden legislation. Other council members were expected to sign on. Their co-signatures provide enough support for passage, but not for a mayoral veto override. As of this writing Carrion and Fisher were still trying to get the proposed legislation approved by the city council.

Garden activists have engaged in extensive letter-writing, phone, and fax campaigns in order to state their case, refute arguments advanced by the city, correct misrepresentations by the media and public officials, and draw the attention of the public to the struggle. The Internet has been an important communication device, a means of disseminating information, a public forum for exchange of ideas, and a bulletin board for calls for help and action alerts. People from other cities in the United States and from other countries have used the Internet to communicate with the New York City garden community and to express their support.

Direct action campaigns have helped to draw the attention of the public to the struggle and to increase pressure on the city administration. Some have argued that this pressure may have had negative effects, inciting the city administration to proceed more rapidly in some cases, for example, in the decision to proceed against the Jardín de Esperanza. On the other hand, there is little doubt that this strategy was a major element in derailing the May

1999 auction and in getting the New York Restoration Project involved, as a result of which it became harder for the city administration to reject a deal. One month before the scheduled auction the Trust for Public Land had made an offer to the city administration to buy 165 community gardens for $2 million. The city had rejected that offer.

In one such action, protesters released 10,000 crickets at an auction held at Police Headquarters on July 20, 1998, to protest the auction of several community garden lots and a building that houses the Charas/El Bohio Cultural and Community Center on the Lower East Side. Despite the bedlam created by this action, the auction proceeded and the properties in question were sold. Another action involved the so-called Standing Our Ground Rally and Conference held on April 9-10, 1999, to educate the general public about community gardens. Organizers had brought together an impressive array of speakers, including two state senators, and members of the city council and the state assembly in addition to representatives of numerous supportive organizations. The rally was enlivened by musical entertainment, dance, and a parade around Bryant Park, the site of the rally.

On May 5, 1999, a demonstration in Lower Manhattan called the Earth Shaking Protest and Civil Disobedience protested the scheduled auction of 112 gardens. About 400 to 500 people participated, chanting, singing, and holding signs. Buckets filled with flowers, a brass band, and street theater enlivened the proceedings. Sixty-two were arrested for nonviolent civil disobedience. At one point people in the streets were chanting exuberantly "No Justice, No Peas," while the paddy wagon filled to overflowing with arrestees bounced up and down as they chanted along with the crowd.

There were many other events, albeit on a smaller scale, such as processions to bring flowers to the mayor, people dressed up as vegetables parading in Lower Manhattan, and fax and phone blitzes, flooding politicians' offices with messages. With an endearing sense of courtesy, activists encouraged participants after such campaigns to send thank-you notes and flowers to hapless secretaries in the respective politicians' offices, thanking them for their efforts.

CONCLUSION

On November 2, 1998, the Garden of Love was bulldozed without any advance warning. This garden at 121st Street and 7th Avenue was associated with the public school across the street and was maintained and planted by children from that school. A schoolteacher and his students were just about to go to the garden, when they encountered the bulldozers. HPD, after several days of vociferous outcries in the press and elsewhere, admitted that the garden was destroyed by mistake and that another nearby garden, the West 129th Street Block Association Garden, was supposed to be bulldozed instead. In response the gardeners from that garden tried to save some of the trees and plants by digging them up and moving them, while the children from P.S. 76 placed candles and wreaths around the perimeter of the former Garden of Love.

In this continuing theater of the absurd, this garden was not bulldozed for over six months, and HPD was not able or willing to provide a clear answer on what was going to happen. It was eventually bulldozed together with four other Harlem gardens in June 1999; in anticipation of this event gardeners in those gardens frantically dug up many of their plants, even trees, and gave them away to other gardens. One gardener told me that a peach tree transplanted from the partially bulldozed J.D. Wilson Memorial Garden, the last remaining garden organized by the neighborhood group Project Harmony, on 122nd Street actually survived in a neighbor's backyard. A year later, the former George W. Brown

Memorial Garden was nothing but a huge crater in the ground; neighbors have repeatedly called the city administration about this hazardous situation. The site of another former Project Harmony garden on 129th Street has been used as a launching place for a series of burglaries, while garbage has been piling up in another.

This event together with others in the following months did much to galvanize the city-wide garden community. One might argue that some of the more spectacularly insensitive actions of the city administration—such as the timing of bulldozing and bulldozing of gardens by mistake—together with the more extreme of Mayor Giuliani's remarks about community gardens and gardeners have actually been helpful, impelling garden supporters into action and making the position of community gardeners appear less extreme and more reasonable and balanced by comparison. Mayor Giuliani has told community gardeners that they were not living in a realistic world and were "stuck in the era of communism" (Fuerbringer 1999). City press releases referred to community garden sites as being "among the last unimproved, derelict, and vacant lots in their communities." In reaction to this stance as well as in reaction to activism, the media and politicians have become more supportive.

The existence of the Nemore report, combined with the support of state senators John Sampson and Velmanette Montgomery, State Attorney General Eliot Spitzer, Brooklyn Borough President Howard Golden, city council members Ken Fisher and Adolfo Carrion, and New York State Assemblyman Richard Brodsky, among others, signals the effectiveness of activism on behalf of community gardens. A list of supporting groups of the direct action events reveals the breadth of interest that the struggle for community gardens has elicited; such groups include the Horticultural Society of New York, the Garden Club of America, the Presbytery of New York, Sierra Club of New York, Brooklyn Green Party, Metropolitan Council on Housing,

The Struggle for Eden

Bedford Stuyvesant Garden Coalition, Project for Public Spaces, Queens Green Party, Manhattan Botanical Garden, Hunger Action Network of NYS, and Urban Arts & Ecology. Various foundations have contributed to the May 1999 rescue acquisition by providing funding, including the LuEsther T. Mertz Charitable Trust, the Mary Flagler Cary Charitable Trust, the Lily Auchincloss Foundation, the Frances & Benjamin Benensen Foundation, the Geoffrey C. Hughes Foundation, the Rose and Sherle Wagner Foundation, the New York Foundation, and the New York Community Trust.

Some legal and legislative efforts may bear fruit in the future, time has been gained, some gardens have been removed from auction lists, some gardens have been transferred to the New York City Department of Parks, and the public has become aware. Some deals have been struck, saving portions of individual gardens; for instance, Brooklyn Borough President Howard Golden brokered a deal with the developer of the Brooklyn Bears Garden site in Boerum Hill, saving 5,000 square feet of an 8,000 square feet garden. However, the reality is that since May 1999, more than 12 gardens have been razed, over 100 community garden sites have moved through the administrative process releasing them for development, another 400 gardens are just as vulnerable, and there is as yet no concrete handhold to block their destruction nor is there a general policy in place with regard to the preservation or creation of community gardens in New York City.

Charles Lott, Baptist minister at the community garden on Glenmore Avenue and Barbey Street, one of East New York's first community gardens, argues that gardens are a place to begin urban renewal. "How do you rally people to fight back? You start a garden" (Hickey 1994: 49). This statement reflects the fact that community gardens ultimately represent far more than green space; for people involved in these initiatives the connection to other essential components of life of social, cultural, and economic significance is immediate and compelling. In the language of community activists, gardens express the notion of battle on all fronts, a fight for an entire way of life rather than single issues.

This fight for a way of life above all involves the right to design one's individual garden plot, one's garden, or one's community—within parameters that do not infringe upon others or upon the environment. These parameters are continually redefined, but recurring themes are a resistance to standards and styles imposed from above and to domination by the market economy at various levels of existence and the need to create spaces for community life, however defined, within the urban maelstrom.

To be sure, these efforts are fraught with conflicts at many levels, beginning with individual gardens' internal politics and continuing to different visions for the community. Both long-term residents and newcomers to the area over the past two decades have embraced and defended community gardens. Other residents and the city administration have criticized and attacked the gardens as an obstruction to affordable housing construction. Some have conceptualized the gardens as a Trojan horse—a vanguard of gentrification; some view gentrification as a positive development while others consider it with dismay. Others look to the gardens as the bastion and last hope for community life for low-income people. Poised on the edge of an ideological sword in their contradictory roles in political, economic, and social changes and in their diverse class and cultural compositions, community gardens are both an expression of and the embodiment of resistance to processes of gentrification of the neighborhood.[17] Analysis of community gardens and garden activism on the Lower East Side reveals the fragmentation in these struggles. Nonetheless, efforts on behalf of the gardens represent a remarkable instance of locally based initiatives, supported by highly idiosyncratic and diverse groups. These initiatives have grown to include the entire city and in fact draw on this expanded base as a source of strength.

NOTES

1. Mayor Giuliani made this pronouncement when asked to comment about the bulldozing of the Esperanza garden in February 2000 (Chivers 2000).
2. This letter was written by Santa Gomez, a young resident on the block, after the J.D. Wilson Memorial Garden on 122nd Street between 7th and 8th Avenues was partially destroyed by bulldozers in June 1999. This garden, a fifteen-year-old garden also known as the Project Harmony Garden, had earlier filed suit to stop its destruction; however, the city administration proceeded anyway. Over half of the garden was gone before lawyers at the Puerto Rican Legal Defense and Education Fund managed to obtain a temporary restraining order.
3. The terms "squatter" and "homesteader" in this context are used advisedly. It is a way to distinguish between people who have occupied and renovated buildings without sanction from the city administration and people who have renovated buildings as part of an urban homesteading program under the auspices of the city administration. However, squatters at times refer to themselves as homesteaders, rejecting the term squatter as a derogatory term, while others embrace it. In the opinion of some squatters, homesteaders have sold out to the city by accepting the city's terms and obligations. In turn some homesteaders refer to their own history in connection with the particular building that they helped to rehabilitate as having had its roots in squatting and in that context refer to this with pride as an act of resistance. This illustrates some of the complexity of the history of housing struggles on the Lower East Side; this same complexity is reflected

in community garden politics.

4. Before entering politics Lopez had worked as an outreach worker in a social services agency. In the 1970s and 1980s she had been active in the housing movement, had herself been a homesteader, and had worked on the development of a community land trust in order to help safeguard affordable housing in perpetuity. In the 1990s she entered electoral politics and became a member of Community Board 3. She was elected a councilwoman for the district in 1998.

5. For a discussion of social movements see Tilly (1978) and Mauss (1975), also see Melucci (1980) for a discussion of new social movements.

6. Includes African-American, Latino, and Asian-American population as reported in the 1990 U.S. Census.

7. A growing number of psychology and environmental studies have addressed the relationship between physiological and psychological well-being and the environment as well as social dynamics in a neighborhood and the relationship between crime rates and community gardens (for instance, see Francis et al. 1994; Taylor et al. 1998).

8. A gardener explained to me that the name "A BC Garden" must not be mistaken for "ABC" as in "Alphabet City," a name for the Lower East Side not popular among many residents; in the 1970s and 1980s "Alphabet City" carried negative overtones and was associated with a perception of that neighborhood as drug and crime-infested. In those years, as an act of defiance and pride, residents renamed the area "Loisaida," which reflects the "Spanglish" version of Lower East Side, the name of a woman and of a village in Puerto Rico. "A BC Garden" refers to a garden located between Avenues B and C.

9. For an early history of Charas and the role of Buckminster Fuller in the construction of geodesic domes on the Lower East Side see Mottel (1973).

10. Bushville was memorable for its permanently inhabited *casitas*, ingeniously constructed shelters complete with porches and decorative elements. They are portrayed in a photography collection that serves to illustrate the potential for an appropriation of aesthetics in social and economic conflicts (Balmori and Morton 1993). See Deutsche and Ryan (1984) for a discussion of processes of gentrification and an "aesthetics of poverty" that represented a central component in the attraction of the Lower East Side to the artist community and people in search of a bohemian life style.

11. Community gardens and allotment gardens have been used as tools by other city administrations. For instance, in 1894 in Detroit, during a period of extremely high unemployment rates, allotment gardens were used as a way to assist people while saving on relief expenditures (Warner 1987). Other cities followed suit in subsequent years. This "assistance" involved the temporary or long-term removal of land from the market to make it available free of charge or at low cost to city gardeners.

12. Santiago describes the poetry and songs associated with *jíbaro* cultural traditions as conveying a message that life involved struggle and hardship, but was "rewarded by a life of independence and contemplation, a closeness to nature coupled with respect for its intractability, and a deeply rooted and proud nationalism" (Santiago 1993: 12).

13. A prominent member of Charas in the 1980s and 1990s was Armando Perez. Perez also was a member of Community Board 3 and the neighborhood's elected democratic district leader. He was murdered in an unresolved crime in another part of New York City in April 1999. At the time of his death he was involved in the fight for the space housing the Charas/El Bohio Cultural Center. Deeply mourned on the Lower East Side, he has been raised to a status akin to that of a patron saint of the community garden struggle on the Lower East Side. In the outpouring of emotions over the death of Armando Perez, garden activists have identified with activists

struggling to fight the eviction of Charas from its building, arguing that it is part of the same struggle.

14. Joe Hill was a member of the Industrial Workers of the World (I.W.W.), known as Wobblies, involved in a labor dispute between copper mining companies and their workers in the second decade of the 20th century.

15. The Natural Resources Defense Council (NRDC) is a national non-profit organization of scientists, lawyers, and environmental specialists, with over 400,000 members nationwide.

16. UDAAP enabled the city to transfer "vacant lots" or "blighted land" to a private development group such as the New York City Housing Partnership without an environmental review.

17. Also see Martinez for a discussion of the dynamics of class on the Lower East Side (Martinez 2001).

The Struggle for Eden

Primavera, Father Winter, Gaia, And Other Restless Spirits: Cultural Constructions of Community

> *But when he had now reached that far-off isle, he went forth from the sea of violet blue to get him up into the land, till he came to a great cave, wherein dwelt the nymph of the braided tresses: and he found her within. And on the hearth there was a great fire burning, and from afar through the isle was smelt the fragrance of cleft cedar blazing, and of sandal wood. And the nymph within was singing with a sweet voice as she fared to and fro before the loom, and wove with a shuttle of gold. And round about the cave there was a wood blossoming, alder and poplar and sweet-smelling cypress. And therein roosted birds long of wing, owls and falcons and chattering sea-crows, which have their business in the waters. And lo, there about the hollow cave trailed a gadding garden vine, all rich with clusters. And fountains four set orderly were running with clear water, hard by one another, turned each to his own course. And all around soft meadows bloomed of violets and parsley, yea, even a deathless god who came thither might wonder at the sight and be glad at heart.*[1]

INTRODUCTION

Marooned in Calypso's world, on her enchanted island, Odysseus mourns for home. This is a quintessentially human yearning and one of the most moving episodes in this tale of cunning, heroic feats, and mind-numbing slaughters. At another level, it pits a world of pragmatic realism against a world of the imagination, a world where dreams and fantasy throw shimmering cloths of gold over old rags and cover deadened landscapes and hollow tree trunks with flowering garlands, a world where a rich and vibrant inner landscape transforms our surroundings. Odysseus leaves, choosing peril in action in a world of concrete facts over an existence in which he has to listen and to be receptive to internal dreams and images and the world around him.

Confronted with community gardens, bulldozers like city administrations have little patience with fantasy landscapes or the transformative power of a world of the imagination, blindly rolling across hand-made garden angels, scarecrows assembled out of urban debris, and flowering bulbs buried in weedy plots in the middle of winter. Indeed, how could they? Their treads are not made for sight.

While the struggle over community gardens is largely defined by market-driven exploitation of real estate and the politics of space, it also is defined by a struggle over competing visions. As such it reflects a gap of understanding and a profound clash of worlds and languages. For an understanding of the "language" of community gardeners, various perspectives offer starting points. One perspective is the way in which art and aesthetics are perceived and handled in community gardens. In this context one can also consider the *casitas*, Puerto Rican temporary shelters created for outside use. Another perspective is the "new tradition" of annual pageants on the Lower East Side in celebration of the gardens. Another important dimension is the impact on and role of children in community gardens. Finally, it is necessary to examine the ideological themes associated with urban community gardening, in particular the concept of community as it is constructed and reconstructed by gardeners. This is partially derived from and inspired by self-described philosophical antecedents.

COMMUNITY AS PRAXIS

The community garden movement on the Lower East Side takes much of its impetus from a self-conscious concern with and creation of "community." Conceptualizations of "history," "memory," and "tradition" together with a perceived unity in the struggle provide common identification markers for a group of individuals highly diverse in class, race, age, gender, and cultural backgrounds. The community garden movement also involves a self-conscious juxtaposition of notions of spontaneous and constructed action with equally self-conscious playing out of roles of victims and actors. In this context, "community" is praxis; it is identical with the process of "community making" and thus both the emergent goal and the dynamic and interactive process of reaching that goal.

The emerging conceptualization of "community" links the seemingly bounded and local character of "community" with the notion of a "community" extending across physical barriers and distances. The linkage between these two notions of community represents a creative and dynamic process particular to urban settings in the late 20th century. The politics of identity making and the creation of "community" are local and site-specific and at the same time city-wide not only in their import but also in the self-perception and self-depiction of participants in the community garden movement and in their conscious efforts at marshaling support and staging initiatives of resistance.

Beginning as small-scale efforts by a few individuals on a block, the community garden movement has evolved into a city-wide effort, seeking to compel the city administration to reconsider its position with regard to vacant lot administration and community gardens in all boroughs in New York City. In a sense the community garden movement preempts the "socially inclusive urban landscape history" called for by Dolores Hayden. According to Hayden, such a history is to assist in the development of new approaches to urban planning and design, which would acknowledge and pay tribute to the social diversity of the city as well as to the need for communal uses of spaces (Hayden 1995:12). Systemic forces and developments impose limitations on individuals' ability to affect outcomes, yet gardeners and activists across New York City have been actively engaged in representing their history and their ideas for a city of the future to the public and in that process shifting the course of events as self-conscious observers and actors in it.

Two vignettes serve as instructive points of departure, one a description of an exhibit of artists' work at the Henry Street Settlement and the other a description of a pageant that is regularly held on the Lower East Side. Both the pageant and the exhibit started out as local in significance and authorship; both ended up reaching out to the city and holding forth a vision of a city of the future while at the same time grappling with concepts of "community" that hark back to more traditional notions of boundedness and continuity.

VISIONS FOR COMMUNITY LIFE IN CITIES

In the winter of 1994–1995 there was an exhibition in the Henry Street Settlement on the Lower East Side called "In-Sites: Lower East Side Artists Re-Think Neighborhood Spaces."[2] For the exhibition artists had created individual visions for the Lower East Side. These highly diverse designs reflected a sense of space where ecology, history, social, cultural, and political dynamics were seen as interacting. A unifying goal was the perceived need to change the existing relationship to the environment. One example is the creation of a marshland fence or belt along a restored East River

Park. The artist Olivia Beens explained her design: "I have designed a fence that reflects the indigenous flora, fauna, birds and fish of the area. An educational component is built into the fence, and the community will be invited to contribute drawings that may become an integral part of the fence." Jody Culkin envisioned the creation of a "Liquid Mall" along the entire length of Allen Street, with designs of tiles, bridges and other ornamental elements emphasizing the many cultures that live in or have passed through the Lower East Side. As a public space, it was supposed to provide a place for both solitude and recreation.

Recurring themes in the exhibition were the creation or reflection of a sense of the past, the creation of islands within the urban maelstrom, the creation of symbolic centers where the diversity of the area could be brought out and celebrated, the creation of a place to feel awe, and the creation of a sanctuary, a place to feel safe. The exhibit connected locally bounded urban planning constructs with concepts for the entire city. Local artists acted as urban landscapers and creators of anchors for community life that seek to transform rather than to exclude the city. In these designs a notion of "community" comes to the fore that involves the recognition and even inclusion of the surrounding city environment. "Community" becomes a resting stop or stepping stone in a river rather than an enclosed or separate enclave.

THE WINTER CANDLE LANTERN PAGEANT

On a chilly Saturday evening in January 1995, I attended the first Winter Candle Lantern Pageant on the Lower East Side in Manhattan. This event, in support of community gardens in the neighborhood, was organized by a coalition of environmentalists, activists, and gardeners, with participation from local schools and churches. Since that day the pageant has taken place annually, with more than 500 gardeners, artists, and neighbors participating every year.

Setting out from the 6th Street Community Center between Avenues B and C, the pageant went around Tompkins Square Park and finally reached the 6th Street Community Garden. There were giant puppets, among them Esmeralda, the Water Ice Princess, with a blue face and a coat of silver tinsel, Primavera, with a green face and billowing green arms and hands, and Father Winter, with an androgynous white face and staring eyes over long, flowing, silvery veils. Gaia, the Earth Mother, sat on a raft, a female torso in white lace, reminiscent of a Virgin Mary, under an arch of dried roses and miscellaneous earthy things. Dancers in blue and in silver-white garb represented icicles and snowflakes. Adults and children carried glowing lanterns in the shape of suns, stars, and moons, as well as bells, wood chimes, and smaller puppets. Several pedi-cabs accommodated individual members of the procession, especially children, throughout the long evening. Interestingly attired individuals came out of buildings and joined the procession as it passed through the streets.

At the final stop, in a community garden on Avenue B, there was a dance performance on the stage in the center of the garden. The procession was arrayed around the stage amid snow-covered flower and vegetable beds and fruit trees. In silence and darkness, a scantily clad dancer slowly came to life in the bitter cold to symbolize earth's awakening. A shaman performed a blessing ceremony, blowing seeds into the four winds. This was followed by a musical offering, an "Aria for Winter," and a performance by fire flame eaters. As the symbolic climax of the evening an "Illuminated Winter Angel," a shimmering wavy construct reminiscent of a white jellyfish, descended along a thin rope from a roof corner six stories high across the street into the garden. The evening concluded with roasted apples, hot cider, and a bonfire.

The brochure handed out that evening contained a description of the myth of the Greek goddess Persephone, who was damned to spend half of the year in the underworld with Pluto. Demeter, her mother and the goddess of fertility, spends the winter mourning the loss of her daughter. The following poem, inspired by this myth, is the gardeners' response to Demeter's lament, to be sung in the procession.

> *We walk through the winter landscape*
> *let the gardens live again*
> *celebrate the winter darkness*
> *let the gardens live again*
> *This wind through my soul blows cold*
> *But we have hope that life will grow.*[3]

This event with its vivid enactment of an imagined community does not eliminate differing notions of community and processes of fragmentation and individuation among the many groups involved in the organization of these gardens. In its construction and content the pageant emphasizes and even celebrates a vision of a community that is not static, but rather emergent, just as the gardens in the context of the seasons are subject to change. The pageant provides a script for a ritualized celebration of contradictions and diversity. It offers a starting point for forging a sense of shared purpose and struggle on behalf of community gardens on the Lower East Side and in New York City.

Both the pageant and the exhibit at the Henry Street Settlement make statements about "community" in an urban environment and the place of individuals within it. These statements revolve around an idealized notion of diversity, a site-specific focus combined with a notion of dynamics linking the specific location with the entire city, and an image of individuals and communities situated in a symbiotic relationship with the environment. In community gardens and in activism on their behalf, the role and place of the individual and the group in society, in the community, and in the environment are constantly examined, negotiated, and defined. Thus, the fight for community gardens is symptomatic of a larger struggle, a search for "place" and for "meaning" in a late 20th century urban existence.

ART AND AESTHETICS AND THE EVERYDAY

Community garden plots are simultaneously private and public spaces. They provide spaces for private creativity and time spent alone or with family and friends. At the same time they are open to the public at regular intervals, on display, visible from the outside, and subject to approbation by the gardening community. Normative concepts of property and ownership are refashioned in community gardens. Plots cannot be bought or sold, yet individuals have limited control over their plots. At times, this becomes an issue difficult to negotiate. In some gardens individual artistic creativity has become a bone of contention. Occasionally it dominates the entire garden, even while physically confined to an individual plot. For instance, the 6th Street and Avenue B Community Garden contains a giant lamppost sculpture known as "Eddie's tower," which consists of rocking horses, propeller blades, flags, clocks, discarded toys, and other elements of daily life. On its 4' x 8' plot the sculpture looms over the other 116 plots of the garden. Factions within the garden are opposed to the tower sculpture; but despite repeated and at times heated discussions at garden meetings, the garden members have not taken positive action against the gardener and his creation.

The question as to who controls the aesthetics of a particular area or an entire garden is constantly renegotiated. Yet, gardens are filled with rich individualistic display precisely because they offer one of the few spaces within an urban environment where people can make a mark on their environment. The American Community Gardening Association has attempted to come up with a definition of a community garden: "Community gardens are neighborhood open spaces managed by and for members of the community" (American Community Gardening Association n.d.). This definition is purposely open-ended in order to account for the unending variety of such spaces. In the late 1990s, this issue occasionally sparked heated debate among gardeners and garden activists in conjunction with discussions about strategy to protect the gardens against the city administration. Some argued that gardens had to be made "acceptable" in terms of general appearance, garden rules, and patterns of utilization. Attempts to draw up such rules that would be applicable to all so-called community gardens drew the ire of many for as many different reasons. The debates over this matter are in themselves instructive about the nature of community gardens and the city-wide struggle on their behalf; they reflect a highly volatile and vocal group of individuals with a great diversity of positions and opinions that ultimately succeeded in shelving the issue in time to turn toward a concerted effort on behalf of the gardens.

At a concrete level, community gardens bring together and give expression to different cultures, not least in the diversity of flowers and vegetables so lovingly tended. In their artistic display, the gardens are collages of different political, economic, and cultural histories. Three different aesthetics exist side by side and overlap in community gardens, the aesthetic of the familiar or home garden, the aesthetic of the fantasy or personal garden, and the recycling aesthetic (Francis et al. 1984). These aesthetic realms are characterized by fluid borders in terms of differences among gardens, within gardens among individual member plots, and in terms of individual behavior that shifts from one aesthetic language to the next according to social context.

One garden contains a miniature version of the 19th century

classical layout of Tompkins Square Park. Another garden contains sculptures composed of objects found by garden members all over the city and transported back to the garden, including lintel pieces and boat dock pilings. The artist Steven Schmerfeld has designed 6' fence panels out of industrial scrap metal—nuts, saw blades, and milling cutters—for the J.D. Wilson Memorial Garden on 122nd Street, half of which was bulldozed in the summer of 1999. In early 2000, the fence was installed to enclose the remainder of the garden. Against the sunlight these panels evoke flowers, leaves, and intricate tracings of tree branches. Situated on top of wasteland, literally debris, gardens incorporate and transform the detritus from our modern existence.

CASITAS

Casitas contain and express many of the contradictions in community gardens. *Casitas* are modeled after the rural, preindustrial bohio dwelling, an 8' x 10' wooden house with a porch and a front yard, common in Puerto Rico. They are often painted in bright colors such as coral, turquoise, or lemon yellow. They are not lived in, but are used for family gatherings, cultural activities, political organization, musical events, classes, and community events (Flores 1992). A description by Sharff shows to what extent *casitas* are focal points for people in the neighborhood in their day-to-day lives:

> 'These were artful miniature houses, porch and all, built from recycled materials, decorated inside and out with 'back home' details: a table covered with an oilcloth and a vase of plastic flowers, lounge chairs, perhaps a giant stuffed panda, slightly the worse for wear. People sat around them in the evenings, the women wearing house dresses and slippers, sipping sodas

from plastic cups, the men in sport shirts and somber slacks, maybe over a domino board that had been set up on an upturned Con Edison wire spool, sipping beer from four-ounce bottles of Miller's High Life" (Sharff 1998: 83).

Casitas, like community gardens, are perched on the fault line between public and private realms. *Casitas* are private dwellings transformed into a public space and a political statement in defense of a way of life.

In individual gardens *casitas* occasionally have been a source of conflict. Sometimes garden members object to a *casita* and its uses on the grounds that it dominates the garden. Others have argued against *casitas* on the grounds of aesthetics. In such instances the conflicts are linked to different class and cultural conceptions about the uses of outdoor spaces and reflect some of the divisions between the Puerto Rican and non–Puerto Rican members in the community. However, these divisions are shifting continuously in the context of shifts of political allegiances. Such a shift was particularly evident in the struggle for the Jardín de Esperanza. In that garden the *casita* was turned into an organizational center used by garden members and supporters from outside the garden during the winter months in anticipation of the bulldozers.

For the city administration *casitas* have represented a convenient means of attacking community gardens; gardens containing such structures fail to meet the official definition of a garden, containing a private space used for familial purposes such as family cookouts. Some activists have argued that *casitas* represent a liability in the struggle for all gardens.

In the fall of 1999, the Rincon Criollo Community Garden in the South Bronx, a garden containing a famous *casita*, received notice from HPD that it was being included in development plans. On December 17, 1999, in response to this development, the Green Guerillas and 11 gardeners from Community Boards 1 and 3 in the

South Bronx held a press conference at Rincon Criollo Community Garden to demand that the land use decision-making process be opened up to the community. For two decades Rincon Criollo has been a popular cultural center and community garden, a gathering place for traditional Puerto Rican music groups as well as for special occasions and holidays. Together with its *casita*, the garden was featured in an exhibition on Puerto Rican culture at the Smithsonian Institute, and in the early 1990s, there was an exhibit about casitas at the Bronx Museum for the Arts.

Accorded recognition by renowned cultural institutions, casitas are transformed from a liability into a potent element of political significance. For the city administration this has reduced the appeal of dismissing these structures as illegal and aesthetically questionable uses of public spaces, when trying to assert control over spaces occupied by *casitas*; instead, the focus has been on legalistic arguments over title to the land. As the struggle over community gardens gained in intensity, fault lines of culture and class, at times expressed by *casitas*, have become blurred, while the emphasis has shifted to the need to work for a common cause, the defense of an entire way of life.

THE RITES OF SPRING

The crowning expression of the community-wide struggle to save the gardens is the annual Rites of Spring Pageant, a twelve-hour long procession through the Lower East Side on Memorial Day. This pageant is the result of a process of construction on many levels. It incorporates diverse religious themes and myths from India, Africa, and Ancient Greece. These in turn were originally suggested and composed as an entity by Felicia Young, the founder of the organization Earth Celebrations.

Since the first pageant in 1991, it has been appropriated by

Primavera, Father Winter, Gaia, And Other Restless Spirits

gardeners and other neighborhood people, who contribute various elements to it every year. It has also been further developed as result of input by artists, actors, and others from all over the city who volunteer in the pageant's preparation and implementation every year. Hence, it is the product of creativity on part of both "outsiders" and "residents" of the neighborhood, rather than something "indigenously" developed. I qualify these terms, in that they are entirely subjective and open to interpretation. The founder of Earth Celebrations had lived on the Lower East Side for over a decade and celebrated her wedding in a community garden. Like many others involved in the pageant, and indeed many others currently self-described as residents of the Lower East Side, she came to the neighborhood from the outside, so to speak.

While many residents on the Lower East Side have been there over several generations, it is—like any other urban neighborhood—subject to shifting populations and patterns of in-and-out migration. Many individuals currently involved in the community garden initiatives came to the neighborhood in the wave of displacement and concomitant gentrification in the 1980s. In those years the city administration tried to make more housing units available to artists and actors as the vanguard to transforming the neighborhood into an upscale residential area to serve the nearby financial district. In the 1970s and 1980s, vacant buildings were crumbling under the years of neglect and were finally demolished by the city administration, leaving scores of debris-filled lots in their wake. Community gardens flourished in the place of buildings that had accommodated residents who were then displaced from the neighborhood. At the same time, community gardens began to emerge as the result of initiatives by neighborhood people who were trying to resist precisely these efforts at gentrification. The pageant expresses and is defined by the destructiveness and fluidity of an urban environment and the fascination with themes of a locally-defined "community." As such the pageant is both "of" the city and "of" the Lower East Side.

The pageants reflect contradictions and changing political allegiances on the Lower East Side. Until 1998, the Rites of Spring Pageant was planned to coincide with the annual Loisaida Festival, a Puerto Rican parade and block party on Avenue C. In fact the two groups joined at one point during the day and proceeded together for a while in symbolic affirmation of shared interests in the Lower East Side. The meeting of Gaia and her cohort with flag-waving drummer bands and cheerleaders in short-skirted uniforms, marching behind jovially smiling community board members and elected officials represented a study in contrasts. In 1999 the two events occurred on different days. The pageant was scheduled for the weekend prior to Memorial Day. According to the organizers the reason for this change was that the Memorial Day weekend had become increasingly impractical—many people were not able to participate because they wanted to spend the weekend out of town. A subtext for the distancing between the two groups was a shift in the political climate. Over the past decade an increasing number of Puerto Ricans had begun to carve out positions of power in electoral politics. Trying to survive in the political process, some were moving away from interest groups that had helped to get them elected and were looking toward other political playing fields. Gardeners in particular were feeling increasingly betrayed and abandoned by individual politicians as well as by Community Board 3, for all that both individual politicians and the community board are ultimately powerless beyond weak attempts at bartering with the city administration and developers over individual projects. Consequently the notion of marching in unison, if only for a few blocks, in the heat of the battle over community gardens was no longer an option.

The Rites of Spring procession is an elaborate and colorful construct, with over 500 people involved in its production. Its central cast of characters, portrayed by people and by puppets carried on floats includes Gaia, the four seasons, the elements, the Earth, Compost, Rainbow, and the Green Man. There are many flowers, garden insects, and other beings associated with gardens and nature. Sun, Moon, Fire, and Water paint their faces and arms and other visible body parts elaborately in the appropriate colors, with costumes and head pieces emphasizing their nature. The so-called mud people, perhaps the ones who have more fun than anyone else in the procession, wear practically no clothes at all, but are coated in pale white mud and wear oversized wobbly full-head masks that only hint at eyes and mouths. The mud people are not assigned to a specific position in the procession. They weave in and out of the line-up and move freely among the spectators, acting as tricksters or clowns of sorts, partially frightening and partially amusing.

Some of the costumes are stunning in their beauty and creativity. In 1999 Summer wore a full-length wide skirt woven with grass that swished softly along with every step and a broad-rimmed hat with grass growing out of it. The Vegetable Goddess wore a crown of carrots and a necklace made of giant radishes. Herbena, as her name indicates representing the world of herbs, wore a fragrant costume decorated with bunches of fresh and dried herbs, cinnamon sticks, cloves, and nutmeg.

The procession moves from one garden to the next and conducts blessing ceremonies at each garden visited. Each garden develops its own welcoming ceremony; in some gardens gardeners read poetry or perform a piece of music. Some gardens offer food and drinks; in one garden I remember the beautifully attired garden mistress of ceremonies standing next to a table set with a tablecloth, a vase, candles, and a tray with a teapot. Gaia, the Earth Mother, sitting on her float under a bower of roses, together with some of garden spirits, enters the garden, while the mournful sound of conch shells fills the air. Inside the garden the mistress of ceremonies takes a tulip bulb out of Gaia's belly and gravely hands it to the gardener in charge of ceremonies at that particular garden. A bowl of clay is constructed throughout the day, as one garden representative after another adds another piece of clay to the bowl and also places a leaf from the garden into the bowl. At the end of the day the "communal salad bowl," as it is referred to in the script, is completely formed and contains an accumulation of diverse greens from all the gardens.

The Rites of Spring Pageant visits the locations of various gardens that have been eliminated over the years, staking out claims to a landscape of place memories, current sites of struggle, and visions for the future. For instance, commemorative stops are made at the sites of the former Garden of Eden, the Jardín de la 10th Street, also known as "Little Puerto Rico," and the A BC Garden; these gardens are referred to as "martyrs."

Throughout the long day, a giant map of the Lower East Side is carried at the front of the procession. At each garden a representative of the garden ceremoniously enters the name of the garden on the map, symbolically correcting the city administration's maps, which only refer to vacant lots or tax lots and housing development proposals, while not recognizing the existence of community gardens, despite the fact that many of these gardens hold leases from the municipal organization GreenThumb and in many instances have occupied their sites for over twenty years.

As the procession makes its way through the Lower East Side, a drama of birth, marriage, struggle, and successful emergence from struggle is enacted. The procession tells the story of the birth of Gaia, the Earth Mother, emerging from a giant pink birth canal, her marriage to the Green Man, and her abduction by developers in black business suits. In this drama Gaia is played by a person. Meanwhile, the Gaia float continues to be carried along throughout the day like a holy shrine. The developers place Gaia on a pickup truck. Throughout the rest of the day at certain intersections one can see the truck roll by with Gaia screaming vociferously from the back of the truck. Eventually in a dramatic battle with the developers, the gardeners, supported by earth and garden spirits, emerge victorious. The developers flee, their business suits in disarray, and several developer spirits, represented by robot-like figures, fall to the ground lifeless, disintegrating into their various components. In the closing ceremony in the Green Oasis Garden on 8th Street between Avenues C and D, children from the garden release butterflies into the spring air.

Since its inception the pageant has taken on a life of its own; the script changes and is adjusted every year. In some gardens visited by the procession, the garden members have prepared dance performances, poetry readings, or musical performances to welcome the procession. During past years the procession repeatedly changed its planned route; several times a gardener suddenly appeared, pointed out the existence of a new garden, and insisted that this garden be included in the blessing ceremony. The physical character of the procession is unique for its fragility and impermanence.

For many months, adults and especially children from the various schools in the neighborhood work on the giant puppets, floats, and costumes for the procession. Everything is made out of inexpensive materials—cardboard, papier-maché, glitter paints, pieces of fabric, face paint, beads, dried herbs, and chains of nuts and sea shells. Reminiscent of the grass bundles that form the basis of women's realm of exchange among the Trobriand Islanders in the Western Pacific, the value of these items in the procession reposes in the fact that they need to be renewed every year and that they express the skill and creativity of the many individuals involved in their production (Weiner 1976). Some individuals identify with particular characters in the procession and craft their own costumes. Flower wreaths to be carried by garden spirits and helpers are prepared the night before in the Community Center on

6th Street. The collages and constructs used in the pageant are remade and repatched lovingly every year. The pageant's inventiveness and creativity proudly proclaim its character as an evanescent handmade product of a labor of love, in affinity with the thriving and equally evanescent gardens.

COMMUNITY GARDENS AND CHILDREN

In community gardens, children and youths are active participants, witnesses, links between generations, and actors in directed scripts for publicizing the plight of the gardens, as victims of a relentless urban environment and symbols of the success of these gardens (von Hassell 2000). Children are critical to the dialectical process of the transformation of "community" along new concepts and themes. Community gardening is a critical factor at the heart of successful community organizing; it involves and grows on children's participation.

On December 31, 1997, upon the order of the current administration of the City of New York, bulldozers razed four community gardens on the Lower East Side in Manhattan. Turned into a wasteland of mud and torn-up vegetation, these now manifestly vacant lots were closed off with large plywood walls. Protesters from the neighborhood attached posters to the walls that showed a child in a winter coat against the background of a razed garden with the words printed underneath: "Daddy, please, please don't let them destroy another garden!"

At the forefront of this struggle is the effort to show that gardens involve children in many different ways. Gardens are portrayed as providing social services at no cost to the city, entertainment, education, and settings in which children can be creatively and constructively connected to the community and the environment.

Primavera, Father Winter, Gaia, And Other Restless Spirits

According to the American Community Gardening Association, a key element in the definition of a community garden is that there must be different generations including children at work side by side (American Community Gardening Association n.d.). This ideal is by no means always realized. Nonetheless, community gardens involve a remarkable level of diversity in terms of age and race and ethnic backgrounds. In community gardens on the Lower East Side and in other neighborhoods in New York City, there are many projects and programs devised for and by children in and around these gardens. While the level of active involvement by children varies from garden to garden, children are granted a degree of freedom and responsibility otherwise difficult to attain in an urban environment.

The garden La Plaza Cultural on Avenue C and 9th Street contains a sculpture garden, an open grass area, a wildflower bed along the border, vegetable plots, and a large paved plaza inside the garden in front of an amphitheater complete with a vine-covered trellis on the top. The wildflower bed was the brainchild of a landscape architect living on the Lower East Side who moved to New York City in 1991. Witness to the squatter scene in that garden in the early 1990s, this man became involved in clearing debris out of one area of the garden along Avenue C. In 1995, with the assistance of a teacher from a local day-care center and preschool, he started a class around the project of setting up a wildflower garden. Approximately 30 children learned about plants, seeds, the environment, and gardens and helped with the planting. For many children this was their first direct experience with plants. A few children still feel a connection to that garden and come by regularly to check on the progress of what they consider to be "their flowers." Similar programs involving local organizations have followed. Nonetheless efforts remain fragmented and hampered by a lack of funds and labor power of committed adults.

The Struggle for Eden

Another project in La Plaza Cultural also was started by adult garden members. Three vegetable plots are currently planted by children with the help of adults. The produce is donated to a neighborhood soup kitchen. There is also a link to a community-supported agricultural project in New Jersey. This project seeks to link consumers in an urban community and local farmers. Children involved in the food production project at La Plaza and others from the Lower East Side have been visiting the farm as part of their summer day camp experience, where they help to plant and harvest.

The Children's Mural Garden on 12th Street and Avenue B is located in a small 20' x 60' lot, originally occupied by a tenement building. It borders on a public playground that has been restored as result of neighborhood activism. Created specifically for children and designed by children, the garden contains a gazebo, a vegetable area, a flower area, and a little waterfall. A solar panel powers the pump underneath the waterfall; as lovely illustration of its operational principle, the water flow stops in the afternoon when the panel is in the shade. Children were involved in the work of designing the actual garden; they were presented with problems and invited to work out solutions. For instance, children designed the storage space underneath the gazebo floor.

The garden is dominated by a mural along the entire back wall, with a river painted down its center so that it seems to merge into the waterfall. Several adults started the Mural Garden project in response to the fact that community gardens are not always welcoming to children. About 150 children were involved in the mural project, with a core group of about 40. Most of these were under 10 years old. The actual work process—preparation of colored drawings on paper, wall priming, transferring drawing outlines onto the wall, and applying paint, together with the challenges of working on a scaffold through cold spells and rainy days, with paint dripping down and the need for speed—is reminiscent of the trials and tribulations of Michelangelo in the Sistine Chapel. It took two years till completion in October 1996, with various groups working on various schedules, during schooldays, on weekends, and in the evenings.

The overall themes were developed by the adults—the underworld, the water world, the sky, the plant world, the vegetable world, and the flower world. Within these themes children contributed freely and creatively. One child drew a flower with a purple dot above and explained that this was the flower releasing its smell. One girl appears in the mural, swimming in the river that bisects the mural and flows into the little rock garden and solar powered waterfall. One child drew seeds with plants growing inside; the symbol on the leaflet for the opening ceremony is a tree inside a seed.

In the Rites of Spring Pageant children play key roles. During one scene, the trash monster, a person covered by a giant mask bedecked with clattering soda cans, is chased and ultimately overcome by children in blue smocks or shirts with little colorful tassels, wearing face masks and carrying homemade tanks marked "air" on their back; in the program they are dubbed "urban jungle recyclers." In the closing ceremony, children dressed as butterflies perform a play and afterward assist in the release of butterflies into the sky.

In the Winter Candle Lantern Pageant, the tone is set by children, who carry glowing lanterns through the dark and wintry streets of the Lower East Side in the procession. Children also participate in demonstrations and marches to protest forthcoming auctions of garden lots or other actions by the city administration; for instance, children carry offerings of flowers and vegetables to the mayor at City Hall. Posters or press photos of such events frequently feature children as a kind of vanguard of all gardeners.

The settings referred to above indicate the diversity of themes linking benefits to children and the continued existence of gardens.

These themes include education, environmental awareness, notions of self-help and community organizing, creativity, self-directed learning, cooperative work, and participation in community life.

The impact of community gardening initiatives on children is not easily quantifiable or measurable. In direct reflection of an extremely fragmented social economic environment, many children involved in community garden projects come from troubled homes and families struggling with unemployment, homelessness, poverty, and attendant consequences. Stories of disappearing children abound, and organizers of projects often are overwhelmed with the difficulty of keeping track of them, not to mention actively assisting children beyond the limits of the particular project. One of the gardens bulldozed in December 1997 was involved in a tutoring program for children from a neighboring shelter. Now the impact of that effort appears impossible to measure, if it has not completely evaporated in the meantime. A garden on 12th Street and 1st Avenue, founded in 1983, is an exception, in terms of its longevity, the length of individual children's involvement, and the amount of follow-up. This garden has been designed, constructed, and planted by and for children, with a minimum of adult guidance. Children continue to manage the garden and work on ongoing projects.[4]

Certainly, a number of community gardens in their struggle to stave off the bulldozers make claims about their various community programs and children's programs in particular that appear overblown. Yet many programs are impressive and memorable, such as the 12th Street Garden or the Children's Mural Garden. Whatever the impact, it is hard to resist the compelling image of children creating art, planting vegetables, designing a garden, or going on a day trip to visit friends from their garden who have gone on to college. The assumed or envisioned impact of community gardening initiatives on children is a cornerstone in the ideological conceptualization of the role of these gardens in the community.

Community gardens are portrayed by their proponents as repositories of community spirit and as having tremendous impact on their respective neighborhoods, providing stabilization, continuity, and arenas for constructive social interaction. Programs and projects for children help to make concrete and further develop ideas for community life and a balance of cooperation and individualism in an urban context. Children are featured as participants, witnesses, and links between the generations. They become actors in directed scripts for publicizing the plight of the gardens—as victims of a relentless urban environment and as symbols of the success of these gardens and by extension of the successful revitalization of a community. Children become the emotional touchstone linking the various themes of environmental justice, education, and community life.

The same element of community organizing inspired earlier initiatives on the Lower East Side. During the 1970s, various organizations linked environmental issues, vacant lot reclamation, and youth organization as central components in a revitalization of the community. In the current struggle on behalf of community gardens, children as actors and unifying goal are pitted against the city administration's position that community gardens at best are no more than private backyards for some extended families or at worst simply vacant lots.

Certainly, children involved in community gardens and associated projects generally are too young to act independently; they are inducted by their families, friends, neighborhood organizations, and schools. Yet children are active contributors on a variety of levels. Ultimately, a debate about the fuzzy borderline between the "actual" and the "constructed" impact—here I refer to visions of a community, children as activists, and the actual or claimed impact of gardens—is irrelevant; community organizing is precisely about that process of transcendence from the "constructed" to the "actual."

PHILOSOPHICAL ANTECEDENTS

Gardeners on the Lower East Side referred me to various writers whom they considered seminal to their ideas about community gardening. Thus instructed I went off to read Simone Weil and Iris Murdoch, Ronald Ableman, and Wendell Berry, a frequently surprising voyage of discovery. These writers are concerned with the contradictions of the demands of the group versus the needs of the individual within a fragile, even damaged environment, seeking to find a constructive and dynamic middle ground between untrammeled individualism and stifling communal rules.

Simone Weil is concerned with the experience of alienation in the industrialized world. "Never has the individual been so completely delivered up to a blind collectivity, and never have men been less capable, not only of subordinating their actions to their thoughts, but even of thinking" (Weil 1977: 27–28). Writing against the background of National Socialism and World War II, Weil expresses her fear of a world in which science is king and where human beings are at the mercy of an industrial concern too vast and too complex for any one person to grasp. Weil argues that individual needs to escape the collective frenzy and that such an escape is possible only through progressive decentralization of social life in conjunction with a place-based focus for individual existence. "Nothing is more impelling in a man than the need to appropriate, not materially or juridically, but in thought, the places and objects amidst which he passes his life. A cook says, 'My kitchen,' a gardener, 'My lawn,' and this is as it should be" (Weil 1977: 62). Weil was not able to find such solace by claiming the world around her. Confronted with the incomprehensible, she chose an escape by waging a herculean struggle of despair; Weil purposely starved herself to death in wartime London in sympathy with French victims of the Holocaust.

More accessible because less overwhelmingly invincible in its moral ethical purity, Iris Murdoch offers a philosophical stance as a more personal way out of the anomie and oppressiveness of modern existence, based on an existentialist embrace of the fact of mortality: "We are what we seem to be, transient mortal creatures, subject to necessity and change" (Murdoch 1970: 79). Like Weil, Iris Murdoch looks at advances in the sciences and technology over the last centuries as a double-edged sword, partially responsible for the growing malaise and sense of life as self-enclosed and purposeless (Murdoch 1970: 79).

Murdoch suggests a way out of this despair of the modern individual locked in on her/himself. She refers to something that she calls, with some sense of the awkwardness of the term, "unselfing." Accordingly it is possible to stop the paralyzing gaze inwards by looking outside oneself, for instance at nature. Describing the experience of seeing a kestrel outside her window, Murdoch writes: "In a moment everything is altered. The brooding self with its hurt vanity has disappeared" (Murdoch 1970: 84). According to Murdoch, this experience of a life outside oneself invigorates and opens the soul. "More naturally, as well as more properly, we take a self-forgetful pleasure in the sheer alien pointless independent existence of animals, birds, stones and trees. Not how the world is, but that it is, that is the mythical" (Murdoch 1970: 85). Murdoch sees this experience as the basis for one's ability to live in the world and with others in a constructive and non-destructive fashion.

Gardeners had referred me to Weil and Murdoch. They might as well have referred me to Charles Taylor, Theodore Roszak, or Amitai Etzioni, who offer philosophical and sociological perspectives as cogent and applicable to the issue of individual and community in modern society as the writing of Weil and Murdoch, if not more so. It is noteworthy that the writers I was told about were women, poets, and farmers, for whom the working out of concepts of community and individuality and the definition of a meaningful human existence held immediate and personal relevance and were not matters to be resolved on another plane of existence.

Charles Taylor offers a critique of contemporary civilization and delineates the challenges faced by individuals in dealing with the experience of fragmentation and alienation in a society dominated by disengaged instrumentalism (Taylor 1989). In a modern-day existence, the individual is "taken out of a rich community life and now enters instead into a series of mobile, changing, revocable associations, often designed merely for highly specific ends. We end up relating to each other through a series of partial roles" (Taylor 1989: 502).

According to Taylor this fragmentation and alienation is not conducive toward creating individuals able to act freely and to participate in society in a constructive fashion. Freedom in society is based on local focal points of self-rule, and the ability to engage in self-rule is not given in "atomic instrumental society" (Taylor 1989: 502). Taylor is interested in the contradictory facets of the modern identity, torn between the need to seek expressive fulfillment and the need to respond to the call for a moral ethical stance, in particular with regard to the ecological irresponsibility of instrumental society.

Roszak analyzes what he describes as a religious renewal in the early 1970s in response to the looming ecological crisis, according to Roszak "the first discernible symptom of advanced disease within" (Roszak 1973: xvii). Amitai Etzioni provides a blue print for a community, specifying a moral-ethical value system within the context of rights and responsibilities on the basis of a communitarian ideology. With this blueprint he tries to provide a framework that allows individuals a maximum of action and creativity within a viable community. Like the other authors cited, Etzioni links the environmental movement and a struggle for a way of life. "The Communitarian movement—which is an environmental movement dedicated to the betterment of our moral, social and political environment—seeks to sort out these principles. And Communitarians are dedicated to working with our fellow citizens to bring about the changes in values, habits, and public policies that will allow us to do for society what the environmental movement seeks to do for nature: to safeguard and enhance our futures" (Etzioni 1993: 2–3).

In the works of Paul Ableman (1993) and Wendell Berry (1985) the preceding philosophical positions are transmuted into a poetic language of concrete experience—the love for the soil, creation, growth and decay, and the cycle of life and death. Ableman writes about the life of the land and the intrinsic value of working the soil; his writing is grounded in concrete descriptions of agricultural techniques in different parts of the world and an examination of the possibilities for farming without many of the methods of industrialized or factory farming used in the 20th century. Wendell Berry, a farmer as well as a poet, gives voice to his philosophy of existence in poetry and prose (Berry 1985).

In anthropology the notion of a dynamic living community with irrevocable associations and relationships between individuals that are not reducible to partial roles, the direct opposite of Taylor's instrumental society, is made concrete in countless ethnographies of pre-industrial societies. For instance, Paul Radin has argued that in societies not yet subsumed by the industrial world the life of the community and the life of fully realized individuals were not diametrically opposed, but rather dependent on each other for their continued vitality (Radin 1971). According to Radin, this potential for rich individuality within a community was founded on an existentialist worldview with a pragmatic awareness and acceptance of the fragility of life, linked with a fundamental respect for the environment. This existentialist worldview acquires a further dimension in anthropology in works that address the question of gender roles in society. It becomes particularly compelling in Weiner's discussion of the manner in which cycles of life and death are woven into the fabric of male and female realms of exchange among the Trobrianders (Weiner 1976).

The philosophers, poets, writers, and anthropologists discussed address the questions associated with the challenge of negotiating a meaningful and fulfilled individual life in the context of modern society, with its trappings of consumerism, anomie, alienation, and environmental degradation. Concern with these questions reappears in community gardens, in the manner in which gardeners speak about the gardens and their fight for the gardens, and in actions and events associated with the gardens. Gardeners, environmentalists, and activists selectively embrace an amorphous set of beliefs and values.

Described as eco-spirituality and eco-feminism in some of the literature on environmentalism (Milton 1996, 1993), it is appropriated from a philosophical, religious and mythological smorgasbord. However, certain basic tenets can be discerned: a rejection of aspects of the modern-day materialistic culture; a partial embrace of alternative notions of property ownership and cooperative management; a profound concern with the future of the environment; a vision of a community that is self-consciously multi-racial and multi-ethnic, extends across age and gender divisions as well as across class lines, and further extends beyond the borders of the local site or area to include the block, the neighborhood, and the entire city; an identification with the struggle of people in other parts of the country such as other community gardeners and regional farmers; an embrace of the notion of sustainability; and finally a conceptual linkage with comparable and related struggles at a global level.

The brochure announcing the Winter Candle Lantern Pageant invites people to join in "the Odyssey of the Earth." By definition an odyssey involves pain and suffering as well as the discovery of beauty. Community gardeners involved in the pageant make a conceptual linkage between a spiritual odyssey, the struggle for the gardens, and the notion of the environment as a place for a spiritual odyssey; in this context nature can explain the nature of suffering and ultimately the meaning of life by providing an experiential setting for coming to terms with the existence of pain.[5]

Modern society in turn is perceived as failing to provide such a setting. One might argue that in this self-conscious embrace of nature and the imbuing of nature with mystical power, joined with a perception of modern society as devoid of such a power, community gardeners seek to return to an idealized concept of community existing in a symbiotic relationship with nature. However, the various ideological strains involved indicate that the ideas behind community gardening are not reducible to a simplistic utopian "back-to-nature" enterprise. Rather, it is necessary to emphasize that community gardeners select only certain aspects from different sets of beliefs and ideologies and combine this with a skillful manipulation of all the means of late-20th-century society at their disposal to achieve their goal. That goal and the strategies to achieve it are multi-faceted, reflecting the diversity of groups involved. The fight for community gardens is a struggle for a way of life that is by no means a return to a "simpler existence," but rather a creation of something new on the basis of existing elements.

This creative construction out of old and new patterns is most apparent in the emerging concept of individuality. A conversation with gardeners in preparation of the Rites of Spring Pageant provides a key for thinking about this concept. I had gone to the Community Center on 6th Street, where people were preparing for the pageant on the following day. Some were sewing costumes, some were making flower wreaths, others were folding brochures that were to be handed out during the procession. I sat on the tar roof and helped to fold brochures. It was hot, and the conversation ranged freely; we talked about jobs, personal lives, the struggle for the gardens, the mayor, and practical matters regarding the pageant.

At some point someone raised the question of communicability of elements in the pageant. This woman, not a gardener but a volunteer assisting with the pageant, argued that no person perhaps other than the original founder, Felicia Young, had a complete understanding of what the various figures and compositions and choreographed scenes were supposed to symbolize; the figures or spirits had their own ideas of what they were to represent, and these individual images could not really be communicated or explicated to others, least of all to people in the audience. A gardener and activist who earlier had argued that the pageant like other art forms has an educative component now qualified that statement. He said that the pageant to a degree is just for those acting in the procession, for those who are doing it, for those that continue from garden to garden all day until the closing ceremony at night, further adding that the principal element was not necessarily about communicating. This statement points at the concept of individuality and the idea of what community gardening means to the individuals involved in it.

The pageant, passing through the streets of the Lower East Side in a seven-hour-long procession, embodies a concept of individuality reflective of existence in late-20th-century society. Only fragments of the whole are visible to the observer and to the self; individual actions are only partially communicable and partially perceived. Creativity at times approaches the nature of an individual vision quest, the portent of which cannot be fully communicated. At the same time the pageant affirms and expresses moments of union, whether through the ritual of blessing ceremonies in every garden or in the opening and closing ceremonies. The pageant reflects a self-conscious awareness of the fragmentary nature of modern existence and in fact celebrates this as a central part of individual experience. Experience is acknowledged as a solitary activity and at the same time as something that can become a vital component in a larger entity. Individuality is not submerged; it is the defining element, while fragile links of meaning between individuals are reaffirmed and renewed repeatedly in ritualized fashion.[6]

The pageant can be described as the brainchild of an individual and is still driven by this person's commitment, but it also has become a collaborative effort. This history echoes the history of many community gardens, started by one or two individuals and quickly expanding to turn into a project that involves a community. Thus, pageants are mirror images of gardens in the manner in which individuality, communicability, and community are linked in a dynamic relationship. Gardens like the pageants embody the notion of impermanence and fragility in terms of nature as much as in social and political terms. Like the pageants, gardens and individual member plots are creations of internal visions that remain imaginary to a degree. In community gardens, ideas for alternative forms of existence in an urban environment are made concrete. Gardens allow space for individual creativity and at the same time offer points of intersection with others. Gardens provide space for different types of aesthetics, even an aesthetic of hopes and internal images that are not necessarily visible to an uninitiated observer.

Finally, gardens provide a space for experiential learning about nature and the individual's place in it. Urban community gardeners are putting into practice some of the notions of individuality and community expressed by writers as diverse as Weil, Murdoch, Taylor, Radin, Weiner, and Diamond. Some gardeners link these notions to an understanding of the fragmentation in modern society that shapes individual experiences. On the Lower East Side, these themes have helped to produce community gardens filled with contradictions and vitality. They have helped to produce pageants in which the dynamic relationship of group choreography and individual expression creates a compelling vivid entity.

CONCLUSION

In the pageants, in individual gardens' "memory walls," and in gardens' self-descriptive statements of purpose, concepts of "community," "history," and "memory" are both the themes of and props for the script. These themes are carefully constructed and displayed. The press is invited to protests, commemorative garden events, and pageants. Photographers and filmmakers associated with Earth Celebrations record the pageant, which in itself represents a construct of spontaneity and a carefully planned and directed performance. The pageants have been covered in the *Village Voice* and the *New York Times*, among others; these and other publications such as *National Geographic* have featured many articles about community gardens and their ongoing struggle over the past years.

Community-based organizations, garden coalitions, and individual garden groups, individual adults, and children act both spontaneously and as self-conscious, directed players in a script, alternating between roles as victims and as empowered agents.

On February 24, 2000, NPR broadcast an interview with José Torres of the former Jardín de Esperanza. Many components of the piece, aired ten days after the destruction of the garden, had been taped earlier. José Torres, the son of Alicia Torres, known as the founder of the garden, talked about the history of the garden. He described the work of cleaning the lot and the efforts to keep out drug addicts in the mid-1970s. He talked about the work of planting and constructing the casita. He named some of the food grown in it, jalapeño peppers, tomatoes, and green beans, and mentioned the grapevine that had been growing on the fence since the first year. "We cooked in the garden. We had Halloween parties there and Easter Egg hunts for the kids." In the background, while Torres was talking, one could hear sounds of activities in the garden, people talking, sounds of hammering, children laughing and playing. The interview was interlaced with cuts of comments from Donald Capoccia, the developer of the lot, also referred to as "serial garden killer" by gardeners. Capoccia was heard saying: "I told them I was going to build a building there—a 7-story building with recessed balconies. It will be a beautiful building." The interview cut back to Torres and a description of the struggle to defend the garden, followed by a description of the morning when the garden was finally razed, with sounds of bulldozers, police sirens, and people crying in the background. Finally one could hear Mayor Giuliani deride the gardeners for "living in an unrealistic world."

The observed is involved in the construction of his own image, staging events and preparing appropriate backgrounds. In turn the observer plays a part. In the construction of "community" in the context of initiatives on behalf of community gardens, the gaze of the observer—both concrete by looking into the semi-private gardens from the outside and conceptual through the media—helps to create and shape the internalized image of community.

In their language and themes, organizational patterns and forms of action, individual gardens, casitas, pageants, and community-based initiatives are urban collages, in which the very precariousness of the constructs becomes a central element in their self-display and appeal, a part of the dialectical process of identity creation. The contradiction between creativity for its own sake and for display and effect is reflective of creative efforts in an urban context, in the artistic sense as much as in the sense of political action. Disparate and contradictory elements are joined to create a whole and to make a statement.

Pageants on behalf of community gardens on the Lower East Side are collages in terms of artistic creation and aspects of strategy. They draw on various myths and religious elements from Africa, India, and Ancient Greece to name a few. They are also collages in terms of the physical construction of floats, puppets, and costumes and in terms of the highly diverse, fluctuating membership. Strategies are based on exploitation of the contradictory elements of spontaneity and construction. Visions for community gardens and for urban communities of the future are based on a rejection and a simultaneous embrace and transformation of urban environments. Pageants weave eclectically assembled images of the past into ideas for the future in a language of struggle that is derived equally from the community housing initiatives of the 1970s and the environmental justice movement of the late 1980s and 1990s.

Participation in community gardening involves a process of self-description and display on the border between public and private domains. Staging of community events, participation in pageants, and creation of memory walls and poetry in celebration of gardens straddle the realms of living in an unself-conscious immediacy and acting for effect as it were, in a play that is part of a giant, borderless campaign. The "subjects" of ethnographic description, the gardeners, are their own ethnographers, in their self-conscious process of coming to terms with the conditions of their own alienation. Every action is immediately subject to the public gaze. Urban community gardening at the end of the 20th century represents a central component in efforts to redefine and recreate the notion of "community." "Community" becomes a theater, with a constantly changing script, a volatile audience, a volatile cast, and changing sources of funding for the theater hall. Instead of characters in search of an author, in this new urban "community in the making," every individual is an author in search of a stage.

On January 28, 2000, the Winter Candle Lantern Pageant featured a new puppet. The Puppet of the Future and the Past consisted of twisted steel pipes linked together to form a pillar of thorns; it was crowned by a huge glowing pink double-faced globe. Recycled glass bottle halves, elaborately painted and with candles inside, were suspended from the many silvery arms of the pillar. The structure was set up on a float. When the procession was getting ready to start, volunteers lit the candles, standing on a ladder to reach the top ones. The illuminated globe seemed to expand as one bottle after the other began to glow. Then the puppet was carefully pulled out onto the street to its assigned place at the very end of the procession. We went from garden to garden, ringing bells and swinging lanterns, accompanied by the sound of drums and enveloped in the haze of incense sticks waved in the air. We made a special stop at the Jardín de Esperanza, where a few garden defenders were getting ready for their nightly vigil. Alicia Torres stood outside with a bunch of roses and explained about the fight for the garden to all curious passers-by. The procession circled Tompkins Square Park and finally arrived at La Plaza Cultural on 9th Street and Avenue C for the ceremonies, the performances, and the baked apples and cider. The puppet followed us, luminous and silent, with the candles gently swinging in their bottle beds.

The ingenuity of this construct, its simplicity and clever use of materials, and the love and imagination that went into its making brought forth a thing of wondrous beauty. Moving along in the wake of the procession, ponderously yet full of grace and light, it appeared to call out the central theme that gardeners in the pageant embrace and try to express—the future is behind them or at least at their fingertips, and the means for bringing it to life are at their disposal. According to its creators, the Puppet of the Future and the Past was initially inspired by the image of the Tree of Life, and it was decorated with candles in remembrance of gardens and as the light of the future.

The bulbous two-faced head of the puppet with its twisted arms and awkward body is reminiscent of a painting by Paul Klee, the "Angelus Novus." Also known as the Angel of History, he looks at the wreckage of the past and flees backward in terror, rushing helplessly into the future.[7] Notwithstanding the unintended resemblance to the "Angelus Novus," the Puppet of the Future and the Past in contrast symbolizes a conscious recognition of what is behind and what is ahead and a determination to grasp and redefine both.

NOTES

1. *The Odyssey by Homer.* The Prose Translation of Samuel Butcher and Andrew Lang, 1879.
2. "In-Sites: Lower East Side Artists Re-Think Neighborhood Spaces." Ellen Wexler, guest curator, Henry Street Settlement, Abrons Arts Center, New York, October 28, 1994, to January 17, 1995.
3. This anonymous poem, written by one of the gardeners, appears in the brochure prepared by the organization Earth Celebrations for the annual Winter Pageant, January 28, 1995.
4. See Chapter 5 for a description of this garden.
5. Also see Stanley Diamond for a discussion of the role of art and ritual in modern society, in particular, what he describes as "the integrated arts of the crisis rite that reunites man, woman, nature, and society and resolves its ambivalence while defending and defining the liberty and potential of the person" (Diamond 1982: 877).

6. Participants in the pageant take on roles and wear costumes, sometimes masks. However, these disguises do not eliminate individuals, but rather gain their depth and multidimensionality from the individuals that assume them. Diamond refers to the need to understand "the actor's mask (all our modern masks) as a reduction of the person to a role—the reverse of primitive masking in a communal ritual—which is the expression of the many aspects of the developed self. The first mask hides an absence; the second mask reveals presence" (Diamond 1982: 856).

7. Walter Benjamin describes Paul Klee's Angelus Novus as someone who appears "as if though he is about to move away from something he is fixedly contemplating. His eyes are staring, his mouth is open, his wings are spread. This is how one pictures the angel of history. His face is turned toward the past. Where we perceive a chain of events, he sees one single catastrophe, which keeps piling wreckage upon wreckage and hurls it in front of his feet. The angel would like to stay, awaken the dead, and make whole what has been smashed. But a storm is blowing from Paradise; it has got caught in his wings with such violence that the angel can no longer close them. This storm irresistibly propels him into the future to which his back is turned, while the pile of debris before him grows skyward. This storm is what we call progress" (Benjamin 1968).

The Struggle for Eden

The Rediscovered Amaranth: Patterns of Production, Distribution, and Consumption in Community Gardens

INTRODUCTION

The agricultural year with its cycles of creation and birth, nurturing and abandonment, droughts and floods, pests and plagues, and life and death is a central metaphor in Miguel Algarín's poetry collection *Love Is Hard Work* (Algarín 1997).

Algarin describes picking peaches grown on East 6th Street, eating them fresh, while watching children play in the backyard, and making preserves to be enjoyed in the winter.[1] Algarín has lived and worked on the Lower East Side for many years. The images of sowing, cultivating, harvesting, and burying become a medium for conveying the ebb and flow of the lives of people on the Lower East Side, the suffering and mortality and also the love and vitality of Algarín's friends and family. In his poetry the personal and individual moment grounded in local meaning is inextricably linked to the political moment defined by the societal context of poverty, illness, discrimination, and alienation in an urban existence where the act of carving out a personal space is an act of defiance. Algarín offers concrete images of the labor of love, the labor of creating meaning, the labor of existing as full human beings.

Community gardens provide settings for another form of poetic praxis, where individual spaces of meaning are excavated and nurtured and where a meaningful linkage between production and consumption of the world around us is sought over and over again throughout the cycles of the year. Community gardening encapsulates an approach to living in an urban environment that rejects fragmentation. Community gardeners strive to address the "whole" process of existence, that is, cradle-to-grave cycles of production, distribution, consumption, and waste management within an environmentally viable framework in the context of a dynamic community. The mushrooming of community gardening initiatives across the country has given concrete expression to the notion of a holistic approach to the problems of poverty. Rejecting single-factor solutions, individual gardening initiatives and diverse urban gardening coalitions have sought to look at education, consciousness raising, organization, and community building in conjunction with food security, environmental issues, and consumerism. I do not wish to privilege the growing of food over the cultivation of flowers in community gardening initiatives; in fact, many community gardeners would remind me that the two are inseparable. Yet, by its very nature, food production is central to existence and as such a compelling symbolic and concrete focus for a broad range of programs and initiatives in urban gardening.

A growing gap between rich and poor, urban sprawl, pollution, vanishing green spaces, inner-city deterioration and gentrification with attendant displacement and decreased standard of living of urban poor and low-income people were characteristic of U.S. urban environments in the late 20th century. In conjunction, these factors have contributed to alienation at many levels, fragmented existences, and disintegration of family and community life. The boom economy of the last decades of the 20th century notwithstanding, portions of the population were subject to food insecurity. According to the U.S. Department of Agriculture (USDA), in the years 1996–1998, 10 million households in the United States or 9.7 percent of all households were food-insecure; that is, they did not always have access to enough food to meet basic needs (USDA 1999). Not surprisingly, the prevalence of hunger was higher than average among racial and ethnic minorities, among households with children, especially those led by single women, and among households with incomes below the poverty line. The number of children in hungry or food-insecure households went from 10.36 million in 1997 to 14.04 million in 1998, and of adults from 15.76 million to 22.21 million (USDA 1999).

The far-reaching impact of the transformation of the U.S. food system over the last century is described in a study prepared under the auspices of the Community Food Security Coalition, an organization that has been pivotal in effecting changes of policy at local, regional and federal levels (Ashman et al. 1993). This study draws attention to the shift from "a decentralized, market-coordinated system of food production and distribution to a transnational capital-intensive system coordinated through ownership and contractual arrangements between conglomerates" (Ashman et al. 1993: 55). Poor and low-income neighborhoods are increasingly subject to a fragmented and unreliable food supply, further exacerbated by the abandonment of the inner-city by supermarket chains, a process called supermarket redlining. In many inner-city neighborhoods little fresh produce is available, and that at exorbitant prices. Residents are dependent on local corner stores that charge anywhere from 42 percent to 64 percent more than discount supermarkets. Such supermarkets mostly are located outside the neighborhood and can only be reached by resorting to costly public transportation or a car.[2] New York City's over 1,200 emergency food centers generally can only offer diets nearly devoid of fresh produce. Feenstra, McGrew, and Campbell point out that in the United States now two systems of agricultural production and distribution exist side by side:

"One of these systems consists of large-scale corporate enterprises and contract production by a few buyers, and features high technology, high capital requirements, proprietary control of information, and global sourcing and marketing. The other system consists of small-to-medium scale farms which rely upon input substitution, diversification, and direct marketing to control costs, minimize environmental impacts, and address consumer and community health concern" (Feenstra, McGrew, and Campbell 1999: I).

The global system of food production, driven by the forces of the market and interests of major corporations, affects the individual inner-city resident who goes to buy a head of wilted lettuce at the corner bodega. It is reflected in the food access crisis in poor neighborhoods in the United States. And it has informed the rhetoric of community gardeners, activists, and coalitions at local, regional, and national levels.

Generations of children in cities are growing up without any understanding of the linkages between food production and consumption. The production of food has become as alien and incomprehensible as the production of cheap consumer goods by workers in maquiladoras across the border in Mexico. To many economists agricultural production represents just one other indicator of the economy and, given that it is no more than 2 percent of the Gross National Product in the United States, a relatively minor indicator at that (Gussow 1999). Such an attitude is based on a notion of the economy that is oblivious to the fact that food must be produced and is not an option.

In this context community gardening, which has been on the upswing in many cities of the United States in the last three decades, has raised alternative themes and challenges. In contradiction to the market economy, community gardening has reinjected a form of subsistence farming into the equation in conjunction with notions of sustainability and the concept of "limited good." The principle of "limited good" was defined by Foster in connection with his discussion of peasant societies. According to this principle "all desired things in life . . . exist in finite and unexpandable quantities" (Foster 1965: 296). This is an expression of the basic conceptual orientation in a society in which wealth is circumscribed by absolute limits and where patterns of interaction are worked out to insure equilibrium. By contrast the principle of unlimited good is based on the assumption that there can be continual growth in wealth and productivity, reflecting a capitalist market economy. Food production in community gardens is predicated on the understanding that food is not an option as consumer goods might be an option and that the resources available for its production are limited. Further, it illustrates on many levels that food has social and cultural significance in terms of by whom, with whom, when, and how it is produced, distributed, and consumed.

These themes are reflected eloquently, directly and indirectly, in actions and words of adults and children in community gardens. In 1996, in the Children's Mural Garden on 12th Street on the Lower East Side, a ten-year-old girl made a drawing of a plant, so that it could then be painted on the garden mural. Asked about the plant, the girl said that she had seen it growing in a garden. Nobody knew what it was until an herbalist happened to identify it from the drawing, which was detailed enough for such identification. It turned out to be a plant of the amaranth genus, which was used by the Aztecs for grain and has the highest protein content of all the grain plants. Eradicated after Cortés came to Mexico in 1519, some efforts are now made to grow this plant again. Sadly this girl herself never knew what she drew; she is one of many children who have disappeared since the formal ribbon cutting in 1996. According to the garden member who told me her story, the young girl had an abusive father. She had lived in a squatter building for a while before she disappeared from the Lower East Side. The garden member and teacher involved in the creation of the mural also pointed out that the amaranth is an imaginary flower that never fades and the Greek symbol of immortality. This comment about permanence served to emphasize even more starkly the fragility of urban existence in conditions of poverty, which community gardening initiatives have sought to counteract.

"I went to the 6th Street Community Center to help with preparations [for the annual Rites of Spring Pageant]. On the way I stopped at 6th and B Garden. There was a lot of low-key activity, some people gardening, kids playing, people on stage preparing something, an older woman with a straw hat selling home-made curried chicken, rice and beans, various spice cakes, banana and bread pudding. She told me that she grows just vegetables in her plot. She apologized for the appearance of her plot: "It is only sticks right now." An older man with a hearing aid was contemplating some sickly-looking roses in a plot. He told me that he has two plots; when I looked at him, he said, "well, one, the other I am working for someone else." Children were playing around the elaborately carved playhouse, in the sandbox and on the stage. Three little girls were "watering"; they kept going over to the barrel and then poured water onto miscellaneous plants and onto the ground. "I am watering the raspberries." "Me too." One girl kept dropping her can in the rain barrel, and it had to be fished out. A woman sat there reading, kept an eye on them, said "Remember, the water is for the plants." A little girl ran up and told another: "There is a real live goose." I don't know where that goose was, maybe on Avenue C in preparation for the Loisaida Street Festival next day" (Fieldnotes: May 23, 1998).

On another day that summer, I stood in front of a bed filled with herbs and vegetables, waiting for a friend. An elderly Puerto Rican man walked up to me and started to tell me about the herbs he was growing in that plot. Pointing to various plants such as comfrey, sage, chamomile, and peppermint, he mentioned their medicinal properties. He bruised some of the leaves so that I could smell them. Their scent stayed with me all that day, until I went home on the 1st Avenue bus.

    These vignettes of life in community gardens evoke some

of the immediate and personal meaning that the activity of food production has for gardeners. It is necessary to contextualize these specific experiences. There is a dearth of data about production, distribution, and consumption in community gardens. Because of the informal nature of the process in many if not most gardens, it is a difficult subject to quantify. Only in some gardens and in some cities have efforts been made to begin keeping records. A few surveys, together with USDA data, compiled in conjunction with U.S. Census data, give an approximate idea of the volume of production in urban gardens, the kinds of produce grown, and the approximate dollar value in various cities.[3] The following discussion makes no claim to remedy this lack of comprehensive quantification and information. Rather, the purpose is to illuminate certain themes and ideas that recur in urban gardening initiatives across the country, in New York City, and on the Lower East Side.

While food production initiatives on the Lower East Side have been relatively limited in scale, these initiatives and the way in which they are linked to other aspects of community gardening provide instructive insights into the potential and limitations of urban food production. Further, they illustrate the manner in which individuals at the local level conceptualize these linkages and position themselves in that context. That is, gardeners on the Lower East Side view their role in symbolic terms as much as in concrete terms of responses to needs; gardening, particularly the activities of organic food production and waste recycling, is a means of symbolically affirming a sense of identification with people in other cities and other countries. The scope of this discussion reflects an argument advanced by food activists and gardeners to the effect that food production is simultaneously a local and a national if not global issue and must be analyzed and understood in those terms.

PRODUCTION, DISTRIBUTION, AND CONSUMPTION

According to a report prepared under the auspices of the United Nations Development Program, in the last few decades there has been increase in the number of urban families engaged in urban agriculture across the world (Smit et al. 1996). In many countries urban food production has become a complex thriving industry. Globally about 200 million urban dwellers are urban farmers, providing food and income to about 700 million people (Mougeot 1994). Urban agriculture had been in decline from the late 19th century on; since the 1970s the trend has been reversing itself. The report points out that urban agriculture has often been minimized as "kitchen gardening"; meanwhile, in the United States in the early 1990s, as much as 30 percent of agricultural products were produced within metropolitan areas (Smit et al. 1996).

In 1980, urban metropolitan areas produced 30 percent of the dollar value of U.S. agricultural production (U.S. Census 1980). By 1990 this figure had increased to 40 percent (U.S. Census 1990). According to a 1995 report about community food security in the context of the 1995 Farm Bill, 56 percent of all food was grown in metropolitan regions and urban-influenced counties (Fisher and Gottlieb 1995). In 1982, according to national survey conducted by the Gallup Organization, 44 million American families or 53 percent grew their own food, totaling $18 billion of fruits and vegetables. Gardeners invested an average of $20, which yielded approximately $470 in food value (Gallup Organization 1982). The USDA estimated that urban gardeners involved in its programs grew $16 million worth of fresh food in 1993 alone (Malakoff 1995). This did not include the many productive gardens not involved in USDA programs. The USDA undersecretary Catherine Woteki explained the goal of USDA programs: "Long-term food security depends on strong connections between people in a community—rural and urban and suburban residents; family farmers and inner-city dwellers. Only by building and strengthening these links will communities be able to provide for their own food and nutrition needs, today and in the future" (Cook 1997).

By the mid-1990s, in response to activism by coalitions across the country, support for urban agriculture programs increased at the federal level. The Community Food Security Coalition (CFSC) spearheaded a nationwide campaign for sustainable agriculture; the impact of this campaign is reflected among others in the Community Food Security Act of 1995, signed into law by President Clinton in April 1996 as part of the Farm Bill of 1996. This was to provide $16 million over seven years in matching grants to non-profit organizations for community-oriented food projects. For community gardeners this could help to replace some of the federal funds lost since 1985, after federal spending on urban agriculture was frozen at $3.5 million.

CFSC projects aim at bringing low-income urban residents and small farmers together in Community Supported Agriculture (CSA) programs, new farmers' markets, community gardens, and other ventures.[4] Such programs involve partnerships between regional farmers and communities in order to provide quality produce at affordable prices to CSA members and a stable customer base to farmers.[5] Scott Chaskey of Quail Hill Farm, a CSA farm in Amagansett, New York, spoke of redefining the relationship between the producer and the consumer, counteracting the pressures of the market and providing the producer with a degree of security and the consumer with access to affordable quality produce. "We know now . . . that family farms without strong local markets cannot survive, and that risk sharing is a tricky business, but it must be defined in relatively concrete terms— between producers and consumers—for CSAs to realize their true potential" (Chaskey 2000). By 2000 there were over 1,000 CSA farms in existence throughout this country; eight were working in partnership with community gardens in New York City. As of this writing there are nineteen CSAs in New York City.

According to a co-founder of the Community Food Security Coalition, Mark Winne, the issue of food security has helped to create a conceptual framework that brings together various issues and themes heretofore treated separately; this includes community gardens, farmers markets, community-supported agriculture, inner-city supermarket development to counter the abandonment of the inner-city by supermarket chains, food policy councils, and micro-enterprises (Fisher 1996). In the last decade of the 20th century over 125 organizations have formed that are working on food and farming issues in conjunction with community organization and urban gardening.[6] For community gardeners the concept of community food security provides a concrete issue around which to focus the development of linkages between urban and rural populations, family farms, farmers' markets, and community gardening.

New York City: Production and Distribution

According to a 1986 survey of 600 community gardens in all boroughs of New York City, the approximate annual monetary value of food produced in New York City urban gardens was $1 million (Operation GreenThumb 1986).[7] Seventy-five percent of the gardeners surveyed rated the desire for fresh vegetables as very important. Forty-two percent reported that they garden to save money. Twenty-five percent said their gardens produced food that they could not otherwise afford. Thirteen percent said that they garden to provide items that are unavailable in local stores. The most popular vegetables grown were beans, tomatoes, peppers, cucumbers, and collards. Gardeners also raised cabbage, squash, eggplant, lettuce, okra, onions, corn, carrots, beets, broccoli, and

The Rediscovered Amaranth

cauliflower. A few gardeners experimented with unusual or exotic vegetables such as asparagus, Jerusalem artichokes, peanuts, radicchio, and calaloo. The survey also showed that geography played a role in the types of vegetables grown. For instance, more eggplant and peppers were grown in areas where Latinos were tending gardens. More collards and greens were grown where community gardeners carried on Southern farming traditions. Thirty-one percent of the gardeners were canning food, and fifty percent were freezing food for winter use. Seventy-three percent reported that they shared their harvest with family, friends, the elderly, and sick people in the neighborhood (Operation GreenThumb 1986).

Other production figures are provided by the City Farms network and provide a sense of the potential of urban community gardens. In 2001, the City Farms network included fifteen gardens in the five boroughs of New York City, in a network of community gardens that produce and distribute food to the community. Five different non-profit organizations including the Green Guerillas and Just Food are involved in the coordination and assistance of the various programs. Despite the city administration's negative stance with regard to community gardens in the 1990s, the City Farms network gained four new gardens between 1997 and 1999 that actively participate in the food growing effort. Two City Farms gardens in the Bronx are about 1.5 acres in size; two others in Queens are located adjacent to each other and occupy four to five acres. The others are all much smaller, some less than a quarter of a city block. In one City Farms garden, members include homeless people who are actively participating in the production of their own food.

Six City Farms network gardens have been marketing their products. Some have established relationships with farmers from upstate New York for marketing and purchasing produce. Several markets are operated by local teenagers. The proceeds from such markets in turn are used to benefit these teenagers with various programs, education, and salaries for their work. In 1998, gardens participating in the City Farms network began to keep records of food produced. In 1999, the fifteen participating gardens produced an approximate total of 8,000 pounds of produce. Gardeners donated about 50 percent of this total to local soup kitchens, marketed another 33 percent, and used the remainder at home (Green Guerillas 1999). If one were to extrapolate from these figures, 600 food growing community gardens would produce approximately 319,800 pounds of produce annually or 533 pounds of produce per each garden.

There are no reliable figures for food production in the many other gardens in New York City. In any event, these figures ultimately are not very informative; in order to determine the amount actually saved through community garden food production, after the subtraction of invested material and labor, one would have to determine how much gardeners spend on food on an annual basis. And even then, any resulting figures would not provide a sufficiently contextualized result; that is, the attendant health, social, and educational benefits are impossible to quantify. Essentially, the impact of community gardening is hard to measure. However, the quantifiable amounts and/or the quantifiable impact is not the issue here. Rather, the significance lies in the ambitiousness, range and multi-dimensionality of programs and initiatives developed over the last two decdes in conjunction with community gardening.[8]

Despite the paucity of comprehensive quantitative data, a picture of remarkably prolific production activities in community gardens emerges. These activities range around certain themes that serve as inspirational goals or goads to action, in particular:

- environmental justice
- organic food production
- food security
- entrepreneurship
- education
- employment
- sustainable agriculture

These themes, which focus on the resolution of concrete and tangible problems, are linked to more conceptual themes such as the notion of countering alienation by active participation and involvement in the production of one's own food supply and visions for an alternative society. The themes overlap and reinforce each other in programs and initiatives in New York City and in other cities in the United States.

Efforts to create linkages between urban consumers and regional growers and at the same time to improve community access to regional products are reflected in many initiatives in New York City as well as in other cities. Many of these efforts revolve around the concept of CSA (Community Supported Agriculture), the creation of community markets, and the establishment of links to restaurants, in a layered marketing strategy to ensure that participating farmers would have reliable marketing opportunities. For instance, in 1998, El Puente, a community-based organization and public high school working with the Latino community in Southside, Williamsburg, developed and ran a cooperative vendors' market in their neighborhood. El Puente also worked with the Walter Rogowski Farm in Pine Island, New York, to develop a CSA cooperative. In June 1999 the cooperative had 25 members. Members pay for shares on a sliding scale based on their ability to pay. There is also an option to pay with food stamps. Several City Farms gardens have established close relationships with their neighborhood soup kitchens and seek to respond to specific needs and food preferences by shifting production to certain items. For instance, some gardens have begun to produce more collard greens in response to a call for such vegetables by a predominantly African-American population in the local soup kitchens. In turn, regional farmers respond to the food preferences of their CSA clients, for instance, the Rogowski Farm has begun to include more peppers in their production plan for the benefit of their predominantly Latino customers.

Another City Farms garden is the Tapscott & Union Street Garden in Brownsville, Brooklyn. This garden is involved in the Green Guerillas' Summer Youth Employment Program. Youth work in gardening and engage in art projects. In the late 1990s they created a mural as part of the Green Guerillas' Youth Mural Project. The garden also created a special children's area where young gardeners will be able to grow vegetables, flowers, and herbs.

The Enchanted Garden in Kingsbridge in the Bronx is also a City Farms garden. It was conceived of and created by students from the John F. Kennedy High School Environmental Club. Starting in 1995, the students transformed a vacant lot next to the school into a garden that even includes a reconstructed wetlands area with cattails, marsh marigolds, and swamp willow. In 1998 the garden operated a farm stand and introduced herb sales in the school cafeteria. The students grew vegetables, herbs, and fruits in addition to perennial and annual flowers in over two dozen beds. The students have been expanding the food-growing part of the garden and plan to share their harvest with a nearby residence for homeless children, a community center that provides meals for poor and elderly people, and a soup kitchen. The students also have developed a web site about their garden.

Many community gardens throughout the United States, especially gardens associated with schools, have their own web sites. For instance, the Orchard School in Indianapolis has created a web site dedicated to environmental education that is designed to promote connections and sharing of information between teachers, students, and any organization involved in environmental education. It further provides links to workshops, events, and informational resources available from organizations such as the Purdue Extension, Soil and Conservation Service, Indy Parks, and Master Gardeners.

There are many similarly creative programs in other cities. The Food Project in Lincoln, Massachusetts, provides employment and training to young people and bridges communities through growing and distributing food in metropolitan Boston. It farms on 2 acres of remediated land in inner-city Boston and manages 21 acres in Lincoln on a site located 15 miles outside Boston. The produce is served by the youth at shelters, sold at their inner-city farmers' markets, and distributed to their CSA shareholders in Lincoln. In 1999, 80 youth (60 employed full-time in the summer and 20 during the academic year) plus 1,000 volunteers produced 127,000 pounds of produce. The Food Project is increasing its commitment to enterprise by erecting a greenhouse in Lincoln and piloting value-added food products at its markets and the CSA drop-off site.

The San Francisco League of Urban Gardeners (SLUG) educates, trains, coordinates, and acts as facilitator for urban agriculture. Supported by SLUG, the Alemany Youth Farm integrates the fight for environmental justice with a social justice strategy. Youth learn about food production and the operation of a small farm. At the same time they learn about lead hazard reduction as part of a holistic approach for building healthy communities (Fisher and Gottlieb 1998). They have launched the Urban Herbals label in conjunction with a honey, jams, vinegar, and salsa processing business that includes both production and marketing.

Another example is the Farmer's Market Nutrition Program, a joint effort of the University of Illinois Cooperative Extension

Service and the Illinois Department of Public Health Women, Infants, Children (WIC) program. Four community vegetable gardens supported by the Cooperative Extension Service Urban Gardening Program provided the WIC food center with fresh zucchini in July, tomatoes in August, and green peppers in September. WIC recipients can redeem WIC food coupons for the vegetables as well as for fresh fruits. The gardeners receive payment from the WIC program for their vegetables. Thus, low-income mothers shopping at WIC food center can buy fresh vegetables grown in Chicago community gardens.

A community garden in New Orleans has established a relationship with a green market and also sells lettuce directly to restaurants (Pottharst 1995). A community garden in Austin, Texas, is involved in food production for a local food bank. The St. John's Organic Community Garden in Phoenixville, Pennsylvania, is the primary source of in-season produce to the local food bank. Supported by the Los Angeles Regional Foodbank, a community garden in a South Central neighborhood of Los Angeles occupies two square blocks, providing space for 150 plots, and is farmed by the area's low-income residents, predominantly Latinos and African Americans.

The programs are many and endlessly diverse. Most have only fragile sources of financial or municipal support. Many have been in existence for ten years or longer. A picture emerges of actively engaged people in urban low-income communities across the country, working with resilience and persistence on these initiatives. The initiatives are participatory and place-based in their organization. They address multiple issues in an integrative fashion. While retaining their individual organizational character, they also increasingly draw on the support of networks and coalitions across the country.

The Rediscovered Amaranth

Lower East Side: Production and Distribution

Patterns of production and distribution in community gardens on the Lower East Side are hardly representative of New York City or the entire country. The Lower East Side with its particular history—a concentrated amalgam of the impact of immigration, industrialization, deindustrialization, and gentrification on a neighborhood and a complex tradition of activism—has defined the depth and dimensions of community gardening initiatives and the conceptual linkages to other struggles. In other neighborhoods in New York City and in other parts of the country one would be more likely to find only selected aspects of such initiatives as well as a tendency toward greater homogeneity in terms of the demographics of community gardens. However, analysis of community gardens on the Lower East Side provides insights into the limitations, potential, and growing import of food production in urban community gardens in America.

In the early 19th century the Lower East Side appeared almost bucolic:

> "In 1825 the region north of Astor Place was still devoted to farms and orchards, with a grey old barn on the site of Grace Church, and a powder-house on Union Square. The fashionable summer evening resort was the Vauxhall Garden, stretching from Broadway to the Bowery, near the present Astor Library, and famous for its trees and flowers, band-music and fireworks, and cakes and ale. In the triangle where Third Avenue and Fourth Avenue come together, stood the grocery store of Peter Cooper, where the uptown lads exchanged berries picked in the Bleecker Street pastures, for taffy and cakes" (King 1893: 39–40).

Between the time when berries grew in the pastures along Bleecker Street and the present day, there was about half a century—from the 1850s to the early 1900s—during which the

The Struggle for Eden

Lower East Side was crowded to the bursting point. Overcrowding, poverty, unhealthy conditions and occasional epidemics such as typhus and cholera made the area a virtual human hell. Conditions eased after 1924, when immigration to the United States and consequently the influx to the Lower East Side was cut back as a result of legislation. In the 1940s Puerto Ricans started to come to the area in increasing numbers. As a result of the contraction of manufacturing during the late 1950s, the city lost 55 percent of its manufacturing jobs between 1960 and 1975, particularly in industries such as the garment trades and small manufacturing, major sources of employment for Puerto Ricans (von Hassell 1996). The impact on Puerto Ricans on the Lower East Side was enormous. "Their declining market position set the stage for the cycle of disinvestment that followed" (Abu-Lughod 1994: 8).

In the 1970s the New York City administration pursued a policy of "planned shrinkage," essentially the dismantling of services to lower-income communities and the reallocation of housing stock so as to better respond to the needs of the corporate city and to solve the city's fiscal crisis (Tabb 1984: 336). The Lower East Side was effectively abandoned, subject to landlord neglect and arson, while the city administration waited like a spider for its prey's imminent death in order to consume it in peace.[9]

Ironically, however, this policy resulted not only in large numbers of vacant lots but also in sweat-equity housing renovation projects and community gardens as well as active and increasingly well-informed residents. Faced with the deterioration of their neighborhood, a crumbling base of employment, and burning and collapsing buildings all around them, people like Alicia Torres of Jardín de Esperanza founded gardens in empty lots, growing food and painstakingly reconstructing an existence and a community for their families. In 2001, despite the havoc wreaked by the New York City administration on community gardens over the past decade, children were still running around in community gardens thrilled about "real apples growing on our tree!"; this is evidence of the remarkable resilience of these grassroots-based initiatives.

In February 2000 there were about forty gardens left on the Lower East Side; nine had been bulldozed over the past three years. The gardens differed in size, ranging from tiny corner lots to almost a quarter of a block, and usage. Some were devoted predominantly to flowers and other decorative plants; others contained a medley of plants, including vegetables from the mundane to the exotic. In most gardens one would find some vegetables, herbs, and even fruit trees. One garden, La Plaza Cultural at 9th Street and Avenue C, participated in the City Farms network. In the summer months the contrast between the crowded and dirty urban street scape and the vibrant green spaces of the gardens was remarkable. A walk around the neighborhood took one past rambling roses and grapevines on fences, laden fruit trees, pole beans, tomatoes, cucumbers, jalapeño peppers, and other vegetables. The grapevine at the Jardín de Esperanza had been growing on the fence at 7th Street since the garden's founding in 1978. A detour into one of the local supermarkets—poorly stocked, badly ventilated, and with a deplorable selection of fresh fruits and vegetables—reinforced the contrast.

Sixth Street Community Center Farm Project is located at La Plaza Cultural on 9th Street and Avenue C. It occupies about 1,000 square feet of growing space, farmed communally and organically. Harvested food is delivered to the Trinity Lutheran Parish Church soup kitchen at least once a week from June through November. Along with City Farms workshops, La Plaza gardeners also receive technical assistance and materials from Rich Sisti, an organic farmer of Catalpa Ridge Farm in New Jersey. This farm has an ongoing arrangement with the 6th Street Community Center. Part of the CSA farms network, it delivers produce to a food cooperative organized by the Community Center. Members in the cooperative receive fresh produce on a weekly basis.

Mutual dependency as part of a productive relationship between local gardeners and regional farmers is reinforced again and again. For instance, local farmers donate hundreds of pumpkins to the 9th and Avenue C Garden on the Lower East Side for fall harvest celebrations and pumpkin smashes. They teach urban gardeners about organic gardening and composting, and they rely on these same people as customers or members of CSA cooperatives.

Consumption, Recycling, and Waste Management

Patterns of consumption and waste management in community gardens provide some of the most poignant challenges to the market-driven consumer society. The notion of sharing resources is echoed in patterns of consumption of community garden produce. Themes of environmental justice and a conceptualization of "limited good" in terms of the earth's resources inform the increasingly sophisticated understanding of the hazards of various forms of soil, air, and water pollution and the treatment of waste products.

Together with other volunteers I repeatedly worked at the Riverside Valley Community Garden on the Upper West Side of Manhattan. While large portions of the garden were always shaded, the garden was remarkably prolific. The garden had been started by a Dominican woman living in a building across the street. Since its inception in the mid-1980s, its membership expanded; there were many children, and the garden had the feel of a huge extended family. On volunteer work days, a team of about eight volunteers worked alongside gardeners throughout the morning. At midday, the gardeners invited the volunteers to lunch. They had prepared it on charcoal grills in the garden, using their own vegetables, lettuce, and fruit—a veritable feast. The gardeners told me that they had lunch together in the garden on most summer weekends.

Sitting under a tree, with the hum of the West Side Highway nearby, eating roasted potatoes grown in the garden and having a gardener explain to me the benefits of the aloe plant, I reflected on the dynamics of New York City volunteerism. The leading individuals in the garden, Latinos in their fifties and sixties, were intensely knowledgeable about every aspect of their garden, including organic gardening, the effects of soil erosion and ground pollution. The volunteers were all white, young middle-class urban professionals, whom one might well find on another day volunteering in a midtown soup kitchen. Most volunteers had limited experience in gardening and were humbled and amazed by their hosts—by their generosity as much as by their evident expertise and initiative.

Many gardens have informal system of distribution of surplus food grown by their members. For instance, in the Young Devils Garden on 115th Street and Madison Avenue, a garden formed in 1991, gardeners place assorted produce such as tomatoes, eggplant, onions, peppers, and okra on a table outside the garden during the summer and fall, offering them to anyone who would like to use them (Hickey 1994). Some gardens have medicinal herb beds; residents are invited to take cuttings for home use.

Community gardens in urban environments are constructed out of discarded materials, creatively recycled and transformed. Railroad ties serve as borders of individual plots, wood from demolition projects reappears in shed walls, and discarded furniture is turned into lawn furniture in a garden's common area. Compost barrels and compost piles are important features. Rain barrels help to tide gardens over periods of drought. In the spring of 2000, Rolando Politi, a local artist, decorated the fence at La Plaza Cultural on 9th Street with soda cans and coffee tins, cut open and flattened so they looked like colorful sunbursts.

Until 2001 there was a recycling center on 7th Street, the Lower East Side Ecology Center, which existed as part of a community garden. Neighborhood people brought their food scraps, cans, bottles, and plastic containers, and the people running the center gave lessons in composting and maintaining worm bins in apartments. The long-term survival of this recycling center is questionable in view of the pressures of the real estate market.[10] In August 2001 this block contained several renovated buildings, including a former synagogue turned into a condominium, a newly constructed apartment building complete with a doorman, and another new building on the lot formerly known as the Jardín de Esperanza.

The City-as-School High School on Clarkson Street in lower Manhattan spearheaded a program that links waste recycling, education, and community gardening. City-as-School initiated Project Grow, a gardening, horticultural therapy, landscape design, environmental science, environmental art, and entrepreneurship program in 1992. Project Grow has designed and constructed a multicultural, intergenerational, community garden on a vacant lot on the Lower East Side. With the assistance of teachers and students from the New York City Board of Education's School of Cooperative Technical Education, Project Grow also designed and constructed a compost-heated greenhouse. The compost is the product of organic waste collected from school and local sources and recycled by the students. Horticulture and science programs have been conducted in the greenhouse since October 1996.

Brooklyn Green Bridge is the community horticulture program of the Brooklyn Botanic Garden and is linked with over 100 community gardens. Brooklyn Green Bridge, in cooperation with community outreach programs in the Bronx, Queens, and Staten Island, has been contracted to demonstrate composting as part of the New York City Department of Sanitation recycling program. Focusing on Manhattan, the Green Guerillas also have been active in this area, engaged in education as well as assistance with arrangement of delivery sites and other practical matters of composting in an urban environment. For instance, at the end of the Christmas season the Green Guerillas collect discarded trees from all over the city and grind them into woodchips at the Jardín del Paraíso on East 4th Street; the woodchips are made available to those who need them.

These various efforts to recycle wastes in the context of urban gardening are minor in scale, and their significance lies more in their educative value and symbolic import than in the volume handled. At the same time, it is possible to discern trends in cities all over the world to address this issue.

In some cities, for instance in Calcutta and Hubli-Dharwad, India, there are successful experiments with recycling of wastewater and other organic waste materials in urban agriculture (Smit et al. 1996; Bakker et al., eds. 2000). In Mexico City much of the waste is used to feed backyard livestock such as cattle, sheep, goats, pigs, chickens, and turkeys. In Accra, Ghana, urban farmers practice solid-waste recycling (Armar-Klemesu and Maxwell 2000).

In many countries in response to an increasing need attitudes about waste management are shifting to a willingness to reexamine methods used before the 20th century. Over the last two centuries there has been a fundamental shift in waste management in urban environments from a closed (sustainable) loop system to the open (unsustainable) loop system, a change in the composition of waste from largely organic to increasingly inorganic and toxic waste, and the development of large-scale waste management systems that dispose of rather than recycle waste (Smit et al. 1996: 14). As yet, few cities have comprehensive waste recycling systems. However, according to Smit, waste recycling and composting efforts at the community level are promising and could help to reduce municipal costs: "An increase in urban agriculture activities would heighten the possibility for food and fuel production to once again transform urban waste from a problem to a resource" (Smit et al. 1996: 14).

The most astounding such effort and easily the least realistic is portrayed in a documentary about community gardens on the Lower East Side, filmed in the mid-1990s.[11] In one scene Adam Purple of the famous Garden of Eden demonstrates his self-invented system, which involves buckets, layers of newspapers, and holes dug in the ground, of recycling his own body waste in the garden. Adam Purple also used to ride his purple bicycle to Central Park in order to collect horse manure from the roadways and trails in the park, which he then transported to his garden. The surrealistic flavor of this enterprise should not detract from the degree to which community gardeners in New York City and other urban environments are reexamining their own place in the environment and the impact that any human actions have on it. This reexamination is reflected in actions performed by gardeners—carrying potentially hazardous debris out of a garden site and replacing it with soil supplied by greening groups such as the GreenThumb, Council on the Environment of New York City, Bronx GreenUp Program, and the Green Guerillas, choosing to work garden plots without pesticides, or carrying their household trash to a recycling site.

In community gardens every can of water poured onto a plot, every lovingly tended compost bin, every truck tire recycled as a planter, every tomato harvested reflects the perception of the world as a finite and fragile organism with limited resources. This is in sharp contrast to an economic system driven by continued growth and expansion and the resulting increase in the amount of waste of organic and inorganic materials. This mountain of waste includes prepared and unprepared foodstuffs, thrown out by food suppliers, stores, restaurants, and farmers on a daily basis all over the United States.

The Rediscovered Amaranth

In this context, the concept of gleaning appears to be a sensible and time-honored response to waste. Gleaning is defined as the process of collecting produce from fields after the harvest; in the last decades it has been expanded to include the retrieval of any food product deemed to be waste at any point in the food system, from restaurant food leftovers to truckloads of produce rejected by buyers, to day-old bread. Gleaning is being examined and tested out in a number of states, involving a diversity of programs. These programs are designed to help low-income families; they link education, lessons in food preservation, gardening classes, community gardening, and distribution of produce to food banks and soup kitchens.

One such effort is the Gleaning Project in Tacoma, Washington. Volunteers are recruited from low-income families to harvest usable produce, bread, and salmon left in the fields, bakeries, and hatcheries near Tacoma. Volunteers get to keep what they can use. Most of the food is delivered to food banks and hot meal sites.

Gleaners also run their own community garden. Yet, perhaps nowhere more than in the notion of gleaning are the contradictions of food security initiatives over the past decades more poignant. The Community Food Security Coalition has argued against federal support for gleaning as a means to solve hunger. The concept of gleaning is perceived as potentially reinforcing and perpetuating the gulf between the rich and the poor in this country. Other organizations have been equally hesitant, concerned about the quality of the food as well as a perceived lack of dignity associated with this form of food procurement. Yet, some activists in food security coalitions and initiatives across the country link the concept of gleaning to visions of an alternative society, in which waste and reckless consumerism are challenged.

It is a profoundly disturbing experience to watch a person go through garbage bins in the hopes of finding edible food. To be sure, this is removed from formally organized projects making it possible for people to collect produce in fields after the harvest and facilitating the collection and distribution of usable food products that otherwise would be discarded. Yet, the notion of day-old bread being just right for poor and low-income people leaves a bad taste in the mouth. As long as the beneficiaries of gleaning are solely poor and low-income people and this process does not affect the overall structure of food production, distribution, and consumption, it appears to be little more than a sorry palliative. On the other hand, such projects in conjunction with daily practices in community gardens contribute to the process of transforming attitudes about consumption and waste and may well have effects radiating far beyond a few urban gardens.

All over the United States, many vacant parcels in urban areas are designated as "brownfields," containing some amount of soil contamination as a result of past use. Activists have called for coordination with environmental agencies to focus on the hazards of proposed urban garden sites (e.g., proximity to freeways, problems of heavy metal contamination, trace elements of volatile organic chemicals, etc.) and the development of mechanisms for either mitigating problems (e.g., soil removal) or establishing alternative approaches (e.g., restrictions on what to grow) (Fisher and Gottlieb 1995: 25). Community gardeners' awareness of ground contamination and associated hazards is determined by the amount of activism in individual gardens and in the neighborhood. Various greening groups make efforts to educate and inform gardeners about these matters. On the Lower East Side some gardeners are aware of these dangers, others again are oblivious. For instance, a member of a garden on 8th Street between Avenues B and C explained to me at the end of the garden's first season that they had not yet planted any vegetables. He and the other garden members were concerned and worried about what was in the ground. They were planning to have the soil analyzed. In many gardens raised beds with imported soil provide some protection against contaminants in the soil.

At 12th Street and 1st Avenue there is a garden associated with a high school. It is located on the site of a former bus depot, and the soil is heavily contaminated with fuel. The garden is the product of labor by children in the neighborhood. Teenagers are in charge of the organization and planning for the garden and interview new members. They also run the organization Open Road of NYC, Inc., which supports similar projects for young people in the city. With some support from the school and the Trust for Public Land, teenagers began working in various neighborhood gardens as volunteers in 1991 in order to learn about the work involved. The garden was formally started in 1993. Some children have been associated with the garden since its inception. It has become a central part of their lives. This is where they spend much of their free time, working, playing, talking, and writing, and feeling safe, successful, and needed. In the fall of 1998, some of the original members, who had been involved in designing the space, graduated and went on to college, retaining a close connection to the garden and their friends. The sign at the entrance from the street reflects the ambitious and innovative use made of this site:

> "This lot used to be a bus depot. It was made into a garden by the students and faculty of all the schools in the J.H.S. 60 building with the assistance and support of the community, Open Road of NYC, Inc., the Department of Sanitation, the Trust for Public Land, Operation Green Thumb, the Golden Rule Foundation, and Prudential. It has a pond, a greenhouse, organic vegetable and flower beds, compost and worm bins. The entire garden is built on top of a liner covered with a foot of topsoil (75% compost, 25% soil)."

The awareness of the many factors affecting lives in urban environments—social, political, economic, and environmental—is transformed into concrete action in community gardens and also increasingly extends to other factors that are not immediately linked to the gardens. Thus, activists and gardeners are making conceptual linkages with other environmental battles. For instance, in the late fall of 1999 Frogworks, a group involved in the fight to protect the Ballona Wetlands in Los Angeles, performed a dramatic and highly entertaining skit of their struggle at the Jardín de Esperanza. They had come to the Lower East Side to express their support for community gardeners and to ask for support in turn.

In the summer and fall of 1999, the New York City administration engaged in a massive spraying campaign to combat a mosquito-borne illness, first identified as St. Louis encephalitis, but later discovered to be West Nile virus, which causes a milder illness. The city used several pesticides for this purpose. One was malathion, a known neurotoxin; the Environmental Protection Agency is considering reclassifying it as a human carcinogen. The other pesticides, resmithrin and sumethrin, have been found to disrupt normal hormonal functioning and trigger allergies and asthma. Insisting that the products were safe, the administration persisted in blanket spraying from trucks and helicopters.

The outrage over the city's failure to make a full public disclosure of health risks posed by the pesticides and to provide reliable notification about spray schedules, the blatant disregard of the manufacturer's warnings attached to use of the products, and the insistence on forcing this campaign on city residents without obtaining an emergency order has fueled efforts on part of activists to get the Environmental Protection Agency involved and to create a broad-based coalition in order to prevent such spraying in the future. On October 12, 1999, the New York Environmental Law and Justice Project served New York City with a Letter of Intent to Sue on behalf of plaintiffs, including the New York Greens/Green Party and individuals. The Department of

Environmental Conservation and the USDA began to investigate the matter. In April 2000, in response to strong protests and pressure from the public and from greening and environmental organizations, as well as to information from scientists, environmentalists, and others, the city administration decided to desist from spraying with the pesticide malathion and agreed to try alternative methods to combat mosquitoes, agreeing to use helicopter spraying only as a method of last resort.

Activists on the Lower East Side make a conceptual linkage between the malathion case and the policy with regard to community gardens, portraying both as equally oblivious to human rights and equally focused on a naked assertion of power. A similar conceptual linkage is made between the struggle to protect community gardens and the increasing concern with the proposed Con Edison plant on the Lower East Side. The malathion case and the proposed Con Edison plant involve a fight against perceived environmental injustice inflicted on neighborhoods, particularly although not exclusively on low-income neighborhoods. Food security initiatives, whether in community gardens, other projects, or coalitions, also seek to redress system-related inequities. Local concerns and protection of one's immediate environment become united with concerns that ultimately extend to a nationwide and even global level, in terms of the fight for human rights, social and environmental justice, and the quest for alternative approaches to existence in the modern world.

Over the years a number of gardeners on the Lower East Side have chosen to have their ashes buried in their respective garden. In a burial at Green Oasis Garden, attended by most of the members, the ashes of a beloved founding member were ceremoniously mixed with the ashes of his dog; after various rituals and a blessing ceremony, which reflected an eclectic blend of religious beliefs, every garden member including children reached into the urn for a handful of ashes and proceeded to spread them all over the garden. The notion of staking a claim to a piece of land by deciding where one wants to be buried is particularly compelling in this nation of immigrants, with an ideology of freedom from old roots and encumbrances and at the same time a yearning for a sense of continuity if not permanence. There is another component perhaps more important than the idea of staking a claim. The wish to have one's ashes spread in a piece of nature reflects the strong sense of wanting to remain a part of or turn into a living, growing, and much loved organism. It also reflects a perception of human beings as tiny particles in the world rather than as a dominant and controlling force.

CONCLUSION

Community garden food production initiatives can be characterized as integrative, involving multiple layers of problems addressed in conjunction, and as place-based, with a focus on specific geographic communities. The lessons learned by community activists since the 1960s are reflected in the emphasis on integrative and place-based initiatives. Initial efforts of community development in the 1960s and 1970s focused predominantly on "bricks and mortar," that is, the creation of affordable housing. This has given way to the recognition that housing is only one component of an effective community development initiative. Activists argue that the goal, the creation of self-sufficient families in sustainable communities, requires a more comprehensive approach. This has resulted in efforts to integrate typical community development work such as housing development, job training, and environmental justice struggles with community food security work, community gardening, and education (Johnson 1999). It is echoed by a statement that might be described as a mission statement of community food security initiatives:

> "Community food initiatives can empower residents and community-based organizations and institutions by developing opportunities for them to have greater participation in and control over their food systems—including production, distribution, access, consumption, and disposition of food waste. Participation in the food system can also support broader community revitalization efforts that address local economic, cultural, and environmental concerns. While targeting food-insecure residents, Community Food Security can support efforts at the local level (and beyond) that promote broader social change and support environmental and social justice objectives" (Joseph 1999).

The effects of food production initiatives in urban community gardening are both concrete and conceptual. Effects can be seen at local, regional, and national levels. They range from the benefits enjoyed by Lower East Side residents who grow a portion of their fresh produce in community gardens to the increasing number of projects supporting the constructive interdependence of regional farms and urban consumers to shifts in attitudes and policies at the federal level over the last decade of the 20th century. Food production in community gardens has furthered the development of a diversity of models such as farmers' markets and CSA cooperatives for restructuring food access in urban areas and linking initiatives to education, employment opportunities, and entrepreneurship.

The effects extend beyond national borders. Gardeners' concerns about food access and distribution and the threatened environment alike incorporate concerns expressed far beyond the local level. The growing resistance to gene-manipulated seed production is one such example of a linkage of local, national, and global concerns. Activists argue that biotechnology is leading to the privatization of plant life and by extension all life. Genetically engineered food is seen as "changing the nature of nature" (Mann 2000; Teitel and Wilson 1999). Community gardeners follow these debates in the media and on the Internet and frequently join in the chorus of activists and coalitions that are trying to apply pressure to large corporations such as Monsanto, DuPont, and Novartis, engaged in the production of genetically engineered plants and seeds, and are lobbying for policy changes at the federal level to bring about a moratorium on the sale of such seed to farmers in the United States as well as in other countries.[12] Developments have come full circle—the CSA concept originated in a local initiative by a group of 30 women in Japan in the 1960s and has inspired initiatives in the United States; now community gardeners and regional farmers are increasingly aware of the multitude of connections at the global level.

At the demonstrations in connection with the World Trade Organization meeting in Seattle in the fall of 1999, Via Campesina, a worldwide small-farmer organization, carried a banner "Get Agriculture out of the WTO." A food security activist who went to Seattle writes: "Farming communities are being destroyed as corporations tighten their grip on the world food supply and governments promote cheap food exports. A system of industrial farming and food production that destroys topsoil, pollutes groundwater, and confines animals within factory farms, is being exported to other countries as a way to food security" (Mann 2000). Working to strengthen small farmers and to enhance their relationships with urban consumers, community food security initiatives challenge "the monopoly power of agribusiness" (Cook 1997: 9).

Community gardeners involved in cooperative relationships with regional farmers identify with the outrage of demonstrators in Seattle; that outrage reflects experiences in gardeners' own communities in terms of the increasing disparity between rich and poor, while hunger and homelessness increase. For community gardeners, concerned about the quality of food in supermarkets and about the possibility of hazardous pollutants in their gardens, the conceptual jump to an identification with demonstrators in Seattle is a minor one. CSA cooperatives, lessons taught by farmers to urban gardeners, and regular work in community gardens illustrate and reinforce linkages between local struggles and nationwide and global concerns.

A food security activist writes:

"The forces of capital and its agencies, such as the World Trade Organization and NATO, have polarized the situation such that community food security and adequate nutrition for all can be achieved only building self-reliant local food systems, from open-pollinated seed to farmers' markets, from breast feeding to hospital food and school food programs supplied by local farmers, processors and distribution agencies and not corporate caterers" (Kneen 1999).

The ultimate goal—sustainability and equitability of food systems at a global level—is played out in the micro environments of community gardens, where there are no mystifying veils between processes of production, distribution, and consumption.

Conceptually, processes of food production in community gardens have injected new themes of cooperation and interdependence in enterprises and provide lessons in the dynamics of mutual assistance. Initiatives reflect a partial rejection of the consumer society and efforts to inject an element of consumer control into the equation. This is predicated on a moral and ethical framework diametrically opposed to the prevailing value set. Individualism and competitiveness, regardless of economic status, are the major foes of community food security (and within that, of adequate personal nutrition). These two behavioral modes form the moral foundation for the corporate-industrial-capitalist food system (Kneen 1999).

The Struggle for Eden

Processes of food production in community gardens provide critical components and a testing ground for visions of an alternative society. These visions revolve around cooperation, resource sharing, and sustainability in conjunction with a work practice that involves adults of all ages working with children, a notion of education that does not draw sharp borderlines between play, work and learning, a concept of a caring and mutually responsible community, and a perception of one's community situated within a national and global context. The domestic realm, ranging from food preparation and consumption to social interactions and the socialization of children, is magnified, literally taken out into the open onto contested terrain and in that process incorporates and takes control of the public realm, the struggle over space, the environment, food access, and social and political equity.

At a conceptual level, food production, distribution, and consumption in urban community gardening provide concrete illustration of the notion of community building as both a process and a goal (Fisher and Gottlieb 1998). These processes represent activism on the ground, which is then taken into the political realm. They offer education through praxis, and they are subject to constant adjustments and strategy changes in response to shifts in the market and in government policies at local, regional, and national levels. Individual active involvement in food production in community gardens, quintessentially defined by time and seasons, serves as a central building block in the conceptualization of community as emergent rather than as static or imposed from the outside.

At one level, community gardening could be viewed as a feel-good palliative for the urban poor at little cost to municipal, regional, and federal governments, a potentially useful method to enhance food production and distribution among the urban poor that does not impact other structures of the economy. One might argue that ultimately community gardening benefits if not distracts low-income and poor people without affecting their structural position in society and the economy. Yet, while recognizing this argument, it is important to remember other dimensions, equally valid if not more so. First, community gardening initiatives cut across classes in the composition of gardens and of activist organizations on behalf of community gardens; consequently, their ultimate impact extends beyond the confines of a single population group. Second, community gardening initiatives reverberate in global themes and are shaped by global themes in a dynamic process; the respective degrees of contribution and influence are not easily quantifiable; however, their existence cannot be denied. Third, community gardening initiatives impact on regional developments, for instance, in terms of enhancing connections between regional farmers and urban consumers. Fourth, community gardening initiatives impact on local developments, affecting city policies, and they have informed and lent impetus to other social and environmental justice initiatives. Finally, these initiatives and their many dimensions are shaped and defined by community gardeners as active participants in the process.

NOTES

1. Miguel Algarín (1997), *Love Is Hard Work: Memorias de Loisaida*. New York: Scribner Poetry.
2. For a discussion on price comparison surveys see Ashman et al. (1993).
3. Ashman et al. (1993) refer to various surveys, according to which gardeners ranked the top three reasons for gardening as pleasure, growing food, and saving money. According to a national gardening survey conducted in 1981 by Gardens for All, a national

community gardening association, 69 percent of all community gardeners reported saving money as their primary reason for gardening, with better-tasting and more nutritional vegetables rated second (Ashman et al. 1993: 190). Further, they cite an estimate, based on the application of a USDA formula, according to which $600 worth of vegetables can be grown per year in a 4' x 16' raised bed.

4. Greenmarket is a related program, albeit without the emphasis on a connection to community gardens; it was organized by the Council on the Environment of New York City in 1976 to save nearby farmlands and to bring fresh local produce to city dwellers. By 1998 as many as 200 farmers and food producers participated in the Greenmarket program.

5. "The origin of the Community Supported Agriculture (CSA) concept, the partnership between consumers and farmers, can be traced to Japan in the mid-1960s. Homemakers began noticing an increase in imported foods, the consistent loss of farmland to development, and the migration of farmers to the cities. In 1965, a group of women approached a local farm family with an idea to address these issues and provide their families with fresh fruits and vegetables. The farmers agreed to provide produce if multiple families made a commitment to support the farm. A contract was drawn and the 'teikei' concept was born, which translated literally means partnership, but philosophically means 'food with the farmer's face on it.' Clubs operating under the teikei concept in Japan today serve thousands of people sharing the harvest of hundreds of farmers" (Van En 1995: 29). This innovative idea finally was introduced in the United States in the mid-1980s; by the late 1990s there were over 600 CSA projects in the United States.

6. To illustrate the range of activities in the area of community food security, one might consider a report by Feenstra, McGrew, and Campbell (1999) which profiles thirteen community food

systems projects in California. All projects had to satisfy certain requirements to be included. One, each project must have well-developed roots in a geographically distinct community and in a particular place. Two, the project must be defined by a holistic and comprehensive approach to problem solving when addressing such issues as food security, affordability, organic production processes, community economic development, and direct marketing between farmers and consumers. Three, each project must involve the cooperation of multiple organizations and actors. However, this report did not include community gardens, CSA projects, food banks, or farmland protection groups.

7. The results of the Operation GreenThumb survey were announced by Hadley W. Gold, Commissioner of the Department of General Services in New York, in recognition of National Gardening Week in April 1987.

8. A 1993 report under the auspices of the American Community Gardening Association examines five programs across the country, illustrating the range of possibilities for inner-city entrepreneurship in conjunction with urban food production (Frohardt 1993). Located in New York City, San Francisco, Dayton, Ohio, and South Providence, Rhode Island, all are community-based gardening programs that have evolved over the years to include a revenue-generating component. They create linkages between urban agriculture, training and employment for young people, opportunities for entrepreneurship, regional farmers, farmers' markets, and stores and restaurants. They receive some support from foundations, universities, corporations, and the government, and all struggle to be self-supporting, yet according to Frohardt, all have succeeded in creating jobs and opportunities for youth, micro business development, and revenue generation.

9. For a more detailed history see Abu-Lughod 1994; von Hassell 1996.

10. The lot is part of the development project of Donald Capoccia on 7th Street, its fate will be determined in conjuction with the final fate of the bulldozed Jardín de Esperanza (see Chapter 3).

11. Evans, David Hayward (1997), *Dirt: A Year in the Life of Gardens in the East Village*.

12. For instance, the Northeast Food Coalition posted a communication from Ronnie Cummins, Director, Campaign for Food Safety/Organic Consumers Association, on its Internet list serve in March 2000 (Cummins 2000). Cummins provided extensive information on genetically engineered foods and crops, calling for support for, among others, the eventual elimination of factory farming.

Conclusion

INTRODUCTION

In the spring and summer 2000, "bulldozer season" in the words of a gardener, community gardeners all over New York City worked on their gardens and planned events in and around them, evidence of their determination to carry on.

For instance, in May 2000, confronted with the possibility of bulldozing at any time, the Lower East Side garden La Plaza Cultural in cooperation with several other gardens in the neighborhood organized a day-long festival in celebration of the koi, the Japanese carp. Teachers, musicians, artists, and performers together with gardeners created this event. Adults and children were invited to wander from garden to garden to listen to Japanese flutes, participate in art work, and watch dance performances. On June 17, 2000, gardeners from community gardens all over New York City gathered to celebrate the 4th Annual Summer Solstice Celebration at the Clinton Community Garden, located on West 48th Street and to toast the introduction of the community garden legislation proposal to the city council. On June 24, 2000, the gardeners of the J.D. Wilson Memorial Garden held a mulberry festival to celebrate the completed installation of their new fence. Members of that garden have been going to court to try to save the remaining fragment of their garden. One of the founders of the garden, Cynthia Worley, has jars of mulberry jam in her kitchen, made from last year's harvest. Gardeners and supporters of the city-wide garden community joined in the celebration.

This continuing vibrant energy in the face of hovering bulldozers brings to mind the last scene of Goethe's *Faust*. The protagonist looks down at a crowd of people busily working on the construction of a huge drainage canal and a damn to protect their fields and homes and the labor of their hands from flood waters. Deeply moved by this spectacle, Faust decides that it is time to bring to an end his bargain with Mephistopheles—Faust had agreed to surrender his soul to the devil, once Mephistopheles had succeeded in showing him, sated and cynical as he was, something for which he would be willing to give his life and soul. For Faust, the attainment of freedom and a life well lived are inseparable from a life of activity and the work and the process of earning it every day, surrounded by dangers. The sight of New York City's community gardeners, tenacious, diverse, unquenchable, imaginative individuals, who confront their nemesis with flowers and mulberry jam, might have evoked Faust to declare: "To this moment I would say: stay, thou art beautiful."[2]

COMMUNITY GARDENS IN OTHER U.S. CITIES

According to a report based on a National Gardening Association survey (Goodman 2000; American Community Gardening Association 1998), since 1991 there has been a 22 percent increase in community gardens in the country, with a total of gardens reported in 1996 of 1,906 in New York, 1,318 in Newark, New Jersey, 1,135 in Philadelphia, 131 in San Francisco, and 44 in Washington, D.C. Of course, these numbers do not include the losses in New York since 1996 and are misleading. However, if one looks beyond the specific history of New York City, the overall trend indicates an increase of urban community gardening activity. In 1990 the American Community Gardening Association had 250 member gardens; in 2000 there were 900 members, representing approximately 500,000 community gardeners. In data from 38 cities in a 1998 survey the American Community Gardening Association estimated 6,020 community gardens

Conclusion

nationwide, with approximately 2 million community gardeners (Goodman 2000). The increase in sheer numbers and volume of urban community gardening activities in the United States over the last decade is matched by an increase in the scope of these initiatives and the strength and organizational sophistication of coalitions within cities and nationwide.

In various cities in the United States, for instance, in Chicago, Denver, Portland, San Francisco, and Seattle, city administrations have made conscious efforts to include community-managed green spaces in their urban planning programs (American Community Gardening Association 1992, 1998).

For instance, in Seattle Mayor Paul Schell has mandated that up to five new community gardens be built each year, despite a severe shortage of land. In June 2000, the Seattle City Council unanimously approved the Five-Year Strategic Plan for P-Patch Community Gardens. This plan, with a stated emphasis on high density areas, is the beginning of a systematic approach for expanding the community gardening program in the city of Seattle.

Boston is among the most successful in terms of securing its gardens. Over half of Boston's community gardens are owned by land trusts or other non-profits. Garden Futures, an umbrella organization formed in 1994 by the four land trusts, is working on increasing public and government awareness and support. New housing often includes new public gardens. The South End Lower Roxbury Land Trust was set up by the Boston redevelopment Authority, with the help of local developers; their aim has been the preservation of existing gardens as community assets in a neighborhood subject to intense development pressures. Additional gardens were placed within a greenway built into the community on a platform over a railroad cut. Other cities such as Berkeley, California, and Chicago have included community gardens in their comprehensive open space plans (Kirschbaum 2000).

In other cities such as New Orleans, Louisiana, and Madison, Wisconsin, public-private partnerships with strong input from neighborhood groups, garden activists, and greening groups have successfully worked out ways to preserve community gardens and retain community control of state or city-owned surplus land. A study prepared by researchers in Baltimore compares neighborhood open space management in six cities with similar demographics: Atlanta, Boston, Chicago, Detroit, New York, and Philadelphia. According to this report, key ingredients for successful management of small open spaces in urban environs are public-private partnerships with active involvement of community garden groups and government support, vehicles such as land trusts for establishing stability of projects by securing title to properties, and comprehensive open space plans of the respective municipalities (Parks & People Foundation of Baltimore 2000).

The greatest continuing threat to community gardening is insecure land tenure. A 1996 survey indicated that less than 2 percent of gardens were in permanent ownership or in a land trust (American Community Gardening Association 1998). Sally McCabe, outreach coordinator and a board member of the American Community Gardening Association, described the events in New York City in the last years of the 20th century as "a wake-up call" (Goodman 2000). According to activists one of the most important goals for the future is greater visibility of community gardens in open space plans and municipal policy. In order to achieve this goal it will become even more necessary to get involved in local, state, and federal politics. Andrew Stone of the Trust for Public Land said: "You must engage in the political process" (Kirschbaum 2000: 9). In the last years of the 20th century, alerted by events in New York City, a growing number of local governments began to address this issue (Kirschbaum 2000). Gardeners echo this thought, again and again emphasizing the need to network, to get organized, and to become active participants in

Conclusion

local and municipal governments.

BEYOND THE UNITED STATES

Community gardens as described in the preceding pages are specific to the United States. When activists speak of the global context, this involves a conceptualization of environmental concerns, greening and food production activities, and a sense of shared problems and challenges. Certainly, not all community gardens are involved in food production. However, urban agriculture is a central factor in many gardens and critical to the self-conceptualization of urban gardeners; furthermore, it is an important component in arguments advanced by activists on behalf of community gardens.

Recent publications attest to the growing importance of diverse forms of urban agriculture in cities all over the world (see Bakker et al. eds. 2000; Meyer-Renschhausen and Holl, eds. 2000). The concept of urban agriculture comprehends community gardens as well as other forms of growing food within urban environs. Such activities, often marginalized but also increasingly acknowledged in policy agendas of city governments, range from food production for home consumption, social sharing, and marketing purposes to leisure-time greening and beautification of neighborhoods. The positioning of urban agriculture and urban gardening activities vis-à-vis municipal and national policies is dependent on local social, economic, and political conditions as well as preexisting traditions of such activities.

In many Third World countries urban agriculture has become an increasingly important source of income and means of obtaining food (Smit et al. 1996; Bakker et al. eds. 2000). While the particular distribution of problems varies widely, urban agriculture and urban gardening all over the world are subject to the same set of critical issues. These are land tenure, governmental policies, and environmental contamination and degradation. The manner in which these challenges are being met or ignored varies from country to country. Comparative analysis indicates that the factors resulting in viable initiatives in other parts of the world are the same as those one would find in viable community garden initiatives on the Lower East Side, that is, strong local and grassroots-based initiatives that receive support from local governments and public-private partnerships. I offer a few examples from areas around the world to indicate the range of initiatives and their positioning within respective local contexts.

In Canada, as in the United States and European countries, various forms of urban gardening were encouraged during the war years. Like the United States, Canada had victory gardens during both world wars (Buswell 1980). Currently Montreal has one of the most ambitious urban community garden programs; started in the 1970s, it includes over 100 gardens. Two-thirds of Montreal's community gardens are zoned as parks and consequently protected from development and land speculation. The support of community gardens is matched by a strong ecological orientation that defines many other city policies and programs. While there is increased development pressure on open space, the city administration is making concerted efforts to find alternative sites in those cases where a garden has to be eliminated. Toronto like Montreal is characterized by a heterogeneous population with many cultures and ethnicities. In both cities community gardens have begun to shape the physical appearance of the city as much as they express and provide means to transmit diverse cultures and bodies of traditional knowledge (Wekerle 2000). In the late 1990s the City of Toronto Health Department, acting on the premise that community gardening is critical to healthy communities, was engaged in a program to expand community gardening opportunities in that city.

Conclusion

In Russia a tradition of weekend and vacation gardening in cottage gardens on the outskirts of cities and a growing need for produce have contributed to active urban agriculture in the present. In the mid-19th century thousands of rural noblemen moved to the cities in search of employment in civil service and other occupations; these new urban residents began to rent rural houses or dachas with gardens where they could continue aspects of their rural life style and traditions on weekends and during the summer months (Moldakov 2000: 33). The majority of dachas are relatively small (5–6 m²) and located on small plots of land in relatively poor soil. However, thousands of residents spend almost every weekend in these areas from April through October. In 1991 the number of summer dacha residents was over 13 million.

Other forms of urban agriculture in Russia take place in various types of garden communities with or without buildings attached; there also have been some successful experiments with rooftop gardens in St. Petersburg (Moldakov 2000). Principal reasons are the production of a supply of fresh green food, income, and also food free of contaminants. In the face of unemployment and underemployment and a generally depressed economy, for many urban gardeners home-grown produce is often the only reliable source of food. In 1997 over 65 percent Moscow residents were involved in urban agriculture, compared to 20 percent in 1970 (Ford et al. 1997). In St. Petersburg more than half of the population is engaged in urban agriculture (Moldakov 2000). In all of Russia approximately 70 million persons are engaged in urban agriculture. However, the future of urban agriculture in Russia is in question. There is no strong governmental strategy for the development of urban agriculture. The biggest threat is the fee structure; rents, in addition to land taxes, charged by the city administration for gardening plots are prohibitive for many urban gardeners (Moldakov 2000).

In Germany allotment gardening has been built into the fabric of urban existence since the 19th century, providing the industrial working class with an escape from their work places and crowded tenements, an opportunity to experience nature, and the possibility of fresh, homegrown produce. At the end of World War II, in a country where all industry and forms of supply and distribution were at a standstill, the produce grown in allotment gardens helped to tide over many families. In bombed-out cities many residents sought temporary shelter in their little allotment garden huts. After World War II and several years of extreme scarcity, new construction of schools and residential, commercial, and industrial developments swallowed up many allotment gardens.

In Berlin allotment gardens acquired enormous importance in the years of the German Democratic Republic and after the Berlin Wall was built. For West Berliners such gardens represented the only green space that they could easily access within the enclosed part of the city. For East Berliners allotment gardens provided a place for community life and individual initiative not immediately within the constant purview of the East German government. Currently over 80,000 gardeners lease Kleingärten (small gardens) or allotment gardens from the city of Berlin. Today many allotment garden communities are located in the heart of the city and hence are subject to development pressures. In the unified city allotment gardens no longer represent such a singular and vital resource to the residents; however, the emotional attachment is powerful and increasingly closely allied with the interests of environmental advocacy groups and greening groups.

Urban agriculture also is incorporated into the learning program in primary and secondary schools. Learning in gardens has a long tradition in Germany; the first school gardens were started in the late 17th century. In Berlin several so-called school gardens are supported out of the school budget and provide spaces for experiential and practical lessons in agriculture, the environment, design, and engineering. In 1994 the Berlin Senate

Conclusion

approved a land use plan for the entire city that includes a program to secure 85 percent of existing allotment gardens (Aue 2000; Meyer-Renschhausen and Holl eds. 2000).

According to conservative estimates as much as 40 percent of the population in African cities is involved in urban agriculture (Mougeot 1994). Case studies and production figures from cities all over Africa reflect the growing importance of urban agriculture to its residents (Bakker et al. eds. 2000; Diallo 1993; Smit et al. 1996). Generally government policies range from benign neglect to suppression of urban agriculture, but in some countries attitudes are shifting toward a greater willingness to actively support such activities. Case studies from Harare, Zimbabwe, Nairobi, Kenya, and Dar es Salaam, Tanzania, among others, indicate the increasing importance of informal sector activities as necessary survival strategy in conjunction with rising urban poverty and decreasing formal sector employment (Bakker et al. eds. 2000; Smith ed. 1999).

They further point to the importance of considering the relationship between labor markets, economic class, gender roles and distribution of labor, as well as informal versus formal sector work in urban agriculture. In many African countries women are largely responsible for feeding the family and rely on urban gardening for this purpose. Women are less often involved in income-producing aspects of urban agriculture or alternatively are displaced by men under certain circumstances. For instance, in Harare, Zimbabwe, the high rate of unemployment, particularly in the formal sector, has resulted in an increasing number of men active in urban agriculture. "As attitudes towards urban agriculture become more favorable, there might be a danger that men will displace women from an activity in which women have been engaged for years" (Mbiba 2000: 294).

The most well-known and arguably the most successful and comprehensive urban agriculture program can be found in Cuba.

The Struggle for Eden

One-third of Cuba's vegetables are now grown in cities (Murphy 1999). Havana, the largest city in the Caribbean, has thousands of community gardens, three urban dairies, and one of the most ambitious urban reforestation programs to date. Urban agriculture in Cuba is the result of a response to a crisis. Pinched by U.S. sanctions and blockades and international isolation, Cuba has gone further than most countries in developing urban agriculture as a response to food scarcity and widespread malnutrition. In 1991 the Cuban Ministry of Agriculture began promoting self-provision gardens, enabling poor urban residents to grow food on private or state land at no cost. (Cook 1997: 10)

Furthermore, the end of Soviet supplies and subsidies, in particular pesticides and chemical fertilizers, resulted in a wholesale shift to organic production techniques. By 1999 there were over 26,000 organic gardens covering a total of 5,000 acres in the Havana metropolitan area. Many gardens are located on vacant or abandoned lots, often within the immediate neighborhood of people working these pieces of land; others are on state land made available to gardeners at no cost (Moskow 1997). Another interesting factor is the decision by the Cuban government in 1993 to break up most of the large state farms, in their place supporting small farms and small profit-seeking farm cooperatives. Levels of production increased subsequently. Urban agriculture has been income producing, and it has helped to make Cuba more self-reliant.

It is noteworthy that in Cuba the majority of urban gardeners (91 percent) are men. Some argue that this is most likely due to the agricultural background of many of these men (Moskow 1997). However, evidence from other countries indicates that there is a direct relationship, mediated by class and race dynamics, between the value placed by governments on urban agriculture activities and the societal value placed on production activities for subsistence on the one hand and the respective distribution of

Conclusion

involvement by men and women on the other (Bellows 2000).

As another example one might consider the role of women in urban agriculture in the United States during the war years. In the so-called Liberty Gardens (World War I) and the Victory Gardens (World War II), while many men were serving abroad, women played an active role in an activity that was advertised by the government as critical to the nation's ongoing well-being, if not survival. At the end of the respective war years, when national food production no longer was diverted to serve the military forces, urban agriculture no longer had the same value and most of these gardens were abandoned; women found themselves displaced from this activity, as indeed from other jobs, as men returned from the front.

The relatively high proportion of women involved in urban community gardens from the 1970s on is the result of a combination of factors. A central factor is the continued relatively low value placed on such activities by governmental policy makers and by the society. Associated with the domestic and private realm of family reproduction and subsistence activities, urban gardening, particularly if it involves food production, still is largely marginalized and considered of little value in the overall context, the gradually shifting position of the USDA, among others, notwithstanding. The effects of this valuation of urban community gardening work are mediated by the intersecting dynamics of race, class, cultural background, and particular local histories of grassroots activism, creating different scenarios from garden to garden and neighborhood to neighborhood.

In summary, comparative analysis of urban agriculture activities around the world and community gardening in the United States suggests parallels as well as directions for further inquiry. Tenure is generally insecure, subject to shifts in the desirability of given sites. Most urban agriculture and community gardens are situated on land that is abandoned or temporarily declared to be a wasteland or unwanted land. As development pressure increases, community gardeners and urban farmers suddenly find themselves sitting on valuable real estate. In New York City, many community gardens occupy sites that could be developed for commercial or residential uses. Some urban agriculture activities are located on land that is relatively undesirable by most development standards, for instance, land near railroad tracks in East New York; here chances are that people working that land will not be displaced for some time (Nettleton 2000).

Actively supportive governmental policies with regard to urban agriculture and urban community gardens are the exception. As is the case in the community garden movement in the United States, a growing number of private non-profit organizations as well as international development agencies have become involved, working in cooperation with governmental agencies. Analysis of urban agriculture and community gardening also indicates the importance of the understanding that food production for subsistence as well as for income production involves a range of motivations and is driven by a number of factors that cannot be reduced to considerations of use value and cost benefits.

Consideration of production activities in community gardens helps to illustrate that social factors such as sharing of goods and community life are as powerful as economic need. For instance, Bellows in an analysis of urban gardeners in Silesia, Poland discusses the range of motivations that inspire these gardeners to continue growing in food in heavily contaminated soil despite an awareness of the risks involved (Bellows 2000). Motivations include the need to maintain a network of social relations that is cemented and reaffirmed continually by giving gifts and sharing; this network is a form of insurance in a country suffering from economic crises and periods of great deprivation. Further, motivations include the need to engage in an activity that is perceived as pleasurable and productive; it provides individuals

Conclusion

with a modicum of control over their lives. For these psychological, social, and economic benefits, urban gardeners in Silesia are willing to accept the risks of eating vegetables grown on contaminated soil.

BENEFITS, LESSONS LEARNED, AND IMPLICATIONS FOR THE FUTURE OF CITIES

A growing body of literature attests to the diverse benefits of community gardens. A national survey conducted by Kansas State University horticulturalists at 46 different sites around the country indicated a range of quality-of-life benefits associated with gardening by the respondents, including improved self-esteem, social engagement, and psychological well-being (Waliczek, et al. 1996). Many studies report general health benefits as well as benefits specifically to children in urban environments.[3] Other studies report links between community gardens and dropping crime rates (Pottharst 1995; McCarthy 1994). McCarthy points to statistics that show that neighborhoods with thriving community gardens tend to have lower crime rates (McCarthy 1994).

Gardeners report benefits with regard to food production, savings, and availability of fresh food and perceived health benefits in connection with organically grown fresh produce (Lackey and associates 1998). Other economic benefits involve income production by marketing produce. Urban agriculture has resulted in the creation of new market niches, for instance, the growing market for organic produce. It has also facilitated the production of produce that is geared toward particular population groups, such as the production of okra and collard greens by African-American gardeners or the production of certain kinds of peppers by Latino gardeners.

Some benefits of a qualitative nature are harder to define and impossible to quantify. These are the multidimensional role of patterns of exchange in community gardens, the effects on community life, the effects on connections between individual neighborhoods and the entire city, the linkages between urban and rural contexts, and the linkages, both conceptual and actual, between local concerns and concerns of national and global significance.

In community gardens the exchange of produce, tools, knowledge, and labor help to affirm and reaffirm relationships, expanding and improving the social web in a neighborhood and providing a medium for communication. In many gardens produce is given away on a regular basis; it is laid out on tables at the entrance to the garden or collected in boxes and brought to neighborhood soup kitchens. This non-cash economic system coexists with a market-based economy. It represents a form of security or backup system and also suggests alternative models of assistance (also see Bellows 2000).

At another level urban community gardening, in particular food production, is part of the process of social reproduction of family life and the community, offering new dimensions and possibilities for community and family life, work, and education.

Effects on community life include increased communication among individuals within gardens, within a neighborhood and at a city-wide level. This also includes the diverse network of volunteer organizations and individuals from all over New York City that volunteer in community garden initiatives in neighborhoods often far from their own homes. Community gardens provide a range of opportunities for cross-cultural and cross-class contact. In New York City community gardens and activism on their behalf have produced linkages that extend from individual neighborhoods across the city. The Rites of Spring Pageant and other cultural and political events are examples. While the notion of a citywide

Conclusion

community of urban gardeners is more conceptual than actual and certainly does not involve all gardens or even all neighborhoods to the same extent, this notion has begun to acquire concrete shape—in the support extended by one group of gardeners to another, in the joining of forces in citywide demonstrations, and in an increasingly extensive network of communication among community gardeners that cuts across the city.

Daily praxis within gardens, means of communication, and the content of the central message conveyed repeatedly by gardeners and their supporters indicate a conceptual identification with the entire city. Gardeners share food with others outside the garden. Most gardens have regular opening hours. Many gardens schedule events to which the general public is invited. They participate in community board meetings and attend city council hearings. Gardeners make active use of the media to draw attention to their efforts. One of the central means of communication among community gardeners over the past decade has involved networking through the Internet in addition to more traditional means such as the phone and direct communication. As a result individual garden communities reach out beyond their own borders on a regular basis. That city-wide linkage is particularly pronounced during times of crisis, for instance when the city is proceeding against one or a group of gardens; at such times messages, requests for help, advice, information, and supportive comments from gardeners all over the city as well as from the extended community in other cities pour into community garden list serves, the "bulldozer hotline" is on standby, and people are working the phones to apply pressure to the politicians, alert the media, and rally potential supporters.

Such a conceptual identification with the entire city also is reflected in the central theme or message that is conveyed in many different forms again and again. The urban world is perceived as negative, polluted, filled with asbestos and other harmful agents;

in a social and economic sense, it is perceived as destructive and exploitative, alienating and impersonal. However, the concepts and the language used on behalf of initiatives to protect community gardens involve notions of linkage rather than the desire to create a separation between gardens and the city. Activists and gardeners portray these spaces as playing an important role within the city, making a meaningful contribution to city life on many levels. Instead of drawing up a metaphorical wall between intrusive and polluting city surroundings and community gardens, activists portray gardens as cleansing and transforming, as reaching out, as constructively spilling over in their diverse beneficial effects on many levels of life in individual neighborhoods and the entire city—environmentally, socially, and culturally. In community garden initiatives, "community" involves both a bounded and localized vision and at the same time a notion of transcendence across physical space and across cultural, racial, and ethnic barriers—a "virtual urban community."

Community gardens contribute to the expansion of relationships, conceptual and concrete, between urban, suburban, and rural residents. This is reflected in the expanding network of CSA (Community Supported Agriculture) enterprises and various forms of cooperation among urban community gardeners and rural farmers. The Green politics adage, to think globally and to act locally (Coleman 1994), is reflected in the interest with which community gardeners on the Lower East Side follow other open space issues in the city and across the country, environmental justice issues, and environmental issues at a global level. Newsletters such as the *Community Greening Review*, the Neighborhood Open Space Coalition newsletter *Urban Outdoors*, the American Community Gardening newsletter *Multilogue*, and *Just Food News* reinforce such a broader perspective.

One particular set of developments reflects the importance of considering suburban development in conjunction with urban development and open space planning. In Milwaukee, Wisconsin, Hmong immigrants were engaged in urban agriculture on 2,000 plots located in part on Milwaukee County Grounds property and in part within urban neighborhoods. The land on which the 1,003 community garden plots were located was sold to a development firm. Milwaukee County Grounds won the ensuing court case and evicted the gardeners. However, they have given the gardeners access to other land. It is too early to determine how successful this land swap will be (Lackey and associates 1998). This is noteworthy for two aspects. One is the fact that the gardeners received other land in exchange. Second, the very fact of this large community of Hmong engaged in a form of subsistence farming in an urban and suburban environment reflects the context of global flows of people and the complex effects on receiving countries and localities.

In an article in *National Geographic* celebrating the 25th anniversary of Earth Day, one of the featured success stories was the Garden of Eden in Jamaica, Queens (Graham 1995), a small but thriving garden on a vacant lot in a neighborhood populated predominantly by poor and low-income people. The original Earth Day event on April 22, 1970, attracted as many as 20 million Americans, who were riding on a remarkable wave of enthusiasm for trying to roll back global environmental degradation. The author emphasized a conceptual and concrete linkage between Earth Day, an event that took on the mantel of global significance, and a local initiative like the Garden of Eden. Gardeners and activists echo this linkage at many levels in community gardens in New York City and on the Lower East Side; the struggle for a "healthy garden" and a "healthy community" and a "healthy planet" is perceived as one and the same.

Gardeners fight for the space next to their building, for a green and safe place for their children, for a space within which to nurture community life, for a space that helps to support the ecological balance in the urban environment, for the possibility to develop relationships with regional farmers, for the right to produce and consume food that is grown organically, and for protection of the global environment. While it might be no more concrete than a child's entry in her school atlas—Hannah Pushkin, the Boardwalk, Coney Island, New York City, New York State, America, the Western Hemisphere, the World, the Universe—community gardeners situate themselves within the larger context. In turn, the praxis of community gardening, both in terms of creating and taking care of a garden over many years and in terms of the struggle on their behalf, affects and changes gardeners' actions and approach and the manner in which they interact with the urban environment.

Maps matter, and community gardeners are fully aware of this fact. Until 2000 official maps of the City of New York did not show existing community gardens, only vacant lots; there are various initiatives on the Lower East Side to redress this particular form of political obliteration (see also Chapter 1). Meanwhile, Lower East Side community gardeners who go on the Internet find the Green Map web site. The Green Map system is described as a globally connected, locally adaptable framework for community sustainability. Green Map encourages initiatives to chart sites of environmental significance in urban places around the world. There are participants from cities in many countries. Each locally made Green Map is independently produced. Map makers include people of all ages, particularly children. Green Map and its success to date illustrate the powerful symbolic and emotional component associated with maps and the process of mapping one's place. It also illustrates another point, that is, the dialectical relationship between the global and the local. Community gardeners on the Lower East Side are involved in map making and in the struggle to have their gardens included in the city administration maps. They see themselves as acted upon by the world, both in terms of

Conclusion

immediate local surroundings and in terms of global dynamics, and in turn they seek to act upon the world.

In a symposium about the future of cities and the role of urban agriculture within them, Jac Smit discussed the geographic layout of future cities that would most likely produce sustainable urban environments (Smit and Nasr 2000). Such cities of the future would be based on a grid pattern with multi-centric layouts. Within these multiple centers urban agriculture and community gardens would play a vital role in helping to reduce the need for travel and to make individual areas more livable on a number of levels. Such a geographic layout would also be reflected in organizational patterns, for instance, supply and distribution of food and handling of waste products. According to Smit and Nasr a multi-centric geographical and organizational layout would be a critical feature in terms of the viability and vitality of cities of the future.

Sidney Mintz, known among others for his work on the global commoditization of non-nutritious "hunger killers"—sugar, chocolate, tea and coffee—echoes this position from an anthropologist's perspective. Mintz suggests that the creation of viable cities of future would require the restoration of small-scale, sustainable agricultural systems around urban centers as critical to the future food supply (Mintz 1986).[4] He further suggested management strategies in communities as an important area for research, in particular the need to analyze "not what people have, but what they do with what they have." In this context the urban community garden movement in the United States over the past decades of the 20th century can be considered as a component of the future of cities in the making. The community garden movement and individual garden initiatives are characterized by a multi-centric organization, an emphasis on addressing diverse factors—social, environmental, economic—as part of a single struggle, and an emphasis on sustainability as an ultimate goal. Urban community gardeners serve as an instructive example of what people "do with what they have." Experts in "the art of the possible," urban community gardeners find their opportunity in the limitations of place and in its hardship, to paraphrase Kemmis and the poet Wendell Berry (Kemmis 1991: 138).[5]

Study of community gardens can help to throw light on the manner in which the dynamics of historical traditions, social, economic and political context, and gender, race, and class intersect at the local level and how gardeners negotiate these in their daily lives. Analysis of urban community gardens offers insights into the dynamics of grassroots initiatives and activism. It further illustrates local conceptualizations of sustainability and linkages between global and local worlds, both in terms of concrete factors and in terms of the way in which people in specific localities translate the global context into their own lived experiences.

CONCLUSION

The themes and actual as well as perceived benefits associated with urban community gardens are not all represented equally in all cities or, for that matter, among all community gardens on the Lower East Side.

By virtue of its particular history of activism, the Lower East Side contains a concentration of such conceptual awareness among community gardeners and neighborhood activists. Without their prodding I would not have become aware of the many dimensions associated with this movement. Hence, a description of community garden initiatives on the Lower East Side is intended as a starting point for a comparative consideration of basic shared themes and dynamics that interact with specific local historical, economic and social conditions. It is not supposed to be a representative

Conclusion

description of urban gardening in the United States. To imply the latter would be to contradict a point made earlier, that is, the tremendous diversity among community gardens in different neighborhoods and different cities in terms of history, membership, organization, ideological orientation, and politics, each the product of a unique set of circumstances. Furthermore, the strength of the community garden movement is derived from this very diversity. This diversity also partly accounts for the continuing vitality of a movement that straddles so many dimensions—environmental justice, community revitalization, and food security, among others—linked by an emphasis on multidimensional place-based initiatives and an orientation that takes into consideration global impact and dynamics.

The study of community garden initiatives and the political struggle on their behalf indicates four principal reasons that this development has not evaporated despite the lack of support and political pressures to speed its demise. Community garden initiatives are integrative, in terms of the people involved— different cultures, races, age groups, classes—and in terms of the goals—the creation of gardens, social settings for community reproduction, work, food, and educational settings, to name the principal ones. Second, community garden initiatives are truly local grassroots initiatives as opposed to something imposed from above. The degree of active and autonomous involvement on part of residents and garden members largely determines the chances of success for particular initiatives.[6] Third, community gardens offer unmediated experiences and lived experiences of biological life cycles as a balancing counterpoint to an increasingly urbanized, mechanized environment. Finally, community gardens create spaces that facilitate the expression of individuality within the context of a dynamic community. In conjunction these elements have sustained the continued commitment of individuals and organizations, when many other initiatives fail for lack of interest.

The contrast between the following quotes illustrates the extent to which community gardeners have succeeded in obtaining recognition and putting their gardens on the map. It also illustrates the continuing profound gap between two modes of looking at the world. In the most recent available Community District Needs Report about Community District 3, notable for a spurious distinction between middle-income and market-rate housing, the only reference to community gardens is an oblique one:

> "The New York City Partnership Program will be developing middle-income housing on some vacant sites. The remaining sites will be developed as market-rate housing, and, we hope, the small vacant city-owned lots will be retained as open space" (New York City Department of City Planning 1998).

Less oblique is the comment by HPD Deputy Commissioner Mary Bolton at a public hearing in 1996 (Ferguson 1999b). Lower East Side residents and gardeners expressed criticism about development plans for the neighborhood, which involved four-story townhouses with private entrances and backyards in an area of six-story tenements, that is, low-density construction in a neighborhood traditionally characterized by high density, combined with the sacrifice of open space. Residents, questioning the extent to which such a plan addressed the need for housing on the Lower East Side, asked Bolton about the possibility of incorporating community gardens into the development plans. Bolton responded: "Community space is inconsistent with homeownership" (Ferguson 1999b: 69).

On the other hand, an editorial in the *New York Times*, sharply critical of the city administration's actions with regard to community gardens, described the shift of control over the land on which most community gardens are situated from the Department of Parks to the Department of Housing Preservation and Development as "a process that has been abysmally secretive even

Conclusion

by this administration's standards." In the final analysis the editorial stated that "bulldozing a working garden is an act of neighborhood violence" (*New York Times* January 14, 1999).

Sarah Ferguson, a gardener, writer, and activist living on the Lower East Side, expressed her sense of despair upon the destruction of a garden that she had helped to create on 10th Street. She also spoke about her hope that something positive might emerge as a result of this struggle. Taking me to the tiny shaded backyard behind her apartment building, a remnant of the former community garden, she showed me the backyards of the adjoining newly constructed townhouses. Derisively she spoke of "dog kennels," and indeed they seemed exactly like that, sterile narrow runs behind each townhouse slice, carefully separated from each other by shiny high wire fencing. The items seemingly missing were water bowls and a few drainage holes in the cement to rinse out the refuse.

Without wishing to deny the paramount importance of economic factors and associated power struggles, the conflicts over community gardens on the Lower East Side also reflect cultural and class conflicts and a gap of understanding among people existing within the limiting confines of an urban environment. The attempt to impose standards is not restricted to outside agents such as GreenThumb, the Parks Department, or opponents of community gardens; such cultural differences are just as divisive within the garden community and within individual gardens.

The Lower East Side is rich in poignant examples of such tensions. Some garden communities pride themselves on having created proverbial horticultural jewels and frown upon members whose garden plots do not fit that image. Others are less concerned with such striving, which can border on the intensely competitive, and devote their energies to different aspects. In a number of instances the designation "community garden" or "community space" has been subject to heated dispute.

Several vacant lots on the Lower East Side at one time or another were turned into displays described as art or gardens by some and junkyards by others. Until the early 1990s on East 11th Street there was a site known as Anna's Garden, which I referred to in my mind as the teddy bear garden. I never saw anyone in it. Filled with discarded toys and stuffed bears impaled on top of dead tree trunks, seemingly floating amid high weeds, it seemed like nothing so much as a nightmarish scream of despair. Other images come to mind, puzzling, unfathomable and reflecting the splintered urban imagination—pink flamingos between tomato plants in a garden now gone, Eddie's tower on its tiny plot in the garden on East 6th Street, and the rusty remnants of another age arranged on a fence at the corner lot on 3rd Street, a former gas station, permanently festooned with lametta.

Yet the borderline between the acceptable and the unacceptable in outdoor spaces is fluid. One might argue that nowhere else but in community gardens is there such a space for public expression of the anomie of urban existence and for idiosyncratic displays of individual isolation and fragmentation, a space for maddening individuality, and at the same time a means to find "a way back home" and a way to reconnect to the life of the community. There has to be a space for both dimensions of life. Next to the grey and sad-looking teddy bears, next to the soggy Christmas decoration from seasons past, next to frayed existences and desolation, there are gardens filled with flowers and vegetables, children who want to help, teenagers who take responsibility, people who play music and stage plays, and neighbors who talk to each other. Community gardens provide urban residents with spaces within which it is possible to create a little piece of the world, where individuals can try and fail and try again, and where there are endless opportunities for on-the-ground working out of conflicts.

Conclusion

Initiatives on behalf of community gardens are based on conflicting motivations and strategies and must be contextualized and understood as the outcome of complex and contradictory race, class, and gender dynamics and the shifting forces in the city's economy, politics, and real estate market. Gardeners' conflicts within gardens, within the community, and with the city administration reveal differing notions of community and development on the Lower East Side. Community gardens become bargaining chips in the struggle for influence and control that is waged over different models for development and housing.

At the same time, community gardens and associated initiatives on the Lower East Side, in other neighborhoods in New York City and across the country have helped to create a vocabulary of struggle and images of the remaking of neighborhoods and revitalization of communities. The struggle for community gardens is supported by increasingly sophisticated uses of technology, the media, and the political arena, while reaching out to other neighborhoods throughout the city in order to build strong coalitions and networks. Initiatives on behalf of gardens, both at the individual and local level and city-wide, are based on complex visions for an urban environment of the future. These visions, informed by a consciousness of a polluted and damaged environment and the dynamics of the urban real estate market, are creative with a wide margin for diversity and for cultural collages of unimaginable richness.

At the heart of people's struggle to define themselves and to combat alienation, community gardens provide a way to take control of an image, to be involved in something larger than immediate life, and yet to remain on one's home ground. These contested urban spaces help to mediate the ongoing struggle between a desire to return "home"—to cultivate one's own garden—and the need to be part of an effort that extends beyond the private domain. Rooted in a specific locality, however fragile, community gardeners use the urban environment. They claim it and make it their own.

NOTES

1. Johann Wolfgang Goethe (1966), *Faust, Part II, Act V.*, translation by Malve von Hassell.
2. See for instance Francis et al. 1994, Hart 1978, and Noble 1999; for a related bibliography see American Community Gardening Association 1992a.
3. Sidney Mintz made these comments on a panel organized by the Council for Nutritional Anthropology at the annual conference of the American Anthropological Association in 1996.
4. "This is no paradisal dream; its hardship is its opportunity" (Berry, "Work Song," 1977: 32).
5. "Every community garden must be based—from beginning to end—in the desires, dreams, and elbow grease of the neighborhood residents. It simply won't be sustained, if the project and the lot are suggested 'from above,' even when it is proposed as a tool for beautification, crime reduction, or any other social benefit. Neighborhood gardens that continue to work are initiated and run by the same individuals who will put in sweat-equity in return for a good place to garden and gather" (Pottharst 1995: 99).

Photos

Community gardener and child at La Plaza Cultural on 9th Street and Avenue C, summer 2001; in the background on the right one can see a portion of the mural "The Struggle Continues La Lucha Continua." Courtesy of the author.

Children in the Firefighter Marty Celig Memorial Park on 8th Street between Avenues D and C, summer 2001. Courtesy of the author.

Photos

Community gardeners preparing the stage for a performance in the 6th Street and Avenue B Community Garden, Summer 2001. Courtesy of the author.

Rites of Spring Pageant: Wind, Water, and Fire (from left to right); behind the elements, members of the procession carry a map of the Lower East Side that shows the gardens as blank spaces, to be filled in with a green marker by a gardener at each individual garden visited during the pageant, May 1996. Courtesy of the author.

Photos

Children's Mural Garden, with small solar-powered water feature. June 1997. Courtesy of the author.

A little oasis of peace in the Green Oasis Community Garden.

Necrology

NEW YORK CITY COMMUNITY GARDENS BULLDOZED 1984–2000

THE BRONX

Gardeners Partnership, Prospect Beck, 1989
Tiffany Street Tenants, Kelly Tiffany, 1991
Way Out Church Ministries, Brook Avenue, 1991
GreenThumb Garden Club, Hoe Avenue, 1993
Maria Estella Tenants, Westchester, 1993
Crotona Community Garden, 1993
Mapes Avenue Tenants Association, Tremont, 1993
P.S. 139 Gardening Project, Willis Brook, 1994
Little Mount Bethel Church, Longfellow, 1995
North Luba Block Association, Longfellow, 1995
Bronx Second Chance, Hornaday Vyse, 1996
Longwood Fox Block Association, 1996
Pamela Janki Alli Garden, Topping Avenue, 1997
Bronx Alliance of Block School Educators Garden, Fairmount Mohegan, 1997
Lares Garden, Melrose Commons, 1998
The Point Community Farm, Hunts Point, 1999

Total: 16

BROOKLYN

Puerto Rican Community Center of Brownsville, Brownsville,

The Struggle for Eden

1984
Satellite en Orbita, Brownsville, 1984
Williamsburg Around the Bridge Block Association, Williamsburg, 1986
Coney Island Gospel Assembly, Coney Island, 1989
Residents of Blake Avenue, East New York, 1989
Warwick Street Block Association, Coney Island, 1990
La Placita Gardens I, Coney Island, 1990
Decatur 100 Block Association, Bushwick, 1991
Green Oaks Citizens Club, Bedford Stuyvesant, 1991
United Greene Avenue Block Association, Bedford Stuyvesant, 1992
Madison Street Gardeners, Bushwick, 1993
Green Avenue Improvement, Bedford Stuyvesant, 1994
Bleeker Street Improvement Association, Bushwick, 1996
Menahan Street Block Association, Bushwick, 1996
Eastern District High School Gardeners, Williamsburg, 1996
Girl Scout Community Garden, Bedford Stuyvesant/Brownsville, 1996
Garden Grove Block Association, Bushwick, 1996
The Brooklyn Bear's Garden [negotiated/portion returned to gardeners], 1997
The Friendly Garden, Bedford Stuyvesant, 1997
Putnam Community Garden, Bedford Stuyvesant, 1997
Stockholm Street Block Association, Bushwick, 1997
Elton Street Block Association, East New York, 1997
Cleveland Street Block Association, East New York, 1997
Barbey Street Homeowners Association, East New York, 1997
Good Cheer Weirfield Block Association, Bushwick, 1997
Palmetto/Wilson/Knickerbocker Block Association, Bushwick, 1997
Reclaim Our Cities Kids, Bushwick, 1997
Hancock United Block Association I, Bushwick, 1997

Necrology

Hancock United Block Association II, Bushwick, 1997
Messiah Baptist Church, East New York, 1997
Howard's Glenn Garden (a.k.a. Rock Garden), Bushwick, 1997
Down Home Garden, Bedford Stuyvesant/Brownsville, 1998
Warren Street Garden, 4th and 5th Avenues [returned to gardeners, land unsuitable for construction due to high water table], 1998
Sunflower Garden, Williamsburg, 1999
Kosciusco Street Block Association, Bedford Stuyvesant, 1999
Keap Street Garden, Williamsburg, 1999
Flags Garden, Williamsburg, May 1999
Warren Street Garden, Smith and Court Streets, 2000
Church of the Holy Spirit of Guadalupe I, East New York, 2000
Church of the Holy Spirit of Guadalupe II, East New York, 2000
La Placita Gardens II, Coney Island, 2000

Total: 42

MANHATTAN

Garden of Eden, Lower East Side, 1986
Dome Garden, Upper West Side, 1994
Torres Associates, East Harlem, 1996
Mayaguez Garden, East Harlem, 1996
Pentacostal Church of El Maestro, East Harlem, 1996
Latinos Unidos Borinquen, East Harlem, 1996
A BC Garden, Lower East Side, 1996
Pegasus Project Garden, Upper West Side, 1996
Rivington 6th Street Garden, Lower East Side, 1997
2nd Street Garden, Lower East Side, 1997
Mendez Mural Garden, Lower East Side, 1997
Maria's Garden, Lower East Side, 1997
Angels' Garden, Lower East Side, 1997
Jardín de la 10th Street, Lower East Side, 1997

Parker Forge/Sunnyside Garden, Lower East Side, 1998
The Sowers Garden, Harlem, 1998
Dos Blocos Garden, Lower East Side, 1998
P.S. 76 Garden of Love, Harlem, 1998
Umbrella Garden, Lower East Side, 1999
Souls in Motion, Harlem, 1999
130th Street Homeowners, Harlem, 1999
149 West 132nd Street Block Association, Harlem, 1999
Black United Fund, Harlem, 1999
George W. Brown Memorial Garden, Harlem, 1999
Five Star Garden, Harlem, 1999
Striving Together Garden, Harlem, 1999
American Federation of Police Partnership, Harlem, 1999
Project Harmony/J.D. Wilson Memorial Garden [portion still exists], Harlem, 1999
Garden of the Golden Lions, Harlem, 1999
West 129th Street Block Association Garden, Harlem, 1999
Jardín de Esperanza, Lower East Side, 2000
Jardín Bello Amanecer Borencano [portion still exists], Lower East Side, 2000

Total: 32

QUEENS

Good Neighbor Block Association, East Elmhurst, 1995

STATEN ISLAND

No gardens bulldozed as of September 2000

Total number of New York City community gardens bulldozed between 1984 and 2000: 91

Bibliography

Ableman, Paul. 1993. *From the Good Earth: A Celebration of Growing Food Around the World.* New York: Abrams.

Abu-Lughod, Janet. 1994. *From Urban Village to East Village: The Battle for New York's Lower East Side.* Cambridge, MA: Basil Blackwell Ltd.

Algarín, Miguel. 1997. *Love Is Hard Work: Memorias de Loisaida.* New York: Scribner Poetry.

American Community Gardening Association. n.d. *Statement of Purpose and Definition of Urban Community Gardens.* Philadelphia, PA.

———. 1998. *National Community Gardening Survey.* New York: City of New York, Department of General Services, Operation GreenThumb.

———. 1992. *National Community Gardening Survey.* New York: City of New York, Department of General Services, Operation GreenThumb.

———. 1992a. *A Research Agenda for the Impact of Community Greening.* Philadelphia, PA: American Community Gardening Association.

Armar-Klemesu, Margaret, and Daniel Maxwell. 2000. "Accra: Urban Agriculture as an Asset Strategy, Supplementing Income and Diets." In *Growing Cities, Growing Food: Urban Agriculture on the Policy Agenda*, eds. Nico Bakker, Marielle Dubbeling, Sabine Gündel, Ulrich Sabel-Koschella, and Henk de Zeeuw. Feldafing, Germany: Deutsche Stiftung für internationale Entwicklung, Zentralstelle für Ernährung und Landwirtschaft, 183–208.

Ashman, Linda, et al. 1993. *Seeds of Change: Strategies for Food Security for the Inner City*. Los Angeles: Southern California Interfaith Hunger Coalition.

Asner, Eve. 1969. "Philadelphia's Neighborhood Park Program." In *Small Urban Spaces*, ed. Whitney North Seymour, Jr. New York: New York University Press (1969): 169–183.

Aue, Christina. 2000. "Urban Agriculture and Allotment Gardening in Germany." Paper presented at the International Symposium Urban Agriculture and Horticulture: The Linkage with Urban Planning. Domäne Dahlem, Berlin, July 7–9.

Bakker, Nico, Marielle Dubbeling, Sabine Gündel, Ulrich Sabel-Koschella, and Henk de Zeeuw, eds. 2000. *Growing Cities, Growing Food: Urban Agriculture on the Policy Agenda*. Feldafing, Germany: Deutsche Stiftung für internationale Entwicklung, Zentralstelle für Ernährung und Landwirtschaft.

Balmori, Diana, and Margaret Morton. 1993. *Transitory Gardens, Uprooted Lives*. New Haven: Yale University Press.

Bassett, T. J. 1979. *Vacant Land Cultivation: Community Gardening in America 1893–1978*. Berkeley: University of California at Berkeley, M.A. thesis.

Bellows, Anne C. 2000. "Balancing Diverse Needs: Risks and Pleasures of Urban Agriculture in Silesia, Poland." *TRIALOG 65: A Journal for Planning and Building in the Third World* 2: 18–23.

Benjamin, Walter. 1968. *Illuminations*. New York: Harcourt Brace Jovanovich.

Berry, Wendell. 1985. *Collected Poems 1957–1982*. San Francisco: North Point Press.

Bibliography

———. 1977. *Clearing*. New York: Harcourt Brace Jovanovich.

Bienvenida, Matias, and Marci Reaven. 1979. *The Heart of Loisaida (El Corazon de Loisaida)*. Documentary, 29 minutes, black & white, 16mm. New York: Unifilm.

Boston Urban Gardeners. 1979. *A City Gardener's Guide: Growing, Surviving and Reaping the Fruits of our Labor*. Boston: Boston Urban Gardeners.

Boyer, Christine M. 1994. *The City of Collective Memory*. Cambridge, MA: MIT Press.

Brown, Allison. 1980. *Extension Urban Gardening: The 16 Cities Experience*. United States Department of Agriculture Interim Report about the U.S.D.A. Urban Gardens Program.

Buswell, Shirley. 1980. "The Garden Warriors of 1942." *City Farmer* 3 (2).

Carson, Rachel. 1962. *Silent Spring*. New York: Houghton Mifflin.

Castells, Manuel. 1989. *The Informational City*. Cambridge, MA: Blackwell Publishers.

Chaskey, Scott. 2000. "Reflections on the Northeast Community Supported Agriculture Conference II, November 1999." *Just Food News*, January.

Chivers, C. J. 2000. "Stepping Up Turf Battle, City Seizes Garden and Arrests 31."*New York Times*, February 16.

Chodorkoff, Daniel. 1980. *Un Milagro de Loisaida: Alternative Technology and Grassroots Efforts for Neighborhood Reconstruction on New York's Lower East Side*. New York: New School for Social Research, Ph.D. dissertation.

Coalition for the Homeless. 2001. Statement to the Press. New York, August 1.

Coleman, Daniel A. 1994. *Ecopolitics: Building a Green Society*. New Brunswick, NJ: Rutgers University Press.

Cook, Christopher D. 1997. "Cultivating Locally: Community Gardening for Food Security." *Community Greening Review* 7: 2–10.

Cummins, Ronnie. 2000. *Hazards of Genetically Engineered Foods and Crops: Why We Need a Global Moratorium*. Little Marais, MN: Campaign for Food Safety/Organic Consumers Association. http://www.organicconsumers.org.

Daly, Herman E., and John B. Cobb, Jr. 1989. *For the Common Good: Redirecting the Economy Toward Community, the Environment, and a Sustainable Future*. Boston, MA: Beacon Press.

Deutsche, Rosalyn, and Cara Gendel Ryan. 1984. "The Fine Art of Gentrification." *October 31* (Winter): 91–111.

Diallo, S. 1993. *Urban Agriculture in West Africa: Research Review and Perspectives*. Ottawa, ON, Canada: International Development Research Centre.

Diamond, Stanley. 1982. "Subversive Art." *Social Research* 49 (4) (Winter): 854–877.

Dwight, Eleanor. 1990. "Sanctuary." *New York* 23 (3) (August 6): 41.

Dykstra, Gretchen. 2000. Letter to the Editor of the New York Times, February 17.
New York Times, Letters, February 19.

Bibliography

Etzioni, Amitai. 1993. *The Spirit of Community: Rights, Responsibilities, and the Communitarian Agenda*. New York: Crown Publishers.

Evans, David Hayward. 1998. *Dirt: A Year in the Life of Gardens in the East Village*. (55-minute documentary film). New York: Walkabout Release.

Fagles, Robert. 1996. Homer, *The Odyssey*, translated by Robert Fagles. New York: Viking Penguin.

Feenstra, Gail, Sharyl McGrew, and David Campbell. 1999. *Entrepreneurial Community Gardens: Growing Food, Skills, Jobs and Communities*. Venice, CA: Community Food Security Coalition.

Ferguson, Sarah. 1999a. "A Brief History of Grassroots Greening on the Lower East Side." In *Avant Gardening: Ecological Struggle in the City and the World*, eds. Peter Lamborn Wilson and Bill Weinberg. New York: Autonomedia: 80–90.

———. 1999b. "The Death of Little Puerto Rico." In *Avant Gardening: Ecological Struggle in the City and the World*, eds. Peter Lamborn Wilson and Bill Weinberg. New York: Autonomedia: 60–79.

Fisher, Andrew. 1996. "Food Security Unites Community Advocates." *Community Greening Review* 6: 12–13.

Fisher, Andrew, and Robert Gottlieb. 1998. "Community Food Security and Environmental Justice: Converging Paths towards Social Justice and Sustainable Communities." *Community Food Security News*, Summer.

———. 1995. *Community Food Security: Policies for a More Sustainable Food System in the Context of the 1995 Farm Bill and Beyond*. Los Angeles: The Lewis Center for Regional Policy Studies, School of Public Policy and Social Research, University of California, Working Paper No. 11, May.

Flores, Juan. 1992. "Interview with Tomás Ybarra-Fransto: The Chicano Movement in a Multicultural/Multinational Society." In *On Edge: The Crises of Contemporary Latin American Culture*, eds. George Yúdice, Jean Franco and Juan Flores. Minneapolis: University of Minnesota Press.

Ford, Peter, Nicole Gaouette, and Ruth Walker. 1997. "Urban Gardening Spreads and Flourishes Around the World." *Christian Science Monitor*, September 17.

Foster, George M. 1965. "Peasant Society and the Image of Limited Good." *American Anthropologist* 67 (2): 293–315.

Fowler, Edmund P. 1996. "The Link Between Politics, Policies, and Healthy City Forms." In *Local Places in the Age of the Global City*, eds. Roger Keil, Gerda Wekerle and David Bell. St. Paul, MN: Black Rose Press, 221–232.

Fox, Tom. 1990. *Urban Open Space: An Investment That Pays*. New York: Neighborhood Open Space Coalition.

Fox, Tom, Ian Koeppel, and Susan Kellam. 1985. *Struggle for Space: The Greening of New York City 1970–1984*. New York: Neighborhood Open Space Coalition.

Francis, Mark, Lisa Cashdan, and Lynn Paxson. 1984. *Community Open Spaces: Greening Neighborhoods through Community Action and Land Conservation*. Washington, DC: Island Press.

Francis, Mark, Patricia Lindsey, and Jay Rice, eds. 1994. *Healing Dimensions of People-Plant Relations*. Davis: University of California, Davis, Center for Design Research.

Frohardt, Katherine Elsom. 1993. *Case Studies of Entrepreneurial Community Greening Projects*. Philadelphia, PA: American Community Gardening Association, ACGA Monograph.

Bibliography

Fuerbringer, Jonathan. 1999. "Will Streeters' Generosity Bloom?" *New York Times*, May 16.

Gallup Organization. 1994. *National Gardening Survey*. Princeton, NJ: Gallup Organization (prepared for the National Gardening Association, Burlington, VT).

———. 1982. *National Gardening Survey*. Princeton, NJ: Gallup Organization (prepared for the National Gardening Association, Burlington, VT).

Gellner, Ernest. 1998. *Language and Solitude: Wittgenstein, Malinowski and the Habsburg Dilemma*. New York: Cambridge University Press.

Goethe, Johann Wolfgang. 1966. *Faust*. Berlin: Aufbau Verlag.

Golden, Howard. 1999. *City-Owned Properties Report: A Post Conveyance Assessment*. Brooklyn, New York: Brooklyn Borough President's Office.

Goodman, Richard. 2000. *Report on Community Gardening*. Burlington, VT: National Gardening Association.

Graham, Frank. 1995. "Earth Day: 25 Years Old." *National Geographic Magazine*, April.

Green Guerillas. 1999. *Vitis Vine* (Summer). Newsletter of the Green Guerrillas.

Gröning, Gert. 1996. *Politics of Community Gardening*. Paper presented at the American Community Gardening Association conference "Branching Out: Linking Communities Through Gardening," Montreal, Canada, September 26–29.

Gussow, Joan. 1999. "Food Is Invisible." *Just Food News*, June.

Hamilton, William L. 2000. "Visions of Greener Pastures Reinvent the Lower East Side." *New York Times*, January 6.

Hart, Roger. 1978. *Children's Experience of Place*. New York: Irvington Press.

Hassler, David, and Lynn Gregor, eds., with Don Snyder, photographer. 1999. *A Place to Grow: Voices and Images of Urban Gardeners*. Cleveland, OH: The Pilgrim Press.

Hayden, Dolores. 1995. *The Power of Place*. Cambridge, MA: MIT Press.

Heimlich, Ralph E., ed. 1989. *Land Use Transition in Urbanizing Areas: Research and Information Needs*. Washington, DC: The Farm Foundation in Cooperation with the U.S. Department of Agriculture, Economic Research Service.

Herder, Johann Gottfried. 1881. *Sämmtliche Werke*, ed. Bernard Suphan. Berlin: Weldmannsche Buchhandlung.

Hickey, Mary Frances. 1994. "Greening the Mean Streets." *New York* 27 (41) (October 17): 47–53.

Hirsch, Eric. 1995. "Landscape: Between Place and Space." *The Anthropology of Landscape: Perspectives on Space and Place*, eds. Eric Hirsch and Michael O'Hanlon. New York: Oxford University Press, 1–30.

Huff, Barbara A. 1990. *Greening the City Streets: The Story of Community Gardens*. New York: Clarion Books.

Hynes, H. Patricia. 1996. *A Patch of Eden: America's Inner City Gardeners*. White River Junction, VT: Chelsea Green Publishing.

Jacobs, Jane. 1993. "The City Unbound: Qualitative Approaches to the City." *Urban Studies* 30: 827–48.

Bibliography

———. 1961. *The Death and Life of Great American Cities*. New York: Vintage Books.

Jobb, Jaime. 1979. *The Complete Book of Community Gardening*. New York: Morrow.

Johnson, George. 2000. "In Quantum Feat, an Atom Is Seen in Two Places at Once." *New York Times*, February 22.

Johnson, Martin. 1999. "Community Development Perspective." *Community Food Security News*, Summer.

Joseph, Hugh. 1999. "Redefining Community Food Security." *Community Food Security News*, Summer.

Keil, Roger, Gerda Wekerle, and David Bell, eds. 1996. *Local Places in the Age of the Global City*. St. Paul, MN: Black Rose Press.

Kemmis, Daniel. 1991. *Community and the Politics of Place*. Norman: University of Oklahoma Press.

King, Moses. 1893. *King's Handbook of New York City*. New York: Benjamin Blom Inc., Publishers.

Kinzer, Stephen. 1994. "Dread of Builders in a City Woven with Gardens." *New York Times*, February 18.

Kirschbaum, Pamela R. 2000. "Making Policy in a Crowded World: Steps Beyond the Physical Garden." *Community Greening Review* 10: 2–11.

Knack, Ruth Eckdish. 1994. "Dig These Gardens." *Planning* 60 (7) (July): 20–25.

Kneen, Brewster. 1999. "Enough for All." *Community Food*

Security News, Summer.

Knox, Paul. 1982. "The Social Production of the Built Environment." *Ekistics* 49: 291–297.

Kwartler, Michael. 1990. *The Lower East Side Garden Preservation Project*. New York: Michael Kwartler and Associates, report prepared under the auspices of the Green Guerillas and the Lower East Side Technical Assistance Group, August.

Lackey, Jill Florence and associates. 1998. *Evaluation of Community Gardens (A Program of the University of Wisconsin Cooperative Extension)*. Milwaukee, WI: Jill Florence Lackey & Associates.

Landman, Ruth H. 1993. *Creating Community in the City: Cooperatives and Community Gardens in Washington, D.C.* Westport, CT: Bergin & Garvey.

Lerner, Steve, and William Poole. 1999. *The Economic Benefits of Parks and Open Space*. New York: The Trust for Public Land.

Lesser, Ludwig. 1915. *Der Kleingarten: seine zweckmäßigste Anlage und Bewirtschaftung*. Berlin, Germany: Carl Heymann.

Lovelock, James. 1979. *Gaia: A New Look at Life on Earth*. Oxford: Oxford University Press.

Low, Setha. 1996. "The Anthropology of Cities: Imagining and Theorizing the City." *Annual Review of Anthropology* 25: 383–409.

Luhrmann, Tanya M. 1993. "The Resurgence of Romanticism: Contemporary Neopaganism, Feminist Spirituality and the Divinity of Nature." In *Environmentalism and Cultural Theory: Exploring the Role of Anthropology in Environmental Discourse*, ed. Kay Milton. New York: Routledge: 217–232.

Bibliography

Maffi, Mario. 1994. "The Other Side of the Coin: Culture in Loisaida." In *From Urban Village to East Village*, Janet L. Abu-Lughod et al. Cambridge, MA: Basil Blackwell.

Malakoff, David. 1995. "What Good Is Community Greening?" *Community Greening Review* 5: 4–11.

Mann, Peter. 2000. "Beyond Seattle: The Struggle for Food Security." *Just Food News*, January.

Marcuse, Peter. 1987. "Neighborhood Policy and the Distribution of Power: New York City's Community Boards." *Policy Studies Journal* 16 (2): 277–289.

Martinez, Miranda. 2001. *Creating Community: Culture, Difference & Action Among Community Gardeners on the Lower East Side*. New York: New York University, Ph.D. dissertation (forthcoming).

Mauss, Armand L. 1975. *Social Problems of Social Movements*. Philadelphia: Lippincott.

Mbiba, Beacon. 2000. "Urban Agriculture in Harare: Between Suspicion and Repression." In *Growing Cities, Growing Food: Urban Agriculture on the Policy Agenda*, eds. Nico Bakker, Marielle Dubbeling, Sabine Gündel, Ulrich Sabel-Koschella, and Henk de Zeeuw. Feldafing, Germany: Deutsche Stiftung für internationale Entwicklung, Zentralstelle für Ernährung und Landwirtschaft: 285–301.

McCarthy, R. 1994. "Cultivating Community: Urban Gardening and Social Change." *Blueprint for Social Justice* 48 (3) (November).

McClain, James L., John M. Merriman, and Ugawa Kaoru, eds. 1994. *Edo and Paris: Urban Life and the State in the Early Modern Era*. Ithaca, NY: Cornell University Press.

McDonogh, Gary W. 1997. "Citizenship, Locality and Resistance." *City & Society, Annual Review 1997.*

McGowan, Kathleen. 1998. "Cracks Epidemic." *City Limits* (June/July): 13–16.

Mele, Christopher. 2000. *Selling the Lower East Side: Culture, Real Estate, and Resistance.* Minneapolis: University of Minnesota Press.

Melucci, Albert. 1980. "The New Social Movements: A Theoretical Approach." *Social Science Information* 19 (2): 199–226.

Meyer-Renschhausen, Elisabeth, and Anne Holl, eds. 2000. *Die Wiederkehr der Gärten: Kleinlandwirtschaft im Zeitalter der Globalisierung.* Innsbruck, Austria: Studien Verlag.

Milton, Kay, ed. 1996. *Environmentalism and Cultural Theory: Exploring the Role of Anthropology in Environmental Discourse.* New York: Routledge.

———. 1993. *Environmentalism: The View from Anthropology.* London: Routledge.

Mintz, Sidney W. 1986. *Sweetness and Power.* New York: Penguin.

Mitchell, William J. 1999. *E-Topia: "Urban Life, Jim—But Not as We Know It."* Cambridge, MA: MIT Press.

Moldakov, Oleg. 2000. "The Urban Farmers, Gardeners and Kitchen Gardeners of St. Petersburg." *TRIALOG 65: A Journal for Planning and Building in the Third World* 2: 33–38.

More Gardens! Coalition. 1999. *SEEDS: More Gardens = Less Asthma.* New York: More Gardens! Coalition, Spring, Special

Bibliography

Edition.

Moskow, Angela. 1997. "Havana's Self-Provision Gardens." *Community Greening Review* 7: 17–19.

Mottel, Syeus. 1973. *Charas, the Improbable Dome Builders*. New York: Drake Publishers.

Mougeot, Luc J. A. 1994. *Urban Food Production: Evolution, Official Support and Significance*. Ottawa, Canada: International Research Centre, Cities Feeding People Series Report 8.

Mumford, Lewis. 1961. *The City in History*. New York: Harcourt Brace Jovanovich.

Murdoch, Iris. 1970. *The Sovereignty of Good*. London: Routledge & Kegan Paul.

Murphy, Catherine. 1999. *Cultivating Havana: Urban Agriculture and Food Security in the Years of Crisis*. Oakland, CA: Food First, Institute for Food and Development Policy.

Naimark, Susan. 1982. *Handbook of Community Gardens*. New York: Scribner.

Neighborhood Open Space Coalition. 2000 *Urban Outdoors Review*. New York, Spring.

Nemore, Carole. 1998. *Community Gardens in New York City: "Rooted in Community."* Report prepared for the New York State Senate, Senate Minority Program Office, March.

Nettleton, John. 2000. "Regional Economic and Farmers' Market Development in the New York Region." Paper presented at the *International Symposium Urban Agriculture and Horticulture: The Linkage with Urban Planning*. Domäne Dahlem, Berlin, July 7–9, 2000.

New York City Department of City Planning. 1998. *Community District Needs*.

———. 1992. *Community District Needs*.

New York City Environmental Justice Alliance. 1998. *Open Space and Community Gardens by Community District*. New York: New York City Environmental Justice Alliance.

New York State. 1995. *Conserving Open Space in New York State, 1995*. New York: Prepared by the Department of Environmental Conservation and the Office of Parks, Recreation and Historic Preservation.

New York Times. 1999. "For Sale: The Garden of Eden." Editorial. *New York Times*, January 14.

Nijkamp, Peter, and Adriaan Perrels. 1994. *Sustainable Cities in Europe*. London: Earthscan Publications.

Noble, Holcomb B. 1999. "Study Shows a Big Asthma Risk for Children in Poor Neighborhoods." *New York Times*, July 27.

Operation GreenThumb. 1986. *Operation GreenThumb Gardening Survey*. New York: Survey prepared with the assistance of the Cornell University Cooperative Extension.

Parks & People Foundation of Baltimore. 2000. *Neighborhood Open Space Management: A Report on Green Strategies in Baltimore and Six Other Cities*. Baltimore: Parks and People Foundation of Baltimore, Urban Resources Initiatives.

Pennsylvania Horticultural Society. 1989. *Annual Report of the Pennsylvania Horticultural Society's Philadelphia Green Program*, July 1, 1988–June 30.

Pottharst, Kris. 1995. "Partners in Pride: Urban Dwellers and Abandoned Lots." *Parks & Recreation* 30 (9) (September): 94–

Bibliography

102.

Puntenney, Pamela J., ed. 1995. *Global Ecosystems: Creating Options through Anthropological Perspectives.* National Association for the Practice of Anthropology, American Anthropological Association.

Radin, Paul. 1971. *The World of Primitive Man.* New York: E.P. Dutton & Co.

Raver, Anne. 1997. "Houses before Gardens, the City Decides." *New York Times*, January 9.

Reich, Robert B. 1991. "Secession of the Successful." *New York Times Magazine*, January 20.

Robbins, Ira S. 1969. "Tenants' Gardens in Public Housing." In *Small Urban Spaces*, ed. Whitney North Seymour, Jr. New York: New York University Press, 139–147.

Roszak, Theodore. 1973. *Where the Wasteland Ends: Politics and Transcendence in Postindustrial Society.* Garden City, NY: Anchor Books, Doubleday & Company.

Rotenberg, Robert. 1993. "On the Salubrity of Sites." In *The Cultural Meaning of Urban Space*, eds. Robert Rotenberg and Gary McDonogh. Westport, CT: Bergin & Garvey, 17–29.

Rousseau, Jean-Jacques. 1964. *The First and Second Discourses.* New York: St. Martin's Press.

Saalman, Howard. 1968. *Medieval Cities.* Planning and Cities Series, ed. George Collins. New York: George Braziller.

Saint-Exupéry, Antoine de. 1995. *The Little Prince.* Translated from the French by Katherine Woods. [Original translation 1943]. Thorndike, ME: G.K. Hall & Co.

Sánchez, José Ramón. 1989. "Residual Work and Residual Shelter: Housing Puerto Rican Labor in New York City from World War II to 1983." In *Critical Perspectives on Housing*, eds. Rachel G. Bratt, Chester Hartman and Ann Meyerson. Philadelphia: Temple University Press, 202–220.

Sanjek, Roger. 1999. "I'll Take Rational and Romance, but not Globaloney." *City & Society* 11 (1–2): 117–124.

Santiago, Esmeralda. 1993. *When I Was Puerto Rican*. New York: Addison-Wesley.

Schmelzkopf, Karen. 1995. "Urban Community Gardens as Contested Space." *Geographical Review* 85 (3): 364–381.

Scoones, I. 1999. "New Ecology and the Social Sciences: What Prospects for a Fruitful Engagement?" *Annual Review of Anthropology* 28: 479–507.

Seymour, Whitney North, Jr., ed. 1969. *Small Urban Spaces*. New York: New York University Press, 139–147.

Sharff, Jagna Wojcicka. 1998. *King Kong on 4th Street: Families and the Violence of Poverty on the Lower East Side*. Boulder, CO: Westview Press.

Shiffman, Ronald. 1969. "The Vest-Pocket Park as an Instrument of Social Change." In *Small Urban Spaces*, ed. Whitney North Seymour, Jr. New York: New York University Press, 149–158.

Smit, Jac, and Joe Nasr. 2000. "Urban Agriculture and Urban Patterns: Implications for Sustainability." Paper presented at the International Symposium Urban Agriculture and Horticulture: The Linkage with Urban Planning. Domäne Dahlem, Berlin, July 7–9.

Smit, Jac, Annu Ratta, and Joe Nasr. 1996. *Urban Agriculture: Food, Jobs and Sustainable Cities*. Urban Agriculture Network, United Nations Development Program, Report Produced for

Bibliography

Habitat II Conference on Urban Life.

Smith, Olanrewaju B., ed. 1999. *Agriculture Urbaine en Afrique de L'Ouest: Une Contribution à la Sécurité Alimentaire et à l'Assainissement des Villes*. Ottawa, ON, Canada: International Development Research Centre.

Sommers, Larry. 1984. *The Community Garden Book*. Burlington, VT: Gardens for All/National Gardening Association.

Steinfels, Peter. 1990. "Idyllic Theory of Goddesses Creates Storm." *New York Times*, February 13.

Tabb, William K. 1984. *Marxism and the Metropolis*. New York: Oxford University Press.

Taylor, A. F., A. Wiley, F. E. Kuo, & W. C. Sullivan. 1998. "Growing Up in the Inner City: Green Spaces as Places to Grow." *Environment & Behavior* 30 (1): 3–27.

Taylor, Charles. 1989. *Sources of the Self: The Making of the Modern Identity*. Cambridge, MA: Harvard University Press.

Taylor, L., ed. 1979. *Urban Open Spaces*. New York: Cooper-Hewitt Museum.

Teitel, Martin, and Kimberly A. Wilson. 1999. *Genetically Engineered Food: Changing the Nature of Nature*. Rochester, VT: Park Street Press.

Thrush, Glenn. 1997. "7 Deadly Signs of New York City's Unheeded Housing Crisis." *City Limits* 22 (4) (April).

Tierney, John. 1997. "Why It Is Hard to Rent an Apartment." *New York Times Magazine*, May 4.

Tilly, Charles. 1978. *From Mobilization to Revolution*. Reading,

MA: Addison-Wesley.

Trebay, Guy. 1994. "Everyday Purple." *Village Voice* 39 (41), October 11.

———. 1991. "Where the Wild Things Are." *Village Voice* 36 (16), April 16.

U.S. Department of Agriculture. 1999. *Community Food Security Initiative: Measuring Food Security in the United States: Household Food Security in the United States, 1995–1998.*

U.S. Department of Commerce, Bureau of the Census. 1990. *Census of Population and Housing.*

———. 1980. *Census of Population and Housing.*

Van En, Robyn. 1995. "Eating for Your Community." *In Context* 42 (Fall): 29.

Vico, Gianbattista. 1965. *On the Study Methods of Our Time.* New York: Bobbs-Merrill.

Voltaire, François Marie Arouet. 1970. *Candide.* Paris: Librairie Larousse.

von Hassell, Malve. 2000. "The Impact of Community Gardening Initiatives in New York City on Children." Paper presented at the International Symposium Urban Agriculture and Horticulture: The Linkage with Urban Planning. Domäne Dahlem, Berlin, July 7–9.

———. 1998. "Names of Hate, Names of Love: Contested Space and the Formation of Identity on Manhattan's Lower East Side." *Dialectical Anthropology* 23 (4): 375–413.

———. 1996. *Homesteading in New York City 1978–1993: The Divided Heart of Loisaida.* Westport, CT: Bergin & Garvey.

———. 1995. "Father Winter and Primavera in a Garden on the Lower East Side: Urban Community-Based Environmental Efforts." Paper presented at the American Anthropological Association Meetings, Washington, DC, November 15–19.

———. 1981. "Johann Gottfried Herder: A Lost Ancestor." *Dialectical Anthropology* 5 (4): 331–339.

Waliczek, Tina M., Richard H. Mattson, and Jayne M. Zajicek. 1996. "Benefits of Community Gardening on Quality-of-Life Issues." *Journal of Environmental Horticulture* 14 (4) (December): 204–209.

Warner, Sam Bass. 1987. *To Dwell Is to Garden: Histories and Portraits of Boston's Community Gardens*. Boston: Northeastern University Press.

Weil, Simone. 1977. *The Simone Weil Reader*, ed. George Panichas. New York: David McKay Company.

Weiner, Annette B. 1976. *Women of Value, Men of Renown: New Perspectives in Trobriand Exchange*. Austin: University of Texas Press.

Wekerle, Gerda. 2000. "Multicultural Gardens: Changing the Landscape of the City." Paper presented at the International Symposium Urban Agriculture and Horticulture: The Linkage with Urban Planning. Domäne Dahlem, Berlin, July 7–9.

———. 1996. "Reframing Urban Sustainability: Women's Movement Organizing and the Local State." In *Local Places in the Age of the Global City*, eds. Roger Keil, Gerda Wekerle, and David Bell. St. Paul, MN: Black Rose Press, 137–145.

White, K., ed. 1982. *The Community Land Trust Handbook*. Emmaus, PA: Rodale Press (Institute for Community Economics).

Williams, Raymond. 1973. *The Country and the City*. Oxford: Oxford University Press.

Wilson, Peter Lamborn. 1999. "Avant Gardening." In *Avant Gardening: Ecological Struggle in the City and the World*, eds. Peter Lamborn Wilson and Bill Weinberg. New York: Autonomedia, 7–34.

Index

Numbers
12th Street Garden Urban Gardening Program, 162
6th Street and Avenue B Community Garden, 148, 245
6th Street Community Center, 146, 184, 197
6th Street Community Center Farm Project, 197
9th Street and Avenue C Garden, 198
9th Street B/C Block Association, 106

A
Ableman, Ronald, 164
Abu-Lughod, Janet, 87, 196, 216
Accra, 201
Adopt-A-Building, 8
Africa, 152, 174, 225
African Americans, 194
Agriculture, 12, 17, 45–49, 186–188, 191, 201–202, 210, 214, 216, 221, 223–229, 232–233, 235
Alemany Youth Farm, 193
Algarín, Miguel, 114, 179, 213
All Peoples Garden, 84
Allen Street, 145
Allotment gardens, 11, 49, 138, 224–225
Alphabet City, 137
Alternative technology movement, 117
Alternative visions for society, 18–19
Amagansett, 187
Amaranth, 179, 181, 183, 191, 193, 195, 197, 199, 201, 203, 205, 207, 209, 211, 213, 215
American Community Gardening Association, 45–46, 66, 72, 87, 149, 159, 216, 218–220, 242
Amigos Garden, 7
Ancient Greece, 152, 174
Angel's Garden, 92
Angelus Novus, 176–177
Arana, Reinaldo, 7
Armar-Klemesu, Margaret, 201
Armengärten, 49
Artist Homeownership Program, 34–35
Ashman, Linda, 181, 213–214
Asia, 81
Asian-Americans, 137
Asner, Eve, 63
Astor Foundation, 77
Astor Place, 195
Atlanta, 220
Aue, Christina, 225
Austin, 194
Austria, 49–50
Avant Gardening, 18
Aztecs, 183

B
Bakker, Nico, 201, 221, 225
Ballona Wetlands, 206
Balmori, Diana, 138
Baltimore, 57, 220
Banana Kelly, 16–17

Barbey Street, 134, 250
Bassett, T.J., 55–61, 64, 68, 71
A BC Garden, 103, 106, 108, 137, 156, 251
Bedford Stuyvesant, 70, 72, 134, 250–251
Bedford Stuyvesant Garden Coalition, 134
Beens, Olivia, 145
Bellows, Anne C., 115, 227–228, 230
Beltane, 21, 37
Benjamin, Walter, 177
Berkeley, 219
Berlin, 51, 224
Berry, Wendell, 20, 164, 167, 236
BFC Partners, 92–94
Bienvenida, Matias, 116
Biotechnology, 12, 34, 209
Bleecker Street, 195
Boerum Hill, 134
Bolton, Mary, 238
Borinquen, 36–37, 251
Boston, 61, 66, 193, 219–220
Boston Redevelopment Authority, 219
Boulder, 63, 66
Bowery, 34, 41, 195
Boyer, Christine M, 33
Brodsky, Richard, 133
Bronx, 8, 16, 35, 71, 73, 75, 101, 120–123, 128, 130, 151–152, 200, 202, 249
Bronx Garden Coalition, 121
Bronx Green-Up Program, 73
Bronx Museum for the Arts, 152
Bronx United Gardeners (BUG), 120–121
Brooklyn, 28, 69–71, 94, 99, 120–121, 125, 127–129, 133–134, 192, 200, 249–250

Brooklyn Alliance of Neighborhood Gardens (BANG), 28, 120–121, 125
Brooklyn Bears Garden, 134
Brooklyn Botanic Garden, 200
Brooklyn Green Bridge, 200
Brooklyn Green Party, 133
Brown, Allison, 64–65, 86–87
Brownfields, 16, 204
Brownsville, 75–76, 78, 121, 192, 249–251
Brownsville Garden Coalition, 76, 121
Buddhism, 21
Bush, George, 66
Bushville, 108, 138
Bushwick Garden Coalition, Shirley, 121

C

Calcutta, 201
California, 215, 219
Calypso, 141
Campbell, David, 181–182, 214
Campos, Pedro Albizú, 113
Campos Plaza Residence Garden, Canada, 113
Canal Street, 42
Candide, 33, 38
Capoccia, Donald, 92, 95, 122, 173, 216
Carrion, Adolfo, 130, 133
Casa Victoria, 107–108
Casitas, 10, 37, 83, 90, 111, 138, 142, 150–152, 173
Castells, Manuel, 24
Catalpa Ridge Farm, 197
Celtic beliefs, 21
Center for Children's Health and the Environment, 102
Central Brooklyn Coordinating Council, 71

Index

Central Park Conservancy, 54
Chaplin, Ralph, 35
Charas/El Bohio Cultural and Community Center, 118, 131
Charles Young Park, 77
Chaskey, Scott, 187
Cherry Tree Association, Inc., 21, 35, 120, 122–123
Chicago, 57, 61, 71, 194, 219–220
Chico Mendez Mural Garden, 44, 84, 92
Children, 158–163
Children's Mural Garden, 160, 162, 183, 247
China, 47
Chinampas, 47
Chivers, C. J., 33, 136
Chodorkoff, Daniel, 117–118
Christianity, 21
Christy, Liz, 34, 41, 73, 83
Cities Urban Gardening Program, 64
City-as-School High School, 200
City Farms, 189–192, 197
City Limits, 42, 45, 47
Civilian Defense Volunteers, 60
Clarkson Street, 200
Cleveland, 61, 250
Clinton Community Garden, 76, 217
Coalition for the Homeless, 100
Cobb, John B., 15
Coleman, Daniel, 37
Communitarian movement, 167
Community activism, 9, 16, 45, 62
Community Board 3 in the Bronx, 80
Community boards, 75, 87, 121, 151

Community Development Block Grants, 73
Community District 3, 36, 238
Community District Needs Report, 36, 238
Community Food Security Act (1995), 66, 187
Community Food Security Coalition (CFSC), 181, 187–188, 203
Community garden movement, 51–52, 62, 82, 96–97, 143, 228, 235, 237
Community Greening Review, 232
Community land trusts, 37, 74, 124
Community Supported Agriculture (CSA), 187–188, 191–193, 197–198, 209–211, 214–215, 232
Con Edison, 151, 207
Cook, Christopher D., 187, 210, 226
Cooper Square Committee, 42
Cooper Square Urban Renewal Area, 86
Cooperative Extension Service, 64, 194
Coqui, 53, 85, 92
Corlears Hook Park, 68
Cornell Oasis, 61
Cornell University Cooperative Extension, 99
Cortés, Hernán, 183
Council on the Environment of New York City, 73–74, 103, 111, 202, 214
Counterculture, 82
Cozart, Bernadette, 77
Cross-Subsidy Program, 94

Cuba, 225–226
Culkin, Jody, 145
Cummins, Ronnie, 216

D

Daly, Herman E., 15
Dar es Salaam, 225
Dayton, 57, 216
De Colores Community Yard and Garden, 109
Demeter, 147
Denver, 66, 219
Department of Environmental Conservation (DEC), 206–207
Depression, 53, 56, 58–59
Detroit, 56, 138, 220
Deutsche, Rosalyn, 34, 138
Diallo, S., 225
Diamond, Stanley, 176
Dickens, Charles, 81
Direct action, 74, 92, 121, 126, 130, 133
Doe, Jayne, 122
Dominicans, 198
Dowling School Garden, 61
Duane, Thomas K., 129
Dunne, Diane, 8
Dupont, 210
Dykstra, Gretchen, 54–55

E

Earth Celebrations, 120–121, 152–153, 172, 176
Earth Day, 74, 233
Earth First Journal, 17
East Harlem, 69, 251
East New York, 120–121, 134, 228, 250–251
East New York Garden Coalition, 121
Eco-feminism, 168
Eco-spirituality, 168

Ecological counter-culture, 83
Edo (Tokyo), 48
El Puente, 191
El Sol Brilliante, 10
Electoral politics, 137, 154
Empowerment, 21, 65, 87, 117
Enchanted Garden, 192
England, 48, 75
Environmental Action Coalition, 73–74
Environmental justice, 83, 98–99, 101, 117, 127, 163, 174, 191, 193, 198, 207–208, 213, 232, 237
Environmental Protection Agency (EPA), 206
Etzioni, Amitai, 165–166
Europe, 48, 50, 52, 56, 81
Evans, David Hayward, 216

F

Factory farming, 167, 216
Faile Street, 87
Farm Bill (1995), 186
Farm Bill (1996), 66, 187
Farmer's Market Nutrition Program, 193
Faust, 217–218, 242
Federal Emergency Relief Administration (FERA), 59, 68
Federal policy, 36, 53, 181, 209–210, 212, 220
Federal Surplus Relief Corporation, 60
Feenstra, Gail, 181–182, 214
Fenway Gardens, 61
Ferguson, Sarah, 239
Field, Crystal, 44
Fieldwork, 4, 29, 31–32
Fisher, Andrew, iv
Fisher, Ken, 130, 133
Flores, Juan, 150

Index

Food production, 5, 15–17, 24, 51–53, 180–183, 190–195, 204, 208–212, 227–230
Food Project, 187, 193
Food security, 4, 34, 52, 66, 74, 97, 180–181, 186–188, 191, 203, 207–211, 214–215, 237
Ford, Peter, 223
Forsyth Street, 78
Foster, George M., 182
Fourier, Charles, 20
Fowler, Edmund P. Fox, Tom, 16–17
Frances & Benjamin Benensen Foundation, 134
Francis, Mark, 74, 137, 149
Frogworks, 206
Frohardt, Katherine Elson, 216
Fuerbringer, Jonathan, 133
Fuller, Richard Buckminster, 73, 105, 137

G

Gaia, 21–23, 28, 37, 141, 143, 153–157, 159, 161, 163, 165, 167, 169, 171, 173, 175, 177
Gallup Organization, 66, 186
Garcia, Chino, 104, 118
Garden City Plots, 55, 58
Garden Club of America, 133
Garden Club of Laurelton, 46–47
Garden of Eden, the Bronx, 87, 202
Garden of Eden, Jamaica, Queens, 233
Garden of Eden, Lower East Side, 3–7, 39–47, 53–54, 202, 204, 206–207, 209, 238–241, 246, 251–252
Garden Futures, 219
Garden of Love, 132, 252
Gardens for All, 213

Gellner, Ernest, 27
Genetically engineered foods, 216
Geoffrey C. Hughes Foundation, 134
George W. Brown Memorial Garden, 252
German Democratic Republic, 224
Germany, 48–50, 223–224
Gethsemane Garden Baptist Church, 94
Ghana, 201
Giuliani, Rudolph, 5, 33, 79, 89, 94, 100, 133, 136, 173
Gleaning, 203–204
Gleaning Project, 203
Glenmore Avenue, 134
Goethe, Johann Wolfgang, 242
Gold, Hadley W., 215
Golden, Howard, 99, 129, 133–134
Golden Rule Foundation, 205
Gomez, Santa, 136
Goodman, Richard, 60, 218–220
Gottlieb, Robert, 186, 193, 204, 212
Graham, Frank, 87, 233
Green Guerillas, 34, 73–74, 76, 83, 99, 112, 120, 127–128, 151, 189–190, 192, 201–202
Green Map, 28, 234
Green Oasis Garden, 157, 207
Greening of Harlem Coalition, 77
Greenmarket, 74, 214
GreenThumb, 69, 72–73, 78–79, 87, 91, 94, 102, 112, 115, 129–130, 156, 188–189, 202, 215, 239, 249
Gross National Product, 182
Gussow, Joan, 182

H

Hamilton, William L., 6
Harare, 225
Harlem, 69, 71, 77, 89, 123, 125–127, 132, 251–252
Hart, Roger, 242
Havana, 226
Hayden, Dolores, 143
Hell's Kitchen, 76
Henry Street Settlement, 71, 144, 147, 176
Herder, Johann Gottfried, 26
Hickey, Mary Frances, 134, 199
Hill, Joe, 122, 139
Hirsch, Eric, 11, 19, 26
Hmong, 233
Holl, Anne, 49, 221, 225
Homer, 176
Homesteaders, 107, 136
Horticultural Society of New York, 71, 133
Housing Act, 71
Houston Street, 6, 8, 34, 41, 68, 103
HPD, 36, 41, 78–80, 84, 94, 106, 132, 151, 238
Hubli-Dharwad, 201
Hunger Action Network of NYS, 134
Huttner, Richard, 94
Hynes, Patricia, 77

I

Illinois Department of Public Health, 194
India, 47, 152, 174, 201
Indianapolis, 192
Individuality, 25–27, 166–171
Industrial Workers of the World (I.W.W.), 35, 139
Indy Parks, 193
Informational society, 24

J

Jackie Robinson Park, 77
Jacob Riis Houses, 71
Jacobs, Jane, 4
Japan, 210, 214
Jardín Bello Amanecer Borencano, 8–9, 92, 252
Jardín de Esperanza, 53, 84–85, 89–90, 125, 130, 151, 172, 175, 196–197, 200, 206, 216, 252
Jardín de la 10th Street, 92, 156, 251
Jardín del Paraíso, 103, 109–111, 113, 201
J.D. Wilson Memorial Garden, 125, 132, 136, 150, 217, 252
Jes Good Rewards Children's Garden, 76
J.H.S., 205
Jíbaro tradition, 118
John F. Kennedy High School Environmental Club, 192
Johnson, George, 38
Johnson, Martin, 38, 208
Joseph, Hugh, 209
Just Food, 189, 232
Just Food News, 232

K

Kansas State University, 229
Kemmis, Daniel, 236
Kenya, 225
Kingsbridge, 192
Kirschbaum, Pamela R., 219–220
Klee, Paul, 176–177
Kleingärten, 224
Kneen, Brewster, 211
Knox, Paul, 32
Koch, Edward, 34, 82
Kwartler, Michael, 99

Index

L
La Casa del Sol, 35, 123
La Familia Verde, 121
La Guardia Houses, 71
La Matta Clark, Gordon, 105
La Plaza Cultural, 28, 103–106, 111, 159–160, 175, 197, 199, 217, 243
Lackey, Jill Florence, v, 229, 233
Latinos, 189, 194, 199, 251
Lefferts Place Park, 70
Leipzig, 49–50
Lerner, Steve, 55
Liberty Gardens, 55, 58, 60, 64, 227
Lily Auchincloss Foundation, 134
Limited good, concept of, 182, 198
Lincoln, 193
Liz Christy Garden, 34, 41, 73, 83
Loisaida, 103, 116–117, 137, 154, 184, 213
Loisaida Street Festival, 184
London, 165
Lopez, Margarita, 92
Los Angeles, 194, 206
Los Angeles Regional Foodbank, 194
Lott, Charles, 134
Louisiana, 220
Lovelock, James, 22, 37
Low, Setha, 33, 115
Lower East Side, 3–7, 9–10, 28–31, 78, 80–81, 217, 222, 232–241, 246, 251–252
Lower East Side Collective (LESC), 120–122
Lower East Side Ecology Center, 200
Lower East Side Garden Preservation Coalition, 120–121
Lower East Side Girls Club, 106
Lower East Side Technical Assistance Group, 99
LuEsther T. Mertz Charitable Trust, 134
Luhrmann, Tanya, 22–23

M
Madison, 199, 220, 250
Madison Avenue, 199
Malakoff, David, 54, 186
Malathion, 206–207
Malinowski, Bronislaw, 38
Manhattan, 5, 31, 75–76, 81, 121, 131, 134, 145, 158, 198, 200–201, 251
Manhattan Botanical Garden
Manhattan United Gardeners (MUG), 121
Mann, Peter, 210
Maquiladoras, 182
Marcus Garvey Park, 77
Marcuse, Peter, 86–87
Maria's Garden, 92, 251
Martinez, Miranda, v, 139
Mary Flagler Cary Charitable Trust, 134
Massachusetts, 193
Master Gardeners, 193
Mauss, Armand L., 137
Maxwell, Daniel, 201, 253
Mayans, 47
Mbiba, Beacon, 225
McCabe, Sally, 220
McCarthy, R., 229
McClain, James L., 48
McGowan, Kathleen, 42–43
McGrew, Sharyl, 181–182, 214
Media, 24–27
Mele, Christopher, 7
Melucci, Albert, 137

Mephistopheles, 218
Metropolitan Council on Housing, 133
Mexico, 182–183, 201
Mexico City, 201
Meyer-Renschhausen, Elisabeth, 49, 221, 225
Michelangelo, 161
Midler, Bette, 79
Milton, Kay, 22, 37–38, 168
Milwaukee, 233
Minneapolis, 61
Mintz, Sidney, 235, 242
Miracle Garden, 7
Mitchell, William J., 24
Moldakov, Oleg, 223
Monsanto, 210
Montgomery, Velmanette, 133
Montreal, 222
More Gardens! Coalition, 2, 21, 35, 120, 122–123
Morton, Margaret, v, 138
Moscow, 223
Moses, Robert, 69
Moskow, Angela, 226
Mott Haven, 21, 122
Mottel, Syeus, 117–118, 137
Mougeot, Luc J. A., 47, 186, 225
Multilogue, 232
Mumford, Lewis, 69
Murals, 40, 105
Murdoch, Iris, 164–165
Murphy, Catherine, 226

N
Nairobi, 225
Nasr, Joe, 235
National Cash Register Company, 57
National Gardening Association, 75, 218
National Geographic, 87, 172, 233
National Public Radio (NPR), 172
National Socialism, 164
Native American beliefs, 21
Natural Resources Defense Council (NRDC), 127, 139
Neighborhood Open Space Coalition (NOSC), 72–75, 119, 232
Nemore, Carole, 128
Nettleton, John, 228
New Amsterdam, 41, 67
New Jersey, 160, 197, 218
New Orleans, 194, 220
New social movements, 96, 137
New York Cares, 106
New York City, 2–3, 5–6, 10–12, 24, 28–29, 32–33, 195–196, 233–234, 238, 241, 249, 252
New York City Board of Education, 200
New York City Charter, 129–130
New York City Coalition for the Preservation of Gardens, 121
New York City Department of City Planning, 36, 238
New York City Department of Environmental Protection, 80
New York City Department of General Services, 79, 215
New York City Department of Housing Preservation and Development, 36, 41, 94, 238
New York City Department of Parks and Recreation, 72, 79–80
New York City Department of Sanitation, 200
New York City Department of Transportation, 80

Index

New York City Environmental Justice Alliance (NYEJA), 101, 127
New York City Housing Authority, 70, 72
New York City Housing Partnership, 127, 139
New York Community Trust, 134
New York Environmental Law and Justice Project, 206
New York Foundation, 134
New York Greens, 206
New York Restoration Project, 74, 79–80, 84, 124, 127, 131
New York State Appellate Division Court, 93
New York State Attorney General, 80, 93, 128, 133
New York State Open Space Plan, 54–55, 61, 63, 68–69, 128–129, 219–220, 233
New York State Senate Minority Program Office, 128
New York State Supreme Court, 80, 85, 127–128
New York Times, 29, 55, 77, 172, 238–239
Newark, 218
Nijkamp, Peter, 14
Noble, Holcomb B., 102
Northeast Food Coalition, 216
Novartis, 210
Nutzgärten, 51

O
Odysseus, 141–142
Ohio, 57, 216
Omaha, 57
Open Road of NYC, Inc., 205
Open Space Greening Program, 74
Open space planning, 54–55, 61, 63, 68–69, 233
Operation Green Thumb, 8, 73, 103, 107, 110, 205
Orchard Alley, 108
Orchard School, 192
Organic food production, 52, 185, 191
Orpheus Orchestra, 119

P
P-Patch Community Gardens, 219
Pabón, Carmen, 8–9, 36
Pageants, 4, 28, 30, 45, 84, 120, 142, 154, 171–174
Paley Park, 69
Paley, William S., 69
Pangloss, 33, 38
Paris, 48–49
Park Association of New York City, 69
Parks & People Foundation of Baltimore, 220
Parque de Tranquilidad, 84, 103
Peachtree Garden, 114
Pennsylvania, 63, 194
Pennsylvania Horticultural Society, 63
Perez, Armando, 104, 138
Perrels, Adriaan, 14
Persephone, 147
Peru, 47
Pesticides, 17, 202, 206, 226
Philadelphia, 57, 63, 66, 218, 220
Philadelphia Neighborhood Park Program, 63
Phoenixville, 194
Pingtree, Hazen S., 56
Planned shrinkage, 196
Pluto, 147
Poland, 228
Politi, Rolando, 199
Pollio, Marcus Vitruvius, 51

Poole, William, 55
Portland, 219
Potato Patch Gardens, 55–56
Pottharst, Kris, 194, 229, 242
Pratt Center for Community Improvement, 70
Presbytery of New York, 133
Project Grow, 200
Project Harmony, 120, 123, 126, 132–133, 136, 252
Project for Public Spaces, 134
Prudential, 205
Public School, 109, 132
Puerto Rican Community Center of Brownsville, 78, 249
Puerto Rican Legal Defense Fund (PRLDF), 127
Puerto Ricans, 6–7, 36, 90, 113, 115, 118, 154, 196
Purdue Extension, 193
Purple, Adam, 202

Q

Quail Hill Farm, 187
Quanda Building, 73
Queens, 46, 77, 87, 134, 189, 200, 233, 252
Queens Botanical Garden, 77
Queens Green Party, 134
Quincy Park, 70

R

Radin, Paul, 167
Raver, Anne, 78
Reagan, Ronald, 66
Reaven, Marci, 116
Reclaiming the Streets, 75
Recycling, 11, 17, 48, 74, 91, 95, 118, 149, 185, 198, 200–202
Regional farming, 168, 187, 192, 198, 209–210, 213, 216, 234
Reiter, Fran, 78

Relief Gardens, 55, 58–60, 68
Resmithrin, 206
Reverend Linnette C. Williamson Gardens and Unity Park, 69
Rhode Island, 216
Riis, Jacob, 71, 81
Rincon Criollo Community Garden, 151–152
Rites of Spring Pageant, 29, 104, 152, 154, 156, 161, 169, 184, 230, 246
Riverside Valley Community Garden, 198
Rivington Street, 78
Robbins, Ira S., 71
Roosevelt, Franklin Delano, 60
Rose and Sherle Wagner Foundation, 134
Roszak, Theodore, 165
Rotenberg, Robert, 50–51
Russia, 223
Ryan, Cara Gendel, 138

S

Saalman, Howard, 48
Saint-Exupéry, Antoine de, vii
Sampson, John, 133
San Francisco, 66, 193, 216, 218–219
San Francisco League of Urban Gardeners (SLUG), 193
Sánchez, José Ramón, 7
Santiago, Esmeralda, 118, 138
Satellite en Orbita, 78, 250
Schell, Paul, 219
Schmerfeld, Steven, 150
School of Cooperative Technical Education, 200
School Gardens, 55, 57, 68, 72, 224
Schreber, Daniel Gottlieb Moritz, 49

Index

Schrebergärten, 49–51
Schrödinger, Erwin, 38
Scoones, I., 14
Seattle, 66, 210–211, 219
Section 8, 6, 36
Seymour, Whitney North, 63, 70–72
Sharff, Jagna W., 10, 83, 150–151
Shiffman, Ronald, 70
Sierra Club of New York, 133
Silesia, 228–229
Sisti, Rich, 197
Smit, Jac, 235
Smithsonian Institute, 152
Social movements, 96, 137
Soil and Conservation Service, 193
Soil contamination, 77, 204
South Bronx, 16, 101, 151–152
South Central, 194
South End Lower Roxbury Land Trust, 219
South Providence, 216
Southside, Williamsburg, 191
Spirituality, 13, 21–24, 168
Spitzer, Eliot, 80, 93, 127, 133
Spraying, 206–207
Squatters, 82, 91, 101, 105, 107–109, 113, 115, 136
St. John's Organic Community Garden, 194
St. Louis, 66, 206
St. Louis encephalitis, 206
St. Petersburg, 223
Stanton Street, 78
Staten Island, 200, 252
Stone, Andrew, 220
Stuyvesant, Peter, 41
Sumethrin, 206
Sunset Garden, 80
Sustainability, 13–17, 21, 168, 182, 211–212, 234–236
Sustainable agriculture, 187, 191
Sustainable communities, 16, 50, 52, 66, 73, 208
Sweat-equity, 91, 103, 113, 196, 242

T
Tabb, William K. Tacoma, 196
Tanzania, 225
Tapscott & Union Street Garden, 192
Taylor, A.F., 137
Taylor, Charles, 165–166
Teitel, Martin, 210
Tenement houses, 67
Tenochtitlan, 47
Texas, 194
Theater for the New City, 44
Thrush, Glenn, 6, 36
Tierney, John, 98, 109
Tilly, Charles, 137
Times Square, 43, 55
Times Square Business Improvement District, 55
Time's Up, 21
Tokyo, 48
Tompkins Square Park, 68, 107, 146, 150, 175
Toronto, 222
Torres, Alicia, 90, 172, 175, 196
Torres, José, 172
Trinity Lutheran Parish Church, 197
Trobriand Islanders, 157
Trust for Public Land, 46, 55, 73–74, 79–80, 124–125, 127, 131, 205, 220

U
Uniform Land Use Review Process (ULURP), 128–129

United Nations Development Program, 186
United States, 4–6, 8, 10, 35, 191–192, 196, 202, 204, 210, 214, 219, 221–222, 227–228, 235, 237
University of Illinois Cooperative Extension Service, 64, 194
Upper West Side, 198, 251
Urban agriculture, 12, 45–52, 66, 123, 186–187, 193, 201–202, 216, 221, 223–229, 233, 235
Urban Arts & Ecology, 134
Urban Beautification Act, 71
Urban Development Action Area Program (UDAAP), 129, 139
Urban homesteading, 91, 99, 136
Urban Homesteading Assistance Board, 99
Urban Outdoors, 232
U.S. Department of Agriculture (USDA), 60, 64–66, 86, 180–181, 185–186, 207, 214, 227
U.S. Department of the Census, 36, 137, 185–186

V

Vacancy rates, 6
Vacant lots, 1, 18, 28, 33–34, 42–43, 63, 72, 133, 139, 156, 158, 163, 196, 234, 240
Vallee, Norman, 7
Van En, Robyn, 214
Van Guard, Lisa, 35
Vest pocket parks, 69–70
Via Campesina, 210
Vico, Gianbattista, 26
Victory Garden, 55, 60–61, 64, 69, 222, 227
Village Voice, 172

Voltaire, François Marie Arouet, 33, 38
Volunteerism, 199
von Hassell, Malve, 242

W

Waliczek, Tina M., 229
Walter Rogowski Farm, 191
War Garden Commission, 58
Warner, Sam Bass, 49, 57, 138
Warren/St. Mark's Garden, 61, 69
Washington, 66, 203, 218
Washington, D.C., 66, 218
Waste management, 15, 73–74, 180, 198, 201
Weil, Simone, 164
Weiner, Annette, 157, 168, 171
Wekerle, Gerda, 14–15, 222
West 129th Street Block Association Garden, 132, 252
West Nile virus, 206
Wexler, Ellen, 176
Williams, Raymond, 16, 19–20, 25
Williamsburg, 191, 250–251
Wilson, Kimberly A., 18, 20, 210
Wilson, Peter Lamborn, 18–20, 210
Winne, Mark, 188
Winter Candle Lantern Pageant, 145, 161, 169, 175
Wisconsin, 220, 233
Wittgenstein, Ludwig, 38
Wobblies, 35, 139
Women, Infants, and Children Program (WIC), 194
Works Project Administration (WPA), 60, 68
World Trade Organization (WTO), 210–211
World War I, 49, 58, 60, 68, 227
World War II, 60–61, 65, 69,

Index

164, 224, 227
Worley, Cynthia, 217
Worley, Haja, 123
Woteki, Catherine, 186
WTO, 210

Y
Young Devils Garden, 199
Young, Felicia, 84, 120, 152, 170

Z
Ziergärten, 51
Zimbabwe, 225

About the Author

MALVE VON HASSELL is a freelance writer, researcher, and translator. She holds a Ph.D. in anthropology from the New School for Social Research. Working as an independent scholar, she published *The Struggle for Eden: Community Gardens in New York City* (Bergin & Garvey 2002) and *Homesteading in New York City 1978-1993: The Divided Heart of Loisaida* (Bergin & Garvey 1996). She has also edited her grandfather Ulrich von Hassell's memoirs written in prison in 1944, *Der Kreis schließt sich - Aufzeichnungen aus der Haft 1944* (Propylaen Verlag 1994). She has taught at Queens College, Baruch College, Pace University, and Suffolk County Community College, while continuing her work as a translator and writer. She has published two children's picture books, *Tooth Fairy (Amazon KDP 2012/2020),* and *Turtle Crossing (Amazon KDP 2023),* and her translation and annotation of a German children's classic by Tamara Ramsay, *Rennefarre: Dott's Wonderful Travels and Adventures* (Two Harbors Press, 2012). *The Falconer's Apprentice* (namelos, 2015/KDP 2024) was her first historical fiction novel for young adults. She has published *Alina: A Song for the Telling* (BHC Press, 2020), set in Jerusalem in the time of the crusades, and *The Amber Crane* (Odyssey Books, 2021), set in Germany in 1645 and 1945, a biographical work about a woman coming of age in Nazi Germany, *Tapestry of My Mother's Life: Stories, Fragments, and Silences* (Next Chapter Publishing, 2021), also available in German, *Bildteppich Eines Lebens: Erzählungen Meiner Mutter, Fragmente Und Schweigen* (Next Chapter Publishing, 2022), and a historical fiction novel, *The Price of Loyalty: Serving Adela of Blois* (Historium Press, 2025, forthcoming). You can find more information on her website https://www.malvevonhassell.com.

www.ingramcontent.com/pod-product-compliance
Lightning Source LLC
Chambersburg PA
CBHW070613030426
42337CB00020B/3782